"*New California Writing* is a mosaic, a collage, a road trip through the California infrequently seen on film or television, though familiar to those of us who have called the Golden State home. Some pieces position themselves as knowing outsiders, like a coroner examining the body politic; others live in the moment, intimate and wide-eyed, exploring the California experiment from within. And then there's Natalie Diaz's piece about the Mojave Barbie, which creates its own category of kickass. Hell, who can resist a book that begins with 'On the boat we were mostly virgins'?"
—Briandaniel Oglesby, author of *Halfway, Nebraska*

"The stories and poems in *New California Writing* erupt out of that moment of contact between people and place. It is the voice of Japanese mail-order brides on the long sea journey to meet husbands known only by fuzzy black-and-white photographs. It is a young Indian woman trained as a Human Bear. It is the Filipino little brother waiting for a sister who doesn't return. It is frustrated writers delivering eviction notices for spare change, prison life, a son in mourning, Bishop pines waiting for wildfires, Mojave Indian Barbie's rebellion, the LA River's turbulence, a postapocalyptic tribe of women in caves, poets vs. cops, and always, always, the gifts and burdens of mythology. California writing is not composed of just one voice; it is the voice of the world, and this collection sings, squawks, hollers, roars, whines, and thrums with California encounters of the best kind."
—Deborah Miranda, author of *Bad Indians*

"To call Gayle Wattawa's choices for *New California Writing 2013* eclectic would do little to prepare the reader for this delicious literary feast. She has brought us writers as diverse as Susan Straight, Gustavo Arellano, David Mas Masumoto, and Joan Didion. And Wattawa has scoured every possible literary nook, including such well-established presses as Knopf and W. W. Norton, journals with names like *PALABRA* and

ZYZZYVA, and websites including *The Indigo Vat* and *Zócalo Public Square*. From Malibu to Sacramento, San Francisco to National City, Palm Springs to Boyle Heights, it's all here in poetry and fiction and reportage, our great, messy ever-evolving State of California."

—Daniel A. Olivas, author of *The Book of Want: A Novel*

"Meet a shipload of brides on their way from Japan to San Francisco, a Coast Miwok girl who became the last person inducted into the ancient Human Bear cult, a Japanese-Cherokee-Irish-African-American boy who loves sushi and black-eyed peas, and other such characters who live side by side in the valleys, cities, and seaside towns of California."

—Lucille Lang Day, author of *Married at Fourteen: A True Story*

"This edition of *New California Writing* has so many things that I miss the most about my home state: a vision of beauty from the redwoods and Point Reyes to the desert; an awareness of the abundance and the human costs of agriculture, through winter deserts and peach orchards; a wicked delight in probing the geographies (and fault lines) of diversity, from Mojave Indian Barbies to sushi and black-eyed peas. Each page-turn gives us another rotation of the maddening and breathtaking kaleidoscope that is California."

—Tamiko Nimura, author and food writer

"According to Walt Whitman, the United States is essentially the greatest poem—which makes California the coolest, craziest stanza within that poem. This third installment of *New California Writing* does an amazing job of demonstrating how the cool and the crazy become the classic."

—Dean Rader, author of *Works and Days*

"If this rich and marvelous collection of writing doesn't establish what a strong literary scene exists in the West, particularly in California, nothing else will."

—Greg Sarris, author of *Grand Avenue*

"I am as moved, charmed, by Lysley Tenorio's and Donna Miscolta's tales straight out of Lemoore and National City—those striving, humble municipalities—as I might be by any from Athens in its glory days or Rome in the flush of its power. I'll take Stephen D. Gutiérrez's metaphorical river running through the City of Commerce over the Euphrates during the reign of Nebuchadnezzar. But you don't have to live in California to be enchanted by this collection of fiction, memoir, and poetry. You don't even have to *like* California. You need only be a lover of damn fine writing."

—Suzanne Lummis, poet and director
of the Los Angeles Poetry Festival

NEW CALIFORNIA WRITING

2013

NEW CALIFORNIA WRITING

2013

Gayle Wattawa, Prose Editor

Kirk Glaser, Poetry Editor

Foreword by Peter Coyote

HEYDAY, BERKELEY, CALIFORNIA
SANTA CLARA UNIVERSITY, SANTA CLARA, CALIFORNIA

This California Legacy book was published by
Heyday and Santa Clara University.

© 2013 by Heyday

Library of Congress Cataloging-in-Publication Data
is available.

Cover Design and Illustration: Lorraine Rath
Interior Design/Typesetting: Leigh McLellan Design
Printing and Binding: Worzalla, Stevens Point, WI

New California Writing 2013 was published by Heyday
and Santa Clara University. Orders, inquiries, and
correspondence should be addressed to:
Heyday
P.O. Box 9145, Berkeley, CA 94709
(510) 549-3564, Fax (510) 549-1889
www.heydaybooks.com

10 9 8 7 6 5 4 3 2 1

CONTENTS

CONTENTS

FOREWORD

Peter Coyote

FOR BUDDHISTS, AWARENESS is recognized by "luminosity," "alive-ness," and "lack of distinguishing characteristics." The Chinese use the same character for *awareness* that they use for *sky*. Awareness is the bedrock on which all (human) mental constructions rest—language, thought, perceptions, and so on. In this absolute realm there are neither forms nor distinctions—"no eyes, no ears, no tongue, no body, no mind," as the *Heart Sutra* clearly explains. Consequently, at first blush, it may appear foolish to present a book on new California writing in 2013 as if there were a "California" awareness, contained by our state's borders, which is somehow different than a Manhattan or Illinois awareness.

We do not live (solely) in the absolute but in the relative, where each person, each leaf, each grain of sand is unique. We are able to discriminate—to catalog—influences, and perhaps even *intentions*. In considering California writers and comparing them (gingerly) to those who live elsewhere, I am not suggesting hierarchies of excellence but distinctions that make a difference.

The geology of the earth itself abets this task. The Hudson River appears as much a psychological and cultural border as a geologic boundary. Having said that, precisely what it separates is trickier to identify. From my remove in California, it often feels as if the western bank of the Hudson insulates America's cultural capital from the penetration of a number of "regional" artistic concerns, philosophies, and attitudes percolating through the ether. I will employ Manhattan as a stand-in for that which is most "other" than

California. Comparing a state to a city might seem like comparing apples and oranges, but Manhattan casts such a broad shadow across our national culture that, for purposes of discussion, it seems fair enough.

Manhattan might be forgiven its cultural entitlement when it opines about the relative merits of *its* cultural expression as opposed to, say, that of San Bernardino, Fresno, Los Angeles, or Grass Valley. Manhattan and its hydra of media and publishing complexes sit stolidly confident as a Dutch burgher in the *center* of the American tectonic plate. Manhattan is insulated from the hip-shaking, turn-the-earth-to-jelly quaking that occurs in California, at the *margins* where three such plates intersect. Perhaps some measurable percentage of Manhattan's confidence derives from regal geologic stability, affording it full confidence in its global influence as a financial hub and the assurance that its achievements and values will be nationally accepted as standards of the desirable.

If I am correct in this assessment, *therein lies its exposed Achilles tendon:* in the face of such apparent stability and scale, it can be easy to forget that things *always* change. In California, we are frequently reminded by the jitters and shudders of the earth that our turbulence begins underfoot. Often dwarfed by such forces of nature, artists in the mountain, coast, and high desert regions appear to concentrate less on and refer less to the eastern behemoth churning out news, information, and cultural patterning on the faraway Atlantic coast. It is neither resistance nor stiff-necked pride but rather the immediacy of different influences that accounts for our local focus.

From the Rocky Mountains, which float like skateboarders over an unmoving sea of basalt below, everything slides west toward the Pacific, rolling downhill in the direction of what geologists refer to as "the Triple Junction." This is the area where three enormous sections of the earth's crust—the Pacific, North American, and Gorda Plates—collide, grind, interpenetrate, and upthrust with all the heat, friction, and propulsive kinetics of a geologic porn film. How could such forces not affect the consciousness of those who live in their surround?

The ground churned up by these collisions is the freshest and newest on the planet. Our mountains are jagged and razor-edged, raw and masculine and quite different from the rounded, feminine swells of the East—the Adirondacks, Alleghenies, and Blue Ridge. Perhaps resonance with our geography inclines California artists to associate with the new, the novel, and the creative. Like our soil and mountains, we are, geologically and culturally, in upheaval. We are edge dwellers.

New Yorkers share the Atlantic Ocean with Europe and culturally refer to its centuries of royal traditions, stratified social structures, and high arts. Californians directly border Mexico and the Pacific Ocean. The "immigrants" currently demonized in national debates are people who have *walked* here and can walk "home" to where they've lived for centuries. Less than two centuries ago, large sections of what we refer to as the United States were theirs.

Californians stare south through a barely Europeanized high desert and jungle corridor into Mexico and Central and Latin America and a vast geography where four hundred million souls, immersed in the history of their own empires and dominance, dance wreathed in copal incense and adorned with parrot and magpie feathers. Street musicians create spontaneous ballads of bullets, bandits, glorious crimes, and deaths. Everyday folk leave skull candies and feed the spirits on Día de los Muertos, follow hallucinogenic dreams in the high Sonoran deserts, and swelter in the lowland fecundity of their jungles. They have seen empires come and go and do not appear to be overly impressed by ours.

The Pacific Ocean grinds California granite and serpentine to sand and deposits the flotsam from Japanese fishing boats on our beaches. Kuroshio, the warm-water artery from Asia that insulates us from frigid winters, once swept ancient fishermen to these shores from the Marianas, Samoa, Tonga, Tuvalu, Tokelau, Hawaii, China, Japan, Korea, and Vietnam. They married and swapped cultural artifacts with West Coast native people, who, because they ruled the seas, remained relatively unvanquished by the invading Russians and Americans. These kingdoms—Haida, Tlingit, Swinomish, and Kwakiutl—and their artists and mythologies thrive and still influence our own.

The Pacific embraces peoples, clans, and tribes from Polynesia, Micronesia, and Melanesia—ancient, sophisticated world travelers who made three-thousand-mile journeys in canoes carrying pigs and cassava. They navigated by starlight and were so internally still and sensitive to the occasional accent of a wave against the prow that the occasional rim-shot accent, occurring every ninety waves, then every eight-nine, moving ever lower in count, signaled to them the approach of a yet unseen shore.

I'm not any more sure *how* such disparate influences alter the creative minds here than I can be certain how the sun, light, and soil express themselves in the East as stately eastern oaks and robins and in the West as the torqued and dancing live oaks and the camp jays of California. Local adaptation to light, soil, climate, and culture is as true of humans as it is of plant and animal species. And it is true for the writers in this book. Their minds are neither more nor less creative than their counterparts in Manhattan and the East, but some combination of bioregional pressures and definitive geologic and climatic borders has evolved different emphases and values, as with subspecies of sparrows differing slightly or greatly, depending on their terrain.

My experiences in the East (where I grew to maturity) lead me to observe that frames of reference there are both more mental and more referential to *human* culture than those in California. To many Californians, the anthropocentric perspective of Manhattan leads to an unrecognized provinciality, walled in by the certainties of empire, where values of the marketplace, density of population, and the grandeur of epic human undertakings serves to insulate Manhattan denizens from the different perspective and not-always-human-centered concerns of Western artists. Perhaps because of the relative uniformity of human concerns, East Coast culture feels more cohesive than that of the West, as well as more competitive, perhaps due to the scarcity of resources. Even Los Angeles, our largest urban center, has under half the population of New York. Less delimited by available space than the island of Manhattan, our cities have more sprawl and ramble and can afford to keep the buildings low, inviting more sunlight and fresh air even as they metastasize over a landscape that many Angelenos consider scrub.

Writing this foreword has made me wonder whether twenty-four-hour-a-day immersion in pyramidal, hierarchal architectural and social structures might steer the mind toward stratification, status competition, and comparative thinking.* In the same way that Californians are sometimes accused of being "laid-back" nature-lovers by Manhattanites, our immersion in the natural world affords us a clear premise and platform from which to distance ourselves from a number of the values and premises of the Empire State. Perhaps California's physical distance from older, longer-established cultural capitals also lends a more revolutionary perspective to our view, as it once did for Thoreau and Whitman, when the East Coast was still new cultural ground in comparison to the English culture it had emerged from not that long before.

---

*Having said this, it is obviously true that many "Eastern" writers do not live in concentrated urban areas, and it is my experience that they—Robert Frost, Wendell Berry, John Hanson Mitchell, and their brethren—more resemble their land-inflected Western counterparts in their receptivity to light, space, and seasons than they do the denizens of Manhattan.

Those of us living west of the Rockies tend toward *horizontal* perspectives. The highest peak is not "better" than the next highest. The most aimless meanders may lead one to the unexpected shock of a vivid little wildflower in an otherwise plainspoken and obscure valley. Such a lack of reference to human social values is a core Western experience.

The writers in this collection, like their Eastern counterparts, have been stamped and forged by place. Like hydrangeas, whose blooms are affected by the acid (or lack of it) in their soil and turn white, pale green, red, or blue depending on the pH of the earth and differences of mineral substrates, our cultural and geological background tonalities, histories of place, and local dissonances and interferences must affect and filter incoming frequencies passing through the awareness of our artists. How could we not think differently here than those in Nueva York?

When the earth shakes, we shake. When the sun sets over an infinite horizon, we expand. Even in downtown Los Angeles, artists' sensibilities interact with magma flows. Fog, wind, tectonic shifts, and trees that sprouted during the time of Christ now rival skyscrapers in scale. We are neighbors with ravens, condors, spotted owls, bobcats, and bears on the back porch, wild salmon still numbering in the millions. The breezes blowing through our windows carry different perfumes.

However one categorizes the nuances, the specifics of these differences comprise the chunky compilation you hold as you read this foreword.

Many of these artists will be recognizable to Easterners—Robert Hass, certainly, although his "Poet-Bashing Police" is infused with our gritty Western radicalism and populism, our instinctive siding with the defenseless against the overarmed. (It may be a legacy of so many "outsiders" arriving in California at the same historical moment that Eastern demarcations of status and class were softened and a more laissez-faire democracy grew among them.)

Michael Lewis, from New Orleans (a Caribbean, not an American, city), has made his bones as a shrewd, observant analyst of the vagaries of Wall Street and the financial giants and their predicaments and chicanery. He chooses to live in Berkeley. Does this remove and distance afford him the clarity to see the picture more clearly than, say, the New York pundits who bring us the nightly "analyses"? I think it may. His contribution here, from a new book, *Boomerang,* delivers the starkest appraisal of what life will be like in America's emerging free-market future as cities bankrupted by debt, and choked off from resources by the armed gourmands we quaintly refer to as "the 1 percent," assume their unimpeded dominance over our domestic life. His radicalism never ventures into the impolite, but his clear-eyed observation could have been written years earlier by Los Angeles cultural radical Leslie Evans.

I was gently upbraided by a friend for asserting, in an earlier draft of this piece, that the motorcycle and its call to freedom is a Western invention. She reminded me that New York poet Frederick Seidel writes about his motorcycles (and about a fabulous woman named Clare Peploe, whom Mr. Seidel and I both admire). She is correct, of course, but the tone and particulars of Seidel's extensive *Harper's* piece about motorcycles is altogether different from Joseph Millar's poem about his scavenged Triumph, which deftly links the story of his busted-up motorcycle with the artist's constant struggle for money and survival. Mr. Seidel's piece is peppered with casual references to his wealth, status, and class, and very different (and much more expensive) motorcycles. This is not the biker symbolism of *Easy Rider.*

Poe Ballantine performs a similar, brokenhearted hat trick with his wry piece "Free Rent at the Totalitarian Hotel," and in the same way that our common sunlight appears different on the Atlantic and

Pacific coasts, Poe's tale about a cheesy West Coast rooming house could not be confused with one about a Manhattan "cheap hotel."

A quick review of the book's table of contents reveals a state that locals express as "diversity" among its authors and their concerns—among them tales about Japanese mail-order brides and transplanted Filipino children adrift in the wastelands of Southern California suburbs. Our multiracial, multicultural reality is pungently expressed in Bill Hutchinson's fine story "From Sushi to Black-eyed Peas." I don't mean to suggest that the reality of Manhattan is not equally culturally diverse but that it rarely appears to be the *point,* as Californians have made it.

Chieun "Gloria" Kim's "Water Cycle" links the identity of self and other directly to the earth, and our ever-present relationship to land unobscured by high-rises and paving. David Rains Wallace's "Point Reyes: Renewed by Fire" is a perfect example of a refined and patient human sensibility requiring no fictional device to make nature its core concern. For Mr. Wallace, nature is not Nature, a concept or metaphor, but an *actual,* compelling, and self-sufficient narrative. Jen Bergmark's gut-wrenching story, "Boyle Heights," chronicles the costs of human cultures and classes ground together in mimicry of tectonic plates—a geological romance. The author makes no specific mention of the earth, yet its force is the scaffolding of her story. And there is water. In this state, in which half the year is afflicted by drought, water appears in these stories everywhere: in rain, in rivers, in creeks, in bays, in oceans.

I am guilty of disservice to every writer in this volume I have not mentioned by name. There's not a clinker in Gayle Wattawa's and Kirk Glaser's editorial selections. I don't mean to suggest by this introduction that to appreciate our California culture we must jettison our affections for the scores of Eastern and European literary giants, living and past, in favor of the Western voices offered here.

As Jane Hirshfield, one of my favorite California poets, observed to me recently discussing precisely this subject, "Some hold up one end of a log, some hold up the other, but it's one log, one American voice."

True. Yet each end of the log, and each inch of its length, is also unique. California writers are intimate with the generosity of the earth and often model its fecundity of invention in their craft. In the same way that the existence of eagles is neither a threat nor a value judgment on hummingbirds, we do not have to choose between the offerings of either coast, nor those of all the voices that live in between, whether in Chicago, Albuquerque, Kansas City, or in smaller towns, rangelands, or prairies. Nor do we need to pretend that they are not different.

You hold the paper in your hand. Your mind is the brush. Dip it into this ink and visualize your own sere, sprawling, corrugated landscapes, your own Mediterranean light, drainages, creeks, giant dawn redwoods, bays and seas, Asians, Mexicans, Native Americans, *cholos,* urban decay, yips, chirps, howls, and roars of your imagined California. Enjoy the dance, and stay out from underfoot when the earth stamps her feet.

Peter Coyote
Mill Valley, California
September 2012

PETER COYOTE has performed as an actor for some of the world's most distinguished filmmakers, including Barry Levinson, Roman Polanski, Pedro Almodovar, Steven Spielberg, and Sidney Pollack. He is an Emmy Award–winning narrator of more than 120 documentary films. His memoir of 1960s counterculture, *Sleeping Where I Fall,* has sold through five printings in hardback. An ordained Buddhist, he has been engaged in political and social causes since his early teens.

ACKNOWLEDGMENTS

FIRST AND FOREMOST, my thanks go to all of the people who nominated pieces or submitted their own work: as our publisher Malcolm Margolin says, we "swim in a sea of beauty" here at Heyday, and we're the luckier for it. My intern Lucas Vasquez deserves special mention for his work on this collection, especially his valuable input on selecting and sequencing the pieces. Thanks also to Michael Hicks and Karen Sorensen for assisting me in my searches for new California writing. Susan Straight always has excellent recommendations for this collection. Peter Coyote's thoughtful foreword was a revelation, and I thank him for his gracious involvement in this project. Lorraine Rath and Leigh McLellan give this collection its snazzy look, and I'm indebted to Emily Park and Lisa K. Marietta for their editorial acumen. My colleagues and enablers at Heyday are a joy to work with, but here's a special shout-out to my mentor, friend, and comrade-in-arms Jeannine Gendar. On a personal note: JP, you are the bee's knees.

—Gayle Wattawa

Thank you to Terry Beers for recommending my participation in *New California Writing* and to the Santa Clara University students who helped research for and select the winner of the first *New California Writing* Student Award.

—Kirk Glaser

from *THE BUDDHA IN THE ATTIC*

Julie Otsuka

O N THE BOAT we were mostly virgins. We had long black hair and flat wide feet and we were not very tall. Some of us had eaten nothing but rice gruel as young girls and had slightly bowed legs, and some of us were only fourteen years old and were still young girls ourselves. Some of us came from the city, and wore stylish city clothes, but many more of us came from the country and on the boat we wore the same old kimonos we'd been wearing for years—faded hand-me-downs from our sisters that had been patched and redyed many times. Some of us came from the mountains, and had never before seen the sea, except for in pictures, and some of us were the daughters of fishermen who had been around the sea all our lives. Perhaps we had lost a brother or father to the sea, or a fiancé, or perhaps someone we loved had jumped into the water one unhappy morning and simply swum away, and now it was time for us, too, to move on.

On the boat the first thing we did—before deciding who we liked and didn't like, before telling each other which one of the islands we were from, and why we were leaving, before even bothering to learn each other's names—was compare photographs of our husbands. They were handsome young men with dark eyes and full heads of hair and skin that was smooth and unblemished. Their chins were strong. Their posture, good. Their noses were straight and high. They looked like our brothers and fathers back home, only better dressed, in gray frock coats and fine Western three-piece suits. Some of them were standing on sidewalks in front of wooden A-frame houses with white picket fences and neatly mowed lawns, and some were leaning in driveways against Model T Fords. Some were sitting in studios on stiff high-backed chairs with their hands neatly folded and staring straight into the camera, as though they were ready to take on the world. All of them had promised to be there, waiting for us, in San Francisco, when we sailed into port.

On the boat, we often wondered: Would we like them? Would we love them? Would we recognize them from their pictures when we first saw them on the dock?

On the boat we slept down below, in steerage, where it was filthy and dim. Our beds were narrow metal racks stacked one on top of the other and our mattresses were hard and thin and darkened with the stains of other journeys, other lives. Our pillows were stuffed with dried wheat hulls. Scraps of food littered the passageways between berths and the floors were wet and slick. There was one porthole, and in the evening, after the hatch was closed, the darkness filled with whispers. *Will it hurt?* Bodies tossed and turned beneath the blankets. The sea rose and fell. The damp air stifled. At night we dreamed of our husbands. We dreamed of new wooden sandals and endless bolts of indigo silk and of living, one day, in a house with a chimney. We dreamed we were lovely and tall. We dreamed we were back in the rice paddies, which we had so desperately wanted to escape. The rice paddy dreams were always nightmares. We dreamed of our older and prettier sisters who had been sold to the geisha houses by our fathers so that the rest of us might eat, and when we woke we were gasping for air. *For a second I thought I was her.*

Our first few days on the boat we were seasick, and could not keep down our food, and had to make repeated trips to the railing. Some of us were so dizzy we could not even walk, and lay in our berths in a dull stupor, unable to remember our own names, not to mention those of our new husbands. *Remind me one more time, I'm Mrs. Who?* Some of us clutched our stomachs and prayed out loud to Kannon, the goddess of mercy—*Where are you?*—while others of us preferred to turn silently green. And often, in the middle of the night, we were jolted awake by a violent swell and for a brief moment we had no idea where we were, or why our beds would not stop moving, or why our hearts were pounding with such dread. *Earthquake* was the first thought that usually came to our minds. We reached out for our mothers then, in whose arms we had slept until the morning we left home. Were they sleeping now? Were they dreaming? Were they thinking of us night and day? Were they still walking three steps behind our fathers on the streets with their arms full of packages while our fathers carried nothing at all? Were they secretly envious of us for sailing away? *Didn't I give you everything?* Had they remembered to air out our old kimonos? Had they remembered to feed the cats? Had they made sure to tell us everything we needed to know? *Hold your teacup with both hands, stay out of the sun, never say more than you have to.*

Most of us on the boat were accomplished, and were sure we would make good wives. We knew how to cook and sew. We knew how to serve tea and arrange flowers and sit quietly on our flat wide feet for hours, saying absolutely nothing of substance at all. *A girl must blend into a room: she must be present without appearing to exist.* We knew how to behave at funerals, and how to write short, melancholy poems about the passing of autumn that were exactly seventeen syllables long. We knew how to pull weeds and chop kindling and haul water, and one of us—the rice miller's daughter—knew how to walk two miles into town with an eighty-pound sack of rice on her back without once breaking into a sweat. *It's all in the way you breathe.* Most of us had good manners, and were extremely polite, except for when we got mad and cursed like sailors. Most of us spoke like ladies most of the time, with our voices pitched high, and pretended to know much less than we did, and whenever we walked past the deckhands we made sure to take small, mincing steps with our toes turned properly in. Because how many times had our mothers told us: *Walk like the city, not like the farm!*

On the boat we crowded into each other's bunks every night and stayed up for hours discussing the unknown continent ahead of us. The people there were said to eat nothing but meat and their bodies were covered with hair (we were mostly Buddhist, and did not eat meat, and only had hair in the appropriate places). The trees were enormous. The plains were vast. The women were loud and tall—a full head taller, we had heard, than the tallest of our men. The language was ten times as difficult as our own and the customs were unfathomably strange. Books were read from back to front and soap was used in the bath. Noses were blown on dirty cloths that were stuffed back into pockets only to be taken out later and used again and again. The opposite of white was not red, but black. What would become of us, we wondered, in such an alien land? We imagined ourselves—an unusually small people armed only with our guidebooks—entering a country of giants. Would we be laughed at? Spat on? Or, worse yet, would we not be taken seriously at all? But even the most reluctant of us had to admit that it was better to marry a stranger in America than grow old with a farmer from the village. Because in America the women did not have to work in the fields and there was plenty of rice and firewood for all. And wherever you went the men held open the doors and tipped their hats and called out, "Ladies first" and "After you."

Some of us on the boat were from Kyoto, and were delicate and fair, and had lived our entire lives in darkened rooms at the back of the house. Some of us were from Nara, and prayed to our ancestors three times a day, and swore we could still hear the temple bells ringing. Some of us were farmers' daughters from Yamaguchi with thick wrists and broad shoulders who had never gone to bed after nine. Some of us were from a small mountain hamlet in Yamanashi and had only recently seen our first train. Some of us were from Tokyo, and had seen everything, and spoke beautiful Japanese, and did not mix much with any of the others. Many more of us were from Kagoshima and spoke in a thick southern dialect that those of us from Tokyo pretended we could not understand. Some of us were from Hokkaido, where it was snowy and cold, and would dream of that white landscape for years. Some of us were from Hiroshima, which would later explode, and were lucky to be on the boat at all though of course we did not then know it. The youngest of us was twelve, and from the eastern shore of Lake Biwa, and had not yet begun to bleed. *My parents married me off for the betrothal money.* The oldest of us was thirty-seven, and from Niigata, and had spent her entire life taking care of her invalid father, whose recent death made her both happy and sad. *I knew I could marry only if he died.* One of us was from Kumamoto, where there were no more eligible men—all of the eligible men had left the year before to find work in Manchuria—and felt fortunate to have found any kind of husband at all. *I took one look at his photograph and told the matchmaker, "He'll do."* One of us was from a silk-weaving village in Fukushima, and had lost her first husband to the flu, and her second to a younger and prettier woman who lived on the other side of the hill, and now she was sailing to America to marry her third. *He's healthy, he doesn't drink, he doesn't gamble, that's all I needed to know.* One of us was a former dancing girl from Nagoya who dressed beautifully, and had translucent white skin, and knew everything there was to know about men, and it was to her we turned every night with our questions. How long will it last? With the lamp lit or in the dark? Legs up or down? Eyes open or closed? What if I can't breathe? What if I get thirsty? What if he is too heavy? What if he is too big? What if he does not want me at all? "Men are really quite simple," she told us. And then she began to explain.

On the boat we sometimes lay awake for hours in the swaying damp darkness of the hold, filled with longing and dread, and wondered how we would last another three weeks.

On the boat we carried with us in our trunks all the things we would need for our new lives: white silk kimonos for our wedding night, colorful cotton kimonos for everyday wear, plain cotton kimonos for when we grew old, calligraphy brushes, thick black sticks of ink, thin sheets of rice paper on which to write long letters home, tiny brass Buddhas, ivory statues of the fox god, dolls we had slept with since we were five, bags of brown sugar with which to buy favors, bright cloth quilts, paper fans, English phrase books, flowered silk sashes, smooth black stones from the river that ran behind our house, a lock of hair from a boy we had once touched, and loved, and promised to write, even though we knew we never would, silver mirrors given to us by our mothers, whose last words still rang in our ears. *You will see: women are weak, but mothers are strong.*

On the boat we complained about everything. Bedbugs. Lice. Insomnia. The constant dull throb of the engine, which worked its way even into our dreams. We complained about the stench from the latrines—huge, gaping holes that opened out onto the sea—and our own slowly ripening odor, which seemed to grow more pungent by the day. We complained about Kazuko's aloofness, Chiyo's throat clearing, Fusayo's incessant humming of the "Teapicker's Song," which was driving us all slowly crazy. We complained about our disappearing hairpins—who among us was the thief?—and how the girls from first class had never once said hello from beneath their violet silk parasols in all the times they had walked past us up above on the deck. *Just who do they think they are?* We complained about the heat. The cold. The scratchy wool blankets. We complained about our own complaining. Deep down, though, most of us were really very happy, for soon we would be in America with our new husbands, who had written to us many times over the months. *I have bought a beautiful house. You can plant tulips in the garden. Daffodils. Whatever you like. I own a farm. I operate a hotel. I am the president of a large bank. I left Japan several years ago to start my own business and can provide for you well. I am 179 centimeters tall and do not suffer from leprosy or lung disease and there is no history of madness in my family. I am a native of Okayama. Of Hyogo. Of Miyagi. Of Shizuoka. I grew up in the village next to yours and saw you once years ago at a fair. I will send you the money for your passage as soon as I can.*

On the boat we carried our husbands' pictures in tiny oval lockets that hung on long chains from our necks. We carried them in silk purses and old tea tins and red lacquer boxes and in the thick brown envelopes from America in which they had originally been sent. We carried them in the sleeves of our kimonos, which we touched often, just to make sure they were still there. We carried them pressed flat between the pages of *Come, Japanese!* and *Guidance for Going to America* and *Ten Ways to Please a Man* and old, well-worn volumes of the Buddhist sutras, and one of us, who was Christian, and ate meat, and prayed to a different and longer-haired god, carried hers between the pages of a King James Bible. And when we asked her which man she liked better—the man in the photograph or the Lord Jesus Himself—she smiled mysteriously and replied, "Him, of course."

• • •

Several of us on the boat had secrets, which we swore we would keep from our husbands for the rest of our lives. Perhaps the real reason we were sailing to America was to track down a long-lost father who had left the family years before. *He went to Wyoming to work in the coal mines and we never heard from him again.* Or perhaps we were leaving behind a young daughter who had been born to a man whose face we could now barely recall—a traveling storyteller who had spent a week in the village, or a wandering Buddhist priest who had stopped by the house late one night on his way to Mt. Fuji. And even though we knew our parents would care for her well—*If you stay here in the village,* they had warned us, *you will never marry at all*—we still felt guilty for having chosen our own life over hers, and on the boat we wept for her every night for many nights in a row and then one morning we woke up and dried our eyes and said, "That's enough," and began to think of other things. Which kimono to wear when we landed. How to fix our hair. What to say when we first saw him. Because we were on the boat now, the past was behind us, and there was no going back.

On the boat we had no idea we would dream of our daughter every night until the day that we died, and that in our dreams she would always be three and as she was when we last saw her: a tiny figure in a dark red kimono squatting at the edge of a puddle, utterly entranced by the sight of a dead floating bee.

On the boat we ate the same food every day and every day we breathed the same stale air. We sang the same songs and laughed at the same jokes and in the morning, when the weather was mild, we climbed up out of the cramped quarters of the hold and strolled the deck in our wooden sandals and light summer kimonos, stopping, every now and then, to gaze out at the same endless blue sea. Sometimes a flying fish would land at our feet, flopping and out of breath, and one of us—usually it was one of the fishermen's daughters—would pick it up and toss it back into the water. Or a school of dolphins would appear out of nowhere and leap alongside the boat for hours. One calm, windless morning when the sea was flat as glass and the sky a brilliant shade of blue, the smooth black flank of a whale suddenly rose up out of the water and then disappeared and for a moment we forgot to breathe. *It was like looking into the eye of the Buddha.*

On the boat we often stood on the deck for hours with the wind in our hair, watching the other passengers go by. We saw turbaned Sikhs from the Punjab who were fleeing to Panama from their native land. We saw wealthy White Russians who were fleeing the revolution. We saw Chinese laborers from Hong Kong who were going to work in the cotton fields of Peru. We saw King Lee Uwanowich and his famous band of gypsies, who owned a large cattle ranch in Mexico and were rumored to be the richest band of gypsies in the world. We saw a trio of sunburned German tourists and a handsome Spanish priest and a tall, ruddy Englishman named Charles, who appeared at the railing every afternoon at quarter past three and walked several brisk lengths of the deck. Charles was traveling in first class, and had dark green eyes and a sharp, pointy nose, and spoke perfect Japanese, and was the first white person many of us had ever seen. He was a professor of foreign languages at the university in Osaka, and had a Japanese wife, and a child, and had been to America many times, and was endlessly patient with our questions. Was it true that Americans had a strong animal odor? (Charles laughed and said, "Well, do *I?*" and let us lean in close for a sniff.) And just how hairy *were* they? ("About as hairy as I am," Charles replied, and then he rolled up his sleeves to show us his arms, which were covered with dark brown hairs that made us shiver.) And did they really grow hair on their chests? (Charles blushed and said he could not show us his chest, and we blushed and explained that we had not asked him to.) And were there still savage tribes of Red Indians wandering all over the prairies? (Charles told us that all the Red Indians had been taken away, and we breathed a sigh of relief.) And was it true that the women in America did not have to kneel down before their husbands or cover their mouths when they laughed? (Charles stared at a passing ship on the horizon and then sighed and said, "Sadly, yes.") And did the men and women there really dance cheek to cheek all night long? (Only on Saturdays, Charles explained.) And were the dance steps very difficult? (Charles said they were easy, and gave us a moonlit lesson on the fox-trot the following evening on the deck. *Slow, slow, quick, quick.*) And was downtown San Francisco truly bigger than the Ginza? (Why, of course.) And were the houses in America really three times the size of our own? (Indeed they were.) And did each house have a piano in the front parlor? (Charles said it was more like every other house.) And did he think we would be happy there? (Charles took off his glasses and looked down at us with his lovely green eyes and said, "Oh yes, very.")

Some of us on the boat could not resist becoming friendly with the deckhands, who came from the same villages as we did, and knew all the words to our songs, and were constantly asking us to marry them. We already *are* married, we would explain, but a few of us fell in love with them anyway. And when they asked if they could see us alone—that very same evening, say, on the tween deck, at quarter past ten—we stared down at our feet for a moment and then took a deep breath and said, "Yes," and this was another thing we would never tell our husbands. *It was the way he looked at me,* we would think to ourselves later. Or, *he had a nice smile.*

One of us on the boat became pregnant but did not know it, and when the baby was born nine months later the first thing she would notice was how much it resembled her new husband. *He's got your eyes.* One of us jumped overboard after spending the night with a sailor and left behind a short note on her pillow: *After him, there can be no other.* Another of us fell in love with a returning Methodist missionary she had met on the deck, and even though he begged her to leave her husband for him when they got to America she told him that she could not. "I must remain true to my fate," she said to him. But for the rest of her life she would wonder about the life that could have been.

Some of us on the boat were brooders by nature, and preferred to stay to ourselves, and spent most of the voyage lying facedown in our berths, thinking of all the men we had left behind. The fruit seller's son, who always pretended not to notice us but gave us an extra tangerine whenever his mother was not minding the store. Or the married man for whom we had once waited, on a bridge, in the rain, late at night, for two hours. And for what? A kiss and a promise. "I'll come again tomorrow," he'd said. And even though we never saw him again we knew we would do it all over in an instant, because being with him was like being alive for the very first time, only better. And often, as we were falling asleep, we found ourselves thinking of the peasant boy we had talked to every afternoon on our way home from school—the beautiful young boy in the next village whose hands could coax up even the most stubborn of seedlings from the soil—and how our mother, who knew everything and could often read our mind, had looked at us as though we were crazy. *Do you want to spend the rest of your life crouched over a field?* (We had hesitated, and almost said yes, for hadn't we always dreamed of becoming our mother? Wasn't that all we had ever once wanted to be?)

On the boat we each had to make choices. Where to sleep and who to trust and who to befriend and how to befriend her. Whether or not to say something to the neighbor who snored, or talked in her sleep, or to the neighbor whose feet smelled even worse than our own, and whose dirty clothes were strewn all over the floor. And if somebody asked us if she looked good when she wore her hair in a certain way—in the "eaves" style, say, which seemed to be taking the boat by storm—and she did not, it made her head look too big, did we tell her the truth, or did we tell her she had never looked better? And was it all right to complain about the cook, who came from China, and only knew how to make one dish—rice curry—which he served to us day after day? But if we said something and he was sent back to China, where on many days you might not get any kind of rice at all, would it then be our fault? And was anybody listening to us anyway? Did anybody care?

Somewhere on the boat there was a captain, from whose cabin a beautiful young girl was said to emerge every morning at dawn. And of course we were all dying to know: Was she one of us, or one of the girls from first class?

On the boat we sometimes crept into each other's berths late at night and lay quietly side by side, talking about all the things we remembered from home: the smell of roasted sweet potatoes in early autumn, picnics in the bamboo grove, playing shadows and demons in the crumbling temple courtyard, the day our father went out to fetch a bucket of water from the well and did not return, and how our mother never mentioned him even once after that. *It was as though he never even existed. I stared down into that well for years.* We discussed favorite face creams, the benefits of leaden powder, the first time we saw our husband's photograph, what that was like. *He looked like an earnest person, so I figured he was good enough for me.* Sometimes we found ourselves saying things we had never said to anyone, and once we got started it was impossible to stop, and sometimes we grew suddenly silent and lay tangled in each other's arms until dawn, when one of us would pull away from the other and ask, "But will it last?" And that was another choice we had to make. If we said yes, it would last, and went back to her—if not that night, then the next, or the night after that—then we told ourselves that whatever we did would be forgotten the minute we got off the boat. And it was all good practice for our husbands anyway.

A few of us on the boat never did get used to being with a man, and if there had been a way of going to America without marrying one, we would have figured it out.

On the boat we could not have known that when we first saw our husbands we would have no idea who they were. That the crowd of men in knit caps and shabby black coats waiting for us down below on the dock would bear no resemblance to the handsome young men in the photographs. That the photographs we had been sent were twenty years old. That the letters we had been written had been written to us by people other than our husbands, professional people with beautiful handwriting whose job it was to tell lies and win hearts. That when we first heard our names being called out across the water one of us would cover her eyes and turn away—*I want to go home*—but the rest of us would lower our heads and smooth down the skirts of our kimonos and walk down the gangplank and step out into the still warm day. *This is America,* we would say to ourselves, *there is no need to worry.* And we would be wrong.

L'AMOUR, CA

Lysley Tenorio

M Y SISTER, ISA, speaks English and Tagalog. But one word, she could say in many languages: *koigokoro, beminnen, mahal, amor.* "It's the most important thing," she used to say, "the only thing. L-O-V-E. *Love.*" So when we learned that we would be moving to California, to a city called L'amour, she called it home, the place where we were always meant to be. I believed her.

This was January of 1974, our final days in the Philippines. Isa was sixteen, I was eight, and we were from San Quinez, a small southern village surrounded by sugarcane fields and cassava groves, with a single paved road winding through. Every house was like ours, made of bamboo and nipa and built on stilts, and every neighbor was somehow family. No one was a stranger where we lived.

Like many Filipino men at the time, my father joined the U.S. Navy, and after he had served in Korea and Vietnam, his request for a transfer to America was finally granted. "Our plan from the very beginning," my father said. My mother stayed silent, rubbing the leaf of a houseplant between her fingers until it ripped. My brother, Darwin, who was twelve, said he didn't care one way or another. But Isa started packing that same day. "L'amour, L'amour," she went on, like it was the name of a special friend she had that others never would. Friends and neighbors called her haughty and boastful; our oldest cousin called her an immigrant bitch. "*American* bitch," Isa corrected her, and called our cousin a village peasant who would never know a bigger world. "You're stuck here forever." As though no place was worse than the one you were from.

This is us on the plane, the day we leave: across the aisle my mother stares ahead, barely blinking, never speaking, and my father rifles through papers, rereading each document as though he can't figure out its meaning. Darwin sleeps next to me, so deeply that I double-check the rise and fall of his chest to make sure he isn't dead. On the other side of me is Isa, and only when she looks at me do I realize I'm crying. She unbuckles my seat belt and lets me sit on her lap, promises me that I'll be fine in L'amour.

We land in San Francisco but we keep moving: as soon as we claim our boxes and bags, we board a shuttle van and head south on the freeway, turn east hours later. I'm lying down for most of the ride, my head on Isa's lap, feeling our speed. We never traveled so quickly or smoothly on the dirt roads back home; I could almost sleep. But suddenly we're slowing, and the driver yawns, "Almost there." Isa looks confused, then panicked, and when I sit up all I see are endless fields of gray stalks, the miles of freeway we leave behind, and, up ahead, we seem to be driving into a cloud. "Fog again," the driver says, and down the road, a sign becomes clearer. WELCOME TO LEMOORE, CA, it says, ENJOY YOUR STAY!

They sound the same—L'amour, Lemoore—but I know they're not. "Lemoore." I tug at Isa's sleeve. "What's that mean?" She doesn't answer.

We exit the freeway, turn into the Lemoore Naval Air Station. We drive through foggy streets to a section of military housing, passing rows of gray and concrete rectangular houses with low, flat roofs, then down a street that ends in a cul-de-sac. "That's ours," my father says, and we pull up to a house with a faintly lit doorway, newspaper-covered windows, a grassless yard. We step out, unload our cargo, drag boxes up the driveway to the front door. Most things are too heavy for me to lift, so I stand by the van to guard our belongings. Across the street, a balding blond man mows his dry, yellow lawn. Two houses over, a lady with a shirt that says RENO! soaps her car, sprays it down, soaps it again.

Then I see a family sitting in folding lawn chairs in a line along the sidewalk, their faces toward the sky. I have never had to *meet* a person before—back home, everyone knew everyone—and now is the time for someone to say *Welcome* or *How are you?* But by the end of the day no one says hello, not even us.

I hate my house. Too many walls make too many rooms, the hallway is long and dark as a tunnel. Nothing scared me back home, and I always knew where we were: you could hear a person breathe in the next room, and the floor shook when someone ascended the bamboo stairs. Now, brownish-orange carpet mutes our footsteps; I never know when a person is coming or going, who's here and who's gone.

And even our bedroom doors have locks, which we never had before. But my mother fears someone could enter the house through our bedroom windows while she's alone and cooking in the kitchen, so she makes my father reverse the bedroom doorknobs; that way, she can prevent anyone who tries to break in through our rooms from entering the rest of the house. "But I want my lock *inside* my room," Isa says, and when my father asks why, she says, "Privacy."

"And what would you be doing in there," my father says, "that you need to lock us out?" Before Isa can answer, he is kneeling on the floor, unscrewing the knob.

Strangers come each day with heavy cardboard boxes on dollies—a refrigerator one morning, a kitchen table the next. When my father breaks down the box for our new oven, I drag it to the garage and build it again, turn it on its side, and wedge it between the washing machine and the wall. I crawl in, close the flaps. I fit perfectly. Minutes pass and I decide that I'm hiding, so I wait to be found, for someone to call out, *Where are you? Where did he go?* But no one searches, even as the afternoon fades and the garage darkens.

Then someone comes. It's Isa. She has a suitcase in each hand, like she's running away. But they're empty, and she drops them to the ground like trash, pushes them against the wall with her foot. Then she paces from one end of the garage to the other, never seeing me, and stops at the driver's side window of our new blue Impala. She stares at her reflection and sighs, then rests her forehead against the glass, clasps her hands together below her chin.

When I pray, I pray for us: my parents, Isa, Darwin, and me. Who knows what my sister prays for? When she's finished, she writes something on the window with her finger, looks it over, and hurries back inside. I wait two seconds so I won't be seen, crawl out of the box, and run to the car window, expecting a message from Isa. But all I see is her name, in fancy cursive letters, underlined twice.

I write my name over hers. I do it again and again, until all the dust is gone. Then I crawl back into my box, thinking how funny that Isa never knew I was here, that I still am.

Finally, we start school. The morning of our first day, Darwin and I are sitting at the kitchen table, eating instant champorado from a packet, a thing I've always hated: rice boiled in chocolate has never made sense to me, and when I say, "We should have left this back there," Darwin socks me in the arm, tells me to not say things like that in front of our mother. I'm about to jab him in the head with my spoon when suddenly Isa appears in the kitchen, and the sight of her dazzles me: her eyelids are as blue as our toothpaste, her cheeks so pink I think rose petals have melted into her skin. I want to tell her, *You are beautiful!* and I'm about to, but Darwin says, "You look like a hooker," and when my mother turns from the sink and looks at Isa, I know that trouble is ahead.

She puts her hand on Isa's cheek, wipes off makeup, then rubs it between her fingers as if it were a strange kind of dust. "It's my first day," Isa says, but my mother takes her apron to Isa's face.

"What will people say about you, when they see you like this? Would you do this back home?" She asks more questions, tells Isa that just because we're in Lemoore doesn't mean she can look like any girl on the street, and she's wiping makeup from Isa's face the whole time, until nothing is left. When my mother is done, she steps backward, leans against the sink. "Go to school," she tells us. She doesn't walk us to the door. She doesn't say goodbye.

We walk out of the house, down the driveway, and out of the cul-de-sac. The sun fades as the fog ahead thickens, and our windbreakers don't keep us warm. "Walk faster," Darwin says, blowing on his hands and rubbing them together. We lose him a block later—his school is in another direction—and when he leaves, he just shrugs and says bye, his teeth still chattering. Isa and I go on, holding hands even more tightly now.

Kids crowd the front steps of my school. Isa leads us through the building, down a hallway to my classroom. The door is barely open. We go in. We find rows of empty desks, blank chalkboards, and no teacher in sight. "Maybe we shouldn't be here."

"No," Isa says, double-checking the room number, "this is right." She bends down to fix my collar, promises that everything about this day will be fine, then looks at the clock above the chalkboard beside the American flag. I look too, thinking about the sixteen-hour difference between Lemoore and San Quinez, how here it's today and there it's tomorrow, but the arms of the clock don't move, not at all. I don't know how to tell time, but I understand that Isa is late and not ready for today. Her windbreaker looks like a plastic trash bag on her body, her face is smeary and gray.

The bell rings. Isa leaves. Kids come running in and around me to their desks, and finally the teacher appears with a stickpin between her fingers. "Wear this," she tells me, pinning a name tag shaped like an apple onto my shirt, then leads me to the front of the class. She stands behind me with her hands tight on my shoulders, telling everyone how far I have traveled, and how lucky we are to be together. Then I tell them what my father told us all to say on our first day: "I am very happy to be here." Two girls giggle and won't stop, and when the teacher asks what's so funny, one says that I said *bery* instead of *very*. So I repeat myself, and now I hear it too. *Bery. Bery.* Back home, my English was perfect; here, I can't get it right. I don't speak the rest of the day.

After school, I watch a janitor sweep the hallway while I wait for Isa outside my classroom. When she arrives, she says nothing, doesn't even ask me how I am, or how my day has been. "Let's go home" is all she says, then turns, exits the school. She stays ahead of me the entire way, her legs so long and fast that I can't keep up, and when I almost do, I catch glimpses of her face, her teary forward stare. *Why do you cry, Isa?* I want to ask. *Did they laugh at you, too?* But before I can get a question out, I fall behind again. Half a block separates us by the time we reach our street, and when I'm finally home, Isa is already in her room, door closed and the radio blaring. In the living room, Darwin is lying on the floor in front of the TV, and in the kitchen my mother is staring at a boiling pot, her arms folded over her chest. When I tell them I'm home, they barely nod. So I go back to the garage and crawl into the box, practicing the word *very* over and over until evening, and time for us to eat.

The next day is not much different. All through class I'm silent, and I spend recess lining up pebbles along the bottom of the playground fence. What saves me from tears is knowing that the school day will end, and that Isa will come for me.

Some better days are ahead. Like those afternoons when Isa picks me up wearing school-spirit chains around her neck, or the time she wandered into a picture on the front page of the school newspaper. Once, I even catch her writing *Isa, Class of '75* on the palm of her hand, as if she has always been and will always be a part of it. But when school is over, the autograph pages in her yearbook are empty and white. No one wished her a happy summer, or good luck for the following year. And though her name is listed in the index, my sister is nowhere in the entire book.

Early June. Summer vacation, and the days drag. Isa is always lying on her bed listening to the radio, and the thump of Darwin's basketball is like the ticking of a slow-moving clock. I spend my time by the living room window, watching kids bicycle and roller-skate by, chasing each other down with water pistols. Once, two kids walking a wolf-faced dog stop in front of our house, and just as I'm about to wave, they shout, *"Vietnamese people eat dogs!"* so I yell back, *"We're not Vietnamese people!"* then shut the window and draw the curtains.

Then something happens: one night at dinner, Isa announces that she's been hired as a cashier at Lanes, the diner inside the Naval Station bowling alley. "It's summertime," she says, "maybe I should work." My mother says no, but my father says (quietly, like he's embarrassed), "We need the money," and he allows Isa to take the job on one condition: Darwin and I must accompany her each day, and stay with her until my father comes for us in the evening. "A girl shouldn't be out there alone," he says. But Isa insists she'll be fine on her own, that nothing is dangerous in Lemoore. "Please let me have this," she says. When no one answers, she goes to the window above the sink, slides it open. "Tell me what's out there. Tell me what to be afraid of." She looks like she might cry.

My father tells Isa to take her seat and finish her dinner. Isa sits, arms folded across her chest. I put my hand on Isa's to comfort her, but now I'm wondering: When did she go to the bowling alley? Did she tell me she was leaving, but somehow I forgot?

"Let *go,*" Isa says to me.

The morning Isa starts her job, I find her in the bathroom, try-ing on her uniform, a mustard-colored bowling shirt with matching slacks, and orange shoes that fail to give her the height she'd hoped for. She checks herself in the mirror, moving her shoulders forward, then back, shifting her waist to the right, to the left. "What do you think," she asks me. "Do I look like Cheryl Tiegs?"

"You look like Nora Aunor." Darwin laughs, walking by the bathroom. "You look like Vilma Santos." He goes on with a list of the corniest Filipina actresses, and Isa gets so mad she douses him with a Dixie cup full of bright blue toilet water. "Immigrant bitch!" he shouts.

"*American* bitch," I correct him.

Isa bends down, puts her hand on my cheek, and says, "I love you."

After breakfast, my father drops us off at the bowling alley. Before Isa can get out of the car, he grabs hold of her wrist. "This is a good opportunity for you," he tells her, "so work hard, and be good. And you two"—he looks at Darwin and me—"watch your sister." But as soon as my father drives off, three boys approach on bikes, and Darwin high-fives each one. They're friends from his school and he goes off with them, tells us he'll be back when my father picks us up in the afternoon. "Have fun being bored," he says. Every day after, he leaves us.

So from the beginning, I am the watcher of Isa and this is what I do: each morning when we arrive, I take a corner booth and watch her ring up meals and wipe tabletops and counters, all day long. I know she wishes I weren't there, so I stay quiet and still as I can, but after a week, I'm a problem. "He's here again," Isa's boss says. "Why is he always here?" Isa moves her arm in fast circles as she wipes off a nearby table, as if she is trying to come up with a story for me. I give her one. "Our mother is dead!" I shout this out to make sure Isa's boss hears me. "No one is home to take care of me!" Isa looks up. I try winking at her but instead I blink, and suddenly tears I didn't plan come streaming.

"I'm sorry," he says, patting Isa on the shoulder. "Sorry." That day, he tells Isa to keep all the money in the tip jar, and says I can eat all the corn dogs and Eskimo Pies I want.

We never talk about the lie. Once it's out, I can't take it back. And why should I? My mother takes good care of us—food is always on the table, our clothes are always clean—but the rest of the time she's sitting in her room, reading and rereading letters that make her weep. When we come home, she never asks how we are, or how we've been, and when I ask about her day, she just says, "You were gone. I was alone."

It's better here with Isa. She smiles for me at least, like when she spells my name in ketchup over a basket of fries, or when old ladies call her "dear" and remark on her beauty and good English. One day Isa tells a customer, "Thank you for coming to Lanes," and she sounds so pleased and finally fulfilled with our life in Lemoore that I need to hear it again. So I run out into the bowling alley to the pay phone by the bathroom, drop a dime, and call the diner.

Isa picks up. "Thank you for calling Lanes," she says.

I whisper, "It's me." I can see her but she can't see me, even as I wave. "It's me," I say again.

"Who?"

We have never spoken on the phone before—we have never been apart—and now I sound like a stranger. "Hello?" she says, turning side to side, as though the person on the other end is somehow with her in the room.

Before she asks who I am again, I hang up and go back, running.

Bowling-alley days get longer, I keep watching Isa, and nothing happens. So, little by little, I start to leave. At first I stick close by the diner door, watching off-duty sailors bowl, and I cheer their strikes and laugh at their gutter balls. Then I walk my fingers along the racks of bowling balls, looking for ones I can lift. I start to go farther: without coins I go to the arcade and pretend to play pinball, or finish abandoned games of air hockey. I like to push buttons and pull knobs on the vending machines, hoping that gum or a bag of chips will fall for free, and one day a roll of Life Savers actually does. I snatch it, look around to check if anyone saw, then run back to the diner to tell Isa about my incredible luck and share my candy with her. But when I get to the diner, Isa isn't at the register or standing behind the counter. Instead, she's in a booth by the jukebox, sitting across from someone, a boy her age with long white arms full of freckles and the reddest hair I have ever seen. I press my hands and face against the glass door. I watch. They're just talking, that's all, but he's holding a cigarette, and when he reaches to move a strand of hair from Isa's face, she flinches, just a little. He keeps his hand there, even as the cigarette burns. I haven't seen anyone touch my sister's face since my mother, months before, the morning we started school.

His name is Malcolm and he's always here. He bowls all morning in the very last lane, then visits Isa at noon, stays until we have to leave. He never brings flowers and they never kiss, but, once, they disappear. Returning from the arcade, I find a note taped to the cash register that says BACK IN TEN MINUTES. But I don't know how long ten minutes is, and despite the clock above the jukebox I still don't know how to tell time. So I go running out of the diner, to the arcade, the women's bathroom, then the diner again, and when there is still no sign of Isa, I run out into the parking lot, up and down the rows of cars. The daylight is so bright I can barely see, and every direction I go is wrong. But finally I find her, sitting on the rear bumper of a sky-blue van, right next to Malcolm. A cigarette burns between her fingers.

I point at her to make her understand: *You were gone! I couldn't find you!* but I'm crying too hard and can't catch my breath. She takes my hand and pulls me close, kisses my cheeks, my nose, the top of my head. "Watch," she says. She takes the cigarette to her lips, closes her eyes like she's gathering courage, and exhales a wave of smoke. "See?" She opens her eyes. I breathe her smoke through my nose, and when it makes me sneeze, Isa starts laughing, Malcolm too, and now so do I. "More," I say, and now Isa is making smoke rings, a thing I've never seen, and I try to break them with my finger before they float away and vanish.

Who knew a person could form circles from smoke? Or cry and laugh at the same time? This is a day of learning new things: I look at Isa looking at me, and I think we are amazing.

Later, when my father picks us up, I tell him, "Nothing happened today," then get into the backseat with Isa, put my head on her lap. I watch her staring out the window, and when she looks down at me, she smiles and sighs, like her longing has ended, and we have finally arrived in the place we were meant to be.

Middle of August. Eight months in America, and Isa will be seventeen. The year before, the whole village celebrated her birthday, and in her white, floor-length dress, Isa looked like a bride. This year, we celebrate at the new Pizza Hut on base, and give small gifts: she gets pink fuzzy slippers from my parents, nothing from Darwin, and an egg-carton caterpillar I made in school, from me. "Next year you'll get more," my father says, and as I'm about to sing "Happy Birthday," my mother shushes me. "People will stare at us," she says. When I try again, Isa takes my hand. "You'll sing to me later," she says. But I never do.

The one who makes her birthday matter is Malcolm. The next day at the diner, he tells Isa he wants to take her out for her birthday, someplace far away from here. "Hanford," he says, "maybe Fresno. Anywhere but Lemoore." He takes the saltshaker and taps grains onto the table. "Goddamn Lemoore."

Isa puts her hand on his wrist, right in front of me. "But Lemoore means love," she says. "In French." Then she says "love" all the other ways she knows—*koigokoro, beminnen, mahal*—and Malcolm lights a cigarette, nodding with every word.

That night at dinner, Isa says her boss needs her for a Friday-night late shift and will pay her double, maybe triple, even drive her home afterward. She says the late shift might lead to a promotion, maybe a raise, but my mother says no. "A girl out at night," she says, doom and threat in her voice.

"Then I'll be with her," I say. I tell my parents how much Isa's boss adores me, how I remind him of his son. "But that boy died. A car crash," I say. "He was crossing the street. A van came…" The story is even better than we rehearsed it, and as I lie I'm picturing Isa in a car at night with the window rolled down, her ponytail like a ribbon in the wind, singing to any song the radio plays, and finally, because a dead child fills them with pity, my parents tell us yes, we can go, just this once. "Thank you," Isa says to them, but she's really thanking me. Beneath the table I squeeze her hand to tell her, *You're welcome.*

Everything is perfect. Darwin has come down with a fever and won't be coming with us. My mother still refuses to leave the house at night, and insists my father stay with her. "We'll be okay," I tell my parents throughout the day. "We take care of each other." They believe whatever I say.

Just before dark, my father drives us to the bowling alley. Before we get out, he makes us kiss him goodbye on the cheek, which we've never done the other times he drops us off. He drives away, and I imagine myself in his rearview mirror, shrinking and shrinking as he travels down the road. I'm still waving even after he's gone.

Isa hurries inside to change in the bathroom. I stay where I am. Then, as if he'd been watching, Malcolm pulls up in his van. He doesn't say hello, doesn't invite me in. He just sits there smoking a cigarette, then flicks it out the passenger window. I watch it glowing on the ground until Isa steps out and takes my hand.

"Let's get him home," Malcolm says. He reaches over and opens the passenger door. The backseat is crammed with boxes and crates, album sleeves, parts of a bike, so I sit in front on Isa's lap. She goes over the plan once more, making sure I remember every step. Her arms are wrapped around my chest and I lean back, my head resting against her shoulder. She's shivering and her knee bounces a little, like a mother trying to calm the wailing baby in her arms. "I'll be fine," I whisper, and Isa says, "I know."

Off we go. Malcolm takes a different route home, and every turn becomes a street I don't know. When we finally reach the end of our block, the fog is so thick I almost don't recognize that this is where we live.

Malcolm pulls over. Isa and I step out. "Count eleven houses," she says, pointing toward home, "and you'll be there." She pulls my hood over my head, tugs at the drawstrings, and as she knots them together she tells me to be brave, though she is the one who cries. Then she tells me that she loves me, and that's the most important thing, the only thing.

She kisses my cheek then steps back, climbs into the van. I let them leave first, watching the red taillights of Malcolm's van until they disappear into the fog, and that's when I see it, for the very first time: my breath in the air. It floats before my eyes like a tiny ghost, and I stand perfectly still, marveling at the fact that I possess the power to project something from deep inside me into the night air. I breathe again, watching my breath and remembering the smoke rings Isa made, and I think we are exactly the same.

I start toward home, counting off houses. I walk up someone's driveway, and though the garage is padlocked shut, I tug at the handle anyway, as though it might open. Then I run a zigzag line from house to house, breathing hard so my breath floats in the air again, and no one ever sees me. I've never been outside by myself like this, so late at night in Lemoore. I'm so brave that I even walk in the middle of the street and shout, just once, "*Hello!*"

I stop at the bottom of our driveway. The living room window glows blue and I move toward it slowly, staying low. I stick close to the wall, peeking in. Darwin is on the floor, wrapped in a blanket, my father dozes on his recliner, my mother leans against the doorway of the kitchen. Even as I move to the center of the window, they still think I'm gone.

My breath fogs the glass. It's cold. I leave my family and hurry over to the side of the garage, find the key and flashlight we hid behind the trash cans, and let myself in, make my way quietly and slowly to my box. I crawl inside. In the corner is a pack of crayons and two foil-wrapped corn dogs from Lanes, a thermos of juice, and the roll of Life Savers that fell for free. Next to it is Isa's watch. She'll be home by 2 A.M., when she'll come into the garage, get me from the box, and together we will enter the house, as if we were never apart. I look at the watch. I see the 2, but I don't know how long I'll have to wait. I don't even know the time now.

I stand the flashlight on its end. The whole box glows. I take a red crayon to draw a picture of Isa's night out, but I'm not sure what's beyond Lemoore, maybe lit-up cities with high-rising buildings, strangers who wave and say *Welcome,* and tell you their names. So, instead of Isa's story, I start drawing ours instead: with blue crayon I make a circle for our cul-de-sac, and inside it I draw five people in a row, tallest to shortest. Then I surround the circle with stars, and I decide our cul-de-sac is the whole world itself, our bodies so big we fill it, as if we are everywhere at once.

There is a line of morning light beneath the garage door when I open my eyes, just enough to help me find my way into the house.

Isa didn't wake me. Maybe she forgot. I go to her bedroom door. I whisper her name and wait for her to whisper mine, so we both know we're here. But there's only silence, and the outside knob is still locked, so I unlock it and step inside. Her bed is still made.

She's not hiding in the closet or under the bed. She's not in the living room, or the kitchen, or the bathroom, and now I'm thinking that I've messed up, that she's on her way home, and I came back too soon. Everyone still sleeps, and I don't know what to do. I climb on top of her bed, wait for her all over again.

I wake the second time to shouting and panic, to my father's face in mine. My mother is behind him, and Darwin is in the hallway, shivering with fever. "What happened last night? What have you done?" My father is shaking me, harder and harder. "Where is your sister?" But I have nothing to tell. All I prepared for was Isa's return, so I wait for it, refusing to speak, even if he hits me.

The answers come, later that night, when Isa calls from a pay phone in a place she won't name, to tell us she's not coming back, that she's sorry but happier this way, that she is with Malcolm and she is in love. I'm listening to this on the telephone in my parents' room, my hand cupped over the receiver so they won't know I'm here.

Isa is gone, and now the house feels too small. No matter where I go, I can hear my parents fight, shouting things I shouldn't know—that my mother never wanted to leave, that my father wishes he was alone in America, free of the worries we cause. *"Our plan,"* she says one night. "Is this what we planned for?" My father doesn't answer. He just stands there, jangling his car keys in his pocket, as if he could leave at any moment.

Darwin never mentions Isa, but once I catch him bouncing his basketball outside Isa's window, staring in. When he sees me, he pops me with the ball so hard that I fall backward to the ground. He walks off, and when I breathe, I hurt.

Isa doesn't call again. We go for help, but the Navy can do nothing. Neither can the police. She's gone, not missing, is what they tell us. I don't know the difference.

We do what we can. One morning, my mother and I go door-to-door through the neighborhood looking for her, but she makes me do the talking. "Did you see my sister?" I'll ask a neighbor, then hold up a picture of Isa on her sixteenth birthday. Sometimes I catch my mother peering into their living rooms, her head turning slowly from side to side, like she is trying to learn how other people live. No one has seen Isa, but we go house to house with her picture the next day and the day after, and people start to know who we are.

My father searches at night. Once, he lets me go with him. I sit in the back, kneeling on the seat with my chin on the headrest, looking out the rear window. We drive for what feels like hours, up and down the same streets over and over, until finally we are outside of town on a long, two-lane road. Suddenly he pulls to the side, and when I turn my father is leaning back, his hands still on the wheel. "I don't know where we are," he says to himself. But I do, only now the fog is gone, the gray stalks are sprouting corn, and behind us is a row of palm trees, almost as tall as the ones back home.

Sooner or later, we stop searching. I don't know when, I don't know why, but my parents decide that we must learn to live this way, and one night at dinner, I find only four settings on the table. "If she wants us, she'll call," my father says, scooping rice onto his plate. And, just like that, things go back to normal: my father sleeps early again to rest for the next day's work, my mother cooks and cleans, Darwin plays basketball and rides bikes with his friends. The busier we stay, the less my parents fight, the less Darwin bullies me, and soon, school begins again. I'm a third grader now, learning things all the time: that our final states are Alaska and Hawaii, that anything times zero equals zero. One morning I wake up and my mother tells me, "You're nine years old today."

Days feel fuller than they ever were, and after dinner, when everyone is tired and almost ready for bed, we gather in the living room, in front of the new TV. It's color but still secondhand, and one night half the picture comes in lines so wavy that they almost hurt my eyes. So I look away toward the window, remembering myself on the other side of the glass, the way I watched my family as they are now: nonmoving and silent, their faces blank and glowing blue from the TV screen. We couldn't be truly happy, but somehow everyone rests easy, as if the fact that we are four instead of five is simply a number, and not a tragedy. No one even cries, and I can't understand why.

I put my head on my knees, close my eyes. Somewhere, Isa is fine without us; here, we are fine without Isa. And this is the truth I don't want to know: that the ones who leave and the ones who get left keep living their lives, whatever the distance between. But not me. When I was outside in the night, I watched my family; I knew they were fine. When she thought she was alone, I watched Isa; I listened to her pray. For the rest of my life, I would be like this. It's the difference, I think, between all of them and me; even when I was gone, I was here.

In the last hours of the school day, during filmstrips about good hygiene, our forefathers, and California history, I daydream of Isa: she zooms down a highway edged with cornfields that become skyscrapers, her face framed in the passenger window of Malcolm's van. Wherever she goes, strangers bid her hello, and I think of her thinking of us: that we're stuck here forever, that we will never know a bigger world.

After school, walking home, I daydream again, always of reunion: I'm at the end of our block when I see her, standing at the bottom of the driveway. At first she can't see me in the fog, but then I emerge from it, and now I'm running to her and she's running to me.

It never happens this way.

In December, on the last day of school before winter vacation, I've just walked in the door when my father calls out from the kitchen. "Come here," he says, and before I can ask why he's home so early, I see Isa sitting in her chair at the table. Her eyes are pink from crying, her lips are pressed together like she's keeping a secret. "Hug your sister," my mother says, so I move closer to Isa, who stares at her lap and whispers "Sorry," over and over. Her face seems wider now, heavier, and one thick strand of hair crosses her forehead and trails down her shoulder to her elbow. I rub it between my fingers, wondering how long it took to grow, and I think I might understand the way time works: how its passing is impossible to see, but when it's gone, you feel it. "You should cut this," I say. Then I do as I'm told and embrace my sister, and that's when I see it: the dome of her belly, bigger than it was the last time we held each other.

This is Isa's story: Malcolm got her pregnant. He didn't want the baby, and then he didn't want her. He paid for a bus ticket from wherever they were to Lemoore, and sent Isa on her way. That's all she told my parents; I never knew more than that. "But you shamed us," my father tells her in a voice so soft he sounds like he's speaking to the dead. "You shamed yourself. And if he shows up at my door—"

"He won't," Isa says, and she's right: I never see Malcolm again and he never calls, but now a baby is inside my sister. I think of its curled-up and freckled body, and wonder what will happen when it's born. Do I feed it when it's hungry? Hold it when it cries? No one talks about it, prepares me for it. This baby is like being in America—a thing that just happens, a thing you learn to live with.

My mother is proof of this. One afternoon I'm lying on my bedroom floor staring at the ceiling when I hear her humming. I run to her room, find her laying out baby clothes, their tiny sleeves and pant legs splayed out like *X*'s across her bed. "You wore these once," she says, then holds the smallest shirt I have ever seen against my chest. "Now look. How big you are." She breathes deeply, sits on the edge of her bed, puts her fingers on my cheek.

"Isa left us," I tell her, in case she forgot.

I haven't hugged or kissed Isa since she's been back. Whole days pass and I won't even say hello. She is the same way, and she joins us only at the dinner table, where all she does is stare at some spot on the table or the wall. Once, her stare is so long and steady she barely blinks, barely breathes, and I get suspicious: maybe she misses wherever she was, and is planning to leave us again.

I slam my hand on the table to bring her back. The forks and spoons rattle on our plates.

"Are you brain-damaged?" Darwin says, and when he kicks me hard under the table, I don't even flinch.

Days before Christmas, at the start of each night, the neighborhood houses glow and blink with colored lights, but ours is dim and plain. "They don't have Christmas trees back home," my father says one morning. "Maybe we should get one?"

They shop for a tree that afternoon, and as they pull out of the driveway I go running to my father's window. "I'll watch Isa," I say. But he barely nods, like he knows I'll fail again.

After they leave, Darwin goes outside to shoot baskets, and I sit in the dark hallway, on the floor in front of Isa's open door. She hasn't felt well all day, so she lies on her bed, facing the wall. But we are alone in the house, just Isa and me, and now is the time for all my questions—where she was all those months and the things she did; if she dreamed of me as often as I dreamed of her; and did she plan, from the very beginning, to leave us, knowing that I would wait for her, inside a box?

"You were gone" is the first thing I say.

She nods her head.

"When you left, nobody talked to me. For a long time. Even though I was here." I stare at the carpet, dig my finger into it. "We drove at night to find you. We couldn't." Outside, Darwin's basketball thumps and thumps, and I dig my finger deeper and deeper. "I walk by myself now. All the way to school. All the way home." When Isa turns to face me, I realize I'm crying, but I keep going, telling her more she doesn't know about me: new words I've learned in school, the teeth I've lost, how now I'm nine years old and can finally say *very* the way you're supposed to, but despite all these facts I always end up saying the same thing: "You were gone."

"But I'm back," she says, trying to smile. "I'm here." She takes a deep breath, sits up, rubbing her sides like the baby takes up too much room inside her. Slowly, she gets to her feet, reaches into her dresser, and from beneath folded dresses she takes out a cigarette and a book of matches. She lights it, breathes deeply, and a ring of smoke floats toward me. "Remember how much you liked these? How they made you laugh?" She breathes and breathes, and more rings float my way, but I let them fade.

She doesn't give up. She takes the cigarette to her lips, takes a long, deep breath, but instead of smoke rings all that comes out is a cough. She tries once more but coughs again, like she's forgotten how to smoke. She stubs out the cigarette against the window screen, sets the butt on the sill, and now she hunches over, holding her belly as though it's suddenly heavier than it was before. "I don't feel right," she says, squinting with pain. She steps toward the bed, sits but misses the edge, falls to the floor. She looks funny and I almost laugh, but then I hear her say, "It hurts," and when she looks down between her legs, spots of blood are on her pink pajama bottoms. She puts her hand there, then looks at the blood on her fingers. "Something's wrong," she says. She tries to stand, but she hurts too much to move.

I get up, step into her room, reach for the box of tissues on her dresser and try handing it to her. But she pushes it away and asks for our mother, our father, then says she should get to a hospital, and now I think this baby will be born now, here. But I'm not ready. I don't want to be.

I pull out a tissue and lay it down by her hand. I tell her I'll get Darwin, that he will know what to do. "Just wait here, okay?" I close the door, tell her not to leave, and then, in case she tries to, I lock it.

I take a step back and listen to her shouting my name. Then the doorknob rattles, and I imagine what my mother feared: a stranger on the other side, trying to break in. "Just wait," I say again, then run to the end of the hallway. "I'll be back." Behind me, I can hear Isa's hand slapping softly against the door.

I head to the living room and walk out of the house. I go down the driveway past Darwin, who keeps bouncing his basketball against the garage door. "Where are you going?" he says, but I keep walking, even when he tells me to stay.

I continue down the sidewalk, count eleven houses. When I reach the end, I cross the street, and at the next house a lady is in the front window, holding a teacup in her hand. She sees me standing at the bottom of her driveway, but instead of drawing the curtain or looking away, she just waves, takes a sip of her drink. I don't wave back or even smile, but I nod to let her know I see her.

Then I turn back toward my street. Night is starting, but the air is warm, all the rooftops blink with colored lights, and Christmas trees full of ornaments and silvery tinsel light up every living room window. Soon, our house will be this way too.

This is what L'amour was meant to be. This is the place my sister called home. Finally, after a long, long year, we're here. And so I go back, walking first, then running fast, because I can't wait to ask her, *Isa, how are you? Isa, how have you been?*

HOME IS WHERE THE WART IS

Donna Miscolta

NATIONAL CITY, CA. Nickname: Nasty City. Notable place names within the city: El Toilet Park, Las Panties Pool, Stinkin' Acres.

My hometown is a wart on the map, a giant canker sore to the naked eye. Or so the purveyors of these nicknames would have you believe. And who are they, these tellers of tales, spreaders of potty-themed tags and obnoxious aliases?

Certainly there are those beyond the city limits, who hold their noses as they speed past on the freeway, south to the bars in Tijuana or north to the marinas of San Diego, who lock their car doors and slump in their seats if they happen to take the wrong exit and find themselves cruising among the homies. Later, safe in their own hood, they swagger with the boast that they have been to Nasty City and lived to tell about it.

But it's us too, those like me who once lived there and those who live there still who utter those nicknames with a reckless, nose-thumbing *sticks-and-stones* mentality.

And yet, who among us has not at one time or another answered the question *So where're you from?* with those two words that signal legitimacy: San Diego. Because who after all has heard of National City? And if they've heard of National City, what exactly have they heard?

But forget hearsay. Let's consider the facts.

HISTORY

Our house was on U Avenue, twenty-one alphabetically named blocks from the western edge of the city. A new development in the mid-sixties, the neighborhood was a repetitive alignment of look-alike homes: single-story, L-shaped, bumpy with stucco in dispassionate, middle-of-the-road tones—gray, beige, brown, an occasional watery yellow. Our house was the mirror image of our neighbors'. We could go in each other's homes and know exactly which drawer in the kitchen contained the knives and which the Saran Wrap, where to find the linen, where to pee.

Except for the cement slab of patio, our backyard remained a dusty, rocky rectangle. A drainage ditch ran the length of it. The far side of the ditch sloped upward and defied planting; even the ubiquitous ice plant with its persistent roots, the ecological nuisance of the region, failed to thrive there. On the near side of the ditch, my father sank the legs of a swing set into the sandy soil and we dug troughs with our toes as we swung, spinning dust into the air, into our hair, mouths and lungs.

My parents planted and did their best to nurture a lawn in the disobliging earth in the front yard of the first, last and only house they would ever own. My mother decorated the shallow-rooted grass with plastic and ceramic fauna—chipmunks, deer and the wholly non-indigenous flamingo—and a statue of St. Francis of Assisi with a pair of pigeons sculpted to him. I suppose they were more rightly considered doves, one on his shoulder, the other poetically on his wrist. Every so often, my mother took a sudsy rag to the whole thing to wipe off the shit left by real birds.

The fake deer in my mother's yard was a joke to us, hooved species having no context in our experience of National City. We didn't know that Spanish soldiers once used the land to graze their horses. The area then was called El Rancho del Rey, the king's ranch, to remind Mexico just who owned the land, never mind that the Spanish had driven off the original inhabitants, the Kumeyaay. After independence from Spain in 1821, Mexico renamed the land Rancho de la Nación, the nation's ranch. Look who owned the land now. Not for long though. In 1845 Governor Pio Pico, in a nepotistic gesture, granted Rancho de la Nación to his brother-in-law John Forster. The Andrew Johnson administration issued the land patent as *The National Ranch*. In 1868, the Kimball brothers, businessmen from New Hampshire, purchased the entire rancho. They called it National City.

When we moved in, the street past our driveway was unpaved. When it rained, gullies formed, the runoff silted the already muddy street, puddles dotted the terrain and we carved a motocross track with our bikes. Next to us was an empty lot that would one day be covered in asphalt for parking and below that a rocky ravine that was destined to be a ball field with a chronically broken scoreboard. Across the street was a block-wide expanse of naked dirt that became El Toyon Park, or more familiarly, El Toilet Park. After the bulldozers came to level the ground of ruts and berms, it was seeded with grass, and spindly young trees were rooted at sparse intervals. Tennis and basketball courts were installed and a cinderblock office with restrooms was plunked down.

Then the action started. Low-riders made their slow and stealthy crawl around the park, music vibrating tinted windows, seeping from beneath bouncing chassis. Deals were made, deals were botched, fists flew, maybe a bullet or two. Somebody's mother, often mine, called the cops.

EDUCATION

My father was a postal clerk, my mother a sales clerk. She had a high school diploma. My father's education stalled at eighth grade back in the Philippines during the Japanese occupation. Later, he earned his GED while I was skirmishing with the New Math in elementary school. My difficulty with set theory was excused. My parents wanted their daughters to learn to type, their son to go to college.

LANGUAGES

My father's constant declaration that we were American.
His reluctance to speak Tagalog with the neighbors.
My mother's limping, fractured Spanish.
My unaccented, monolingual speech.

CRIME

It wasn't long before my father had metal bars installed across all the windows, a chain-link fence erected around the property, and floodlights mounted at the front and back entrances.

Across the street the park office and bathrooms, having been thoroughly vandalized, were permanently locked. The tree nearby that had grown large, many-branched and invitingly shady was slashed with graffiti, clamorous hues and hostile cries affirming National City's standing as the county's perennial leader in violent crime.

ECONOMY

"In the center of it all," reads a city promotional flier. "National City is ten minutes from everywhere and positioned for prosperity." When I was growing up, I was deplorably unaware that I lived in the center of it all—that my city was so poised for richness, that one day it would boast the largest enclosed mall in the South Bay, that its row of car dealerships would extend a literal mile. That National City's Mile of Cars *could* be likened theoretically to New York's Museum Mile. Theoretically.

GEOGRAPHY

There's a bay somewhere. The names of the businesses suggest it exists: South Bay Plaza, The Bay Theater, Bay Vista College of Beauty. The Navy claimed most of the real estate along the water, keeping the bay at bay, making us believe we were landlocked.

DEMOGRAPHICS

At a high school reunion, I overheard a woman remark, "I never knew that I attended a poor school."

I was similarly fooled when it came to racial makeup.

For a long time I believed that I had attended a mostly white high school. All the teachers were white—even the Spanish teachers. I was placed in the "smart" classes, which happened to consist mostly of white students. As if smart was a color.

GOVERNMENT AND POLITICS

The mayor was white, the city council was white, the cops were white. More than half the population was brown.

One of my sisters dated a National City cop she met at her secretarial job at City Hall. It was the early 70s. A young, unarmed Chicano youth had been shot to death by a cop. There was going to be a march. I was planning to go. I watched them side by side on the family couch, my sister and her cop boyfriend, who did not believe in irony.

I dated a black wide-receiver at San Diego State. We spent our evenings playing chess. My mother had a sit-down talk with me. *Think about the children. How they'll look. What people will say.* I doubt she had the same talk with my sister.

RECREATION

Despite lessons and much recreational splashing in the Las Palmas (aka Las Panties) pool, we never quite learned how to swim. It was a congenital defect, born of my mother's fear of drowning. She and her sisters used to go to the beach in San Diego mainly to pose in their swimsuits. One day, though, they were actually in the water, where my mother ventured too far and was hauled away by a wave. A sailor saved her life along with her fear of the water.

Our fear was embryonic, transferred by our mother to the amniotic fluid that suspended us in utero, the last time we would so comfortably float.

ENTERTAINMENT AND PERFORMING ARTS

One summer we put on a play. My older sister, because she was the oldest and because the play was her idea, assumed the role of director. During rehearsals, she yelled "cut" and "action" with great authority. She chose me over Thelma, our next door neighbor and my sometimes best friend, for the lead role of King Midas. She chose me not because I was her sister, but because I could enunciate and project and emote better than Thelma could. But Thelma and her sisters thought otherwise, so they didn't take their supporting roles seriously and tittered their lines. I got to exclaim, "Gold! Silver! Precious jewels sparkling with light! They are mine! All mine!" I made each and every exclamation point count. Even though we were our only audience.

TRADITION

I was the only one among my sisters who didn't march on the high school drill team. Never wore white boots and gloves, never had a tiara glitter upon a hair-spray-stiffened updo, never learned a high-stepping arm-waving routine, never snapped my head smartly in unison with 49 other Devil-ettes dressed in identical red, silver-sequined uniforms topped by a cape. Never wore red lipstick to contain a constant, frozen smile.

I wasn't a marcher, couldn't stay in step, couldn't obey commands. So I watched from the sidelines of the Maytime Band Review, slouching with indifference, sometimes disdain, not even caring, hardly noticing, in fact, the appeal in marching down the street, past the city limits and into the world. If only as far as Compton.

POINTS OF INTEREST: THE BAY THEATER

Before it lost moviegoers to the modern cineplexes to San Diego's Fashion Valley, before it switched to showing Mexican films, many of them Christian-themed, until it just gave up and became a church, before it was vacated and put up for sale, the Bay Theater was our Sunday afternoon escape. It's where we saw the *Ten Commandments, Pollyanna,* and *The Blob.* We would get dressed up to go to the movies in our pleated skirts and patent leather shoes, back when the red carpets were still plush, the velvet curtain untarnished, the sconces still intact. My mother would pick us up after the movie and ask, "Was it in color?" As if such a modern invention had yet to reach our city.

POINTS OF INTEREST: KIMBALL PARK

There were ball fields and picnic tables, of course. Grassy slopes with shrubs that could shield adolescents groping each other. And

I have vague memories of a small zoo. Filthy, flea-ridden monkeys huddled inside a cage that stank of piss and rotting peanut shells. Freakish and exotic. But the main attraction for us was the public library. We went every Saturday after catechism across the street at St. Mary's. We would check out an armful of books and then read until our eyes ached, each page sending us closer to our genetically predisposed myopia.

At a certain age—it might have been twelve—one could progress from the children's section to the adult section, like stepping through the looking glass. It was where I found Thomas Hardy, Henry James, and William Faulkner, who took me to moors thick with heather, to drawing rooms with governesses, to decaying Southern mansions far from Kimball Park.

POINTS OF INTEREST: PLAZA BOWL

Sometimes walking home from Kimball Park, we stopped at the bowling alley. We played the pinball machines, stuck our fingers inside bowling balls for size, checked the pay phones for forgotten dimes, and if we scrounged enough change we bought French fries at the snack shop. One of these days, we thought, we would learn to bowl.

POINTS OF INTEREST: LA VISTA CEMETERY

It's the largest plot of land in tiny Lincoln Acres, an unincorporated shard of San Diego County situated entirely within the boundaries of National City and known unaffectionately as Stinkin' Acres. There's a section of the cemetery known as Rest Haven for which no money is allotted for maintenance. Families themselves pour the slabs that mark the graves, drive into the ground the homemade, tilted headstones, the off-kilter wooden crosses. My uncle is buried in La Vista, but in the endowed section where the gravestones conform in size and are laid in neat rows, where the grass is cut and the flowers discarded on a schedule. I like the low-cost, do-it-yourself option myself, though I've already learned I could never rest in National City.

HEALTH SERVICES

In high school, I became a candy striper at the local hospital run by the Seventh Day Adventists. I escorted new patients to the admissions desk, delivered flowers to their rooms, and when they were discharged, guided them through the lobby to the loading zone. Sometimes I was sent to the neighboring convalescent home to help feed the aged the high-fiber, meatless Seventh Day Adventist diet, or to wheel them outside to fart in the sunshine.

From the hospital lobby, I brought home anti-smoking pamphlets and planted them in my parents' bathroom for my father to see when he brushed his teeth, sat on the toilet, or pulled back the shower curtain. My father threw them in the trash can. I brought more home. He told me I had crossed the line, that I was not to judge him, that cigarettes were his only vice. He was a grown-up.

I was a candy striper, who didn't come close to saving lives.

MEDIA

The *National City Star News* was a thin weekly. It was delivered to our house, but mostly ignored. The news was insubstantial, with a few exceptions. My friend Florence was in it when she won the Miss National City pageant, the first non-white contestant to do so. My nephew was in it when he was a five-year-old practicing T-ball at the first hint of spring. My father was in it when his obituary ran.

EMPLOYMENT

When I was in college, I worked the snack bar at the swap meet. I'd never learned to type, so an office job was out. I was a cyclone of a snack-bar worker. I flipped burgers, bagged hot dogs and fries, rang up greasy purchases at the cash register and counted out change, fast—because that's how I did things. As if I could speed up my life in National City.

TRANSPORTATION

I rode out of National City in a Cadillac.

My cousin Bob was passing through from Texas on his way back to Oregon where he had settled in a double-wide just outside the Salem city limits. Bob was Mexican and Irish. He didn't speak Spanish, just pretended he could and I pretended with him. Once when he was in our garage looking for something to tie down some loose objects that had been banging around in the trunk of his car, he asked, "Tienes ropa?" Even *I* knew that ropa means clothes.

And even though I did in fact have clothes, I said, "No, no tengo ropa."

Bobby was a big drinker, a chain smoker, a talker and a brawler. He had a glass eye that pinned you down with its persistent unsee-ingness.

"I know people," he told me. "I can get you a job."

I didn't believe him, but I did it anyway—got in the Cadillac.

TOURISM

I visit National City about once a year from my home in Seattle. A few times my white husband and biracial daughters have accompanied me. "See," I told them once, "there's where I rode my bike, there's where I waited for the school bus, there's where a friend's dog was run over." They surveyed the neighborhood from inside the chain-link fence of my mother's yard. I know they noticed it—the lack of white people around us. We got in the car and I pointed out the changes—the freeway, the new library, the rebuilt high school, the expanded hospital. I told the jokes about the place names—Nasty City, El Toilet, Las Panties, Stinkin' Acres. They laughed, but something didn't ring right, and I regretted the jokes. "Never mind," I said. "You had to be there."

FREE RENT AT
THE TOTALITARIAN HOTEL

Poe Ballantine

O N MONDAY MORNINGS I modeled for the painters at an old
cannery converted into art studios in Eureka, California.
Laughable as it was for a thirty-two-year-old man to strike nude
poses on a wooden platform, I preferred it to what I usually did
for a living: short-order cooking or unloading trucks. I stood up
there on this particular Monday in 1987 trying not to move for
two hours, suffering muscle cramps and loss of circulation, and,
as always, faintly worried about getting an erection but somehow even more uneasy about the possibility of strangers seeing me
through the windows—as if a roomful of strangers weren't ogling
me already. Meanwhile down the hall my painter friend Jim Dalgee
raved so violently that one of the artists suggested calling the police.

After I dressed and picked up my sixty dollars, I went down the
hall and knocked on Jim's door. The ranting stopped for a moment,
and there was a clatter, followed by the door jerking open and Jim
sticking his head out. He did not let many people into his studio,
but he liked me because we had both wasted our youth, had gotten
off to terribly late starts, held similarly outdated and sentimental
views on art, and showed no signs of ever becoming successful. A
short man in his late forties with a brushed-up shock of black hair
like the crest of a blue jay, Jim wore his standard paint-spattered
work shirt, jeans, and tennis shoes. The room behind him was full

of dense blue cigarette smoke that curled in the sunlight from the southern windows. He smelled strongly of turpentine and beer.

"Jim," I said, "we could hear you shouting all the way down the hall."

"Was I shouting?"

"Yes. At the top of your lungs."

"Come in, man. I've got coffee."

Jim's eight-by-ten, brick-walled studio was furnished with a small fridge and a card table with a coffeepot and a boombox on it. Nine years earlier he had fled his previous life as an LA salesman and migrated six hundred miles north to Eureka to start over as a painter at the age of thirty-eight. Stacked against and hanging from every wall were hundreds of his acrylic paintings, all of which he refused to sell or show. Jim's style was postimpressionism: Matisse, Pissarro, Cézanne. He admired foremost those who had started late, such as the stockbroker-salesman Paul Gauguin and the wretched lunatic Vincent van Gogh. Though I was not qualified to judge Jim's work, I would've liked to own his *Black Cattle against Orange Moon at Dusk* or *Portrait of Camille Benoit Desmoulin's Head in a Basket*.

Though I had quit drinking and doing drugs the year before, I allowed myself the occasional consolation of a few cigarettes with Jim in his studio. I also planned one day to write a story about a fictional Jim jumping from the window to his posthumous fame. I poured myself a cup of coffee while he raged at the people on the street below, calling them "philistines" and "slobs." It was unusual to find him in such a state so early.

"Is everything all right?" I asked.

"The sleepwalkers!" he bellowed like an animal in pain.

"They're going to call the police," I said.

"They'll only be doing me a *favor*!" he shouted, sweeping his arm across the room, as if to indicate all the canvases he'd stretched that morning, the color-blobbed cardboard boxes he used for palettes, and the rows upon rows of acrylic paints in plastic squeeze bottles along the floor.

There was no point in talking to him when he was this far gone. The shouting would soon run its course and be replaced by a desperate apprehension that he didn't have long to live. I drank some coffee, shook a cigarette from Jim's pack, and fell into one of two yellow velveteen swivel chairs, a smoldering pedestal ashtray between them, like a giant clam with indigestion.

"I'm going to buy an albacore today," I said, applying a flame to the tip of my cigarette.

"The sycophants!" he snarled and then whirled from the window. "A what?"

"An albacore tuna, down on the docks. They're only a buck a pound. Do you want one?"

"No, nah." He waved in disdain and began to hunt for the cigarette he had just lit, his brow furrowed. "We need to get some more cigarettes."

Around one that afternoon Tarn McVie rapped lightly on Jim's door and stepped into the room. In his midtwenties, Tarn already had paintings in galleries across the country and routinely sold single works for sums that could've sustained me for an entire year. His gigantic oil canvases awed me, and one sticks in my mind to this day: an orange nude coming at you through the water, flash of white at the knee. In spite of his conventional training, European-museum background, postmodern leanings, and early success without apparent struggle, McVie was the sort of natural, congenial artist that Jim and I both longed to be. He was also one of the few painters who refused to sign the petition presently going around to remove Jim from the building.

"Hello, men," he said. "Hear the news?"

"What news?" Jim said, teeth clamped down on his cigarette, another burning in the colossal ashtray between us.

"Market crashed."

"What market?" I asked.

"Stock market. Dow Jones fell over five hundred points," he said. "Highest point drop in history. There's nothing on TV except talk about it. You can't even watch *General Hospital*. Everyone says we're headed for the next Great Depression." His eyes sparkled as if we were all about to go on a field trip to paint tulips and the bus were waiting downstairs. "They're already calling it 'Black Monday.'"

I had never paid much attention to the Ferris-wheel vicissitudes of the New York Stock Exchange, but when $500 billion in stock value simply evaporates, when nearly 25 percent of the market ceases to exist, when the president of the United States preempts soap operas and game shows to urge everyone not to panic and numerous respected experts explain that the country has seen no comparable financial event since 1929, even the poor take heed. I had also been observing the wastrel, arrogant, and bellicose habits of my country for years, and my sensitive, aesthetic side tended toward portent and hyperbole. So I trusted the news media's Henny Penny proclamations that our Day of Reckoning had finally come.

Heading down the alley away from the artists' studios an hour later, I thought I would remember forever this day of ruin, October 19, 1987, the same way I remembered the assassination of John F. Kennedy. A man in a white shirt and blue tie staggered toward me with a dazed expression, and from the sky above I expected to see falling stockbrokers. I pictured myself on a freight train full of hobos. From every corner came the dire chatter of radios and TVs. Like all the gloomy broadcasters, I was convinced that the next Great Depression was upon us.

The fishing boats were in from their morning runs, and it now seemed imperative that I buy that albacore. Food would soon be in short supply, and there would be mobs in the streets, breaking windows and overturning cars.

The rheumy-eyed fisherman shrugged when I told him the news. "They can't break you if you're already broke," he said.

My fish, cleaned and bled, weighed fourteen pounds, and because albacore spoils rapidly, it was frozen as hard as a chunk of iron. Incongruous as it might seem to walk away from a fishing boat with a frozen fish, you couldn't beat the price, and albacore were much easier to cut into steaks this way. I carried it by the tail with a newspaper so it didn't freeze my hand.

I lived downtown in an apartment complex that, for its Second Empire facade, transient tenantry, and despotic manager, I had dubbed the "Totalitarian Hotel." The manager, Mrs. Vollstanger, was a gouty old Prussian and always wore pearls and thick, embroidered white sweaters. She met me at the top of the grand staircase, arms folded, chin trembling, and glowered down at my fish.

"It's an albacore," I explained.

"Yes," she said. "I saw you coming." Mrs. Vollstanger had a telescope in the window of her third-floor apartment and kept track of all the goings-on below. "I have an eviction notice for you to serve."

I considered asking if she was aware of the stock-market plunge but thought better of it, since bad news seemed only to cheer her. "Who's it for?"

"Hot Pants," she said, meaning my common-wall neighbor, a young woman named Annabelle Taft.

It didn't take Mrs. Vollstanger long to find derogatory nicknames for all her tenants. There was Moon Child and Clydesdale Maria and Porky Pete. I suppose behind my back I was Machine-Gun Typist.

"Annabelle?" I said. "Why?"

"I'm not running a brothel here," she retorted, one of her fondest declarations, along with "I'm not running a crack house/animal shelter/home for unwed mothers here."

"Just let me get this fish in the freezer, and I'll be right up," I said, resisting the urge to salute. "Would you like a couple of tuna steaks?"

"No, thank you," she said.

My apartment was a single room with a set of high, arched, greenish windows, an electric stove, a fridge, a sink, and a very long entryway. Sometimes, when someone knocked, it took me so long to get to the door that my caller would be gone by the time I arrived. My place was full of moths whose origin I could not determine. They were the small, rolled-up type, like pencil shavings. I had liked them at first for their silence and the intricate designs on their delicate wings, but now, with their growing numbers and regular obtrusion into my books, blankets, and bathtub, I considered them a nuisance.

My room was sparsely furnished with items left by the previous tenants, who had vacated abruptly. There was a vinyl-covered recliner and a dining-room table, upon which sat my typewriter, and two chairs that went with the table. There was a television on a stand that I did not often use since it received only two channels, though occasionally I watched *I Love Lucy*—a program I had disliked as a child for all its yelling—and a PBS show hosted by theological psychologist John Bradshaw, who asserted that all my addiction problems could be traced back to my "wounded inner child." (Maybe I was hurt by early exposure to episodes of *I Love Lucy*.)

There were four boxes of *Paris Review*s that Jim had lent me, which I studied at night, especially the interviews with famous authors. Throughout the building the floors were covered with cheap carpet that, with all its gold, green, and red filigree, might've been called "gala," but it was so thin that it wrinkled, and there was no padding underneath, so that if you didn't have a mattress— I didn't—you had to build up a nest of blankets on the floor. The heat was regulated by Mrs. Vollstanger, so it was always cold, and it was best not to sleep by the windows, which had bubbles trapped in their glass and made me feel as if I were a specimen in some intergalactic aquarium.

I set my fish across the sink and promptly began to divide it into two-inch crosscut planks with a handsaw I used only for this purpose. While I worked, I thought about the coming of the next Great Depression and wondered how America would fall apart: Slowly or quickly? From the coasts inward or the middle out? With great fanfare or in a puff of smoke? And in which direction would everyone run this time? I also wondered if it had been wise to quit my job and sell my car.

Sawing up a frozen albacore is not much different from sawing up a green tree trunk. I got about twelve steaks, which I wrapped and stacked in the freezer beside all the wild game that Mrs. Vollstanger had cleaned out of her recently deceased husband's stand-up freezer and donated to me. A big-game hunter, he had labeled all his Cryovacked packages in permanent black marker: ELK, ELEPHANT, BLACK BEAR, ZEBRA, GAZELLE. So far I had been reluctant to try any of it for fear that Mrs. Vollstanger had actually killed, dressed, and Cryovacked her husband.

I also had a twenty-five-pound bag of pink beans, a twenty-five-pound bag of black-eyed peas, a twenty-five-pound bag of brown rice, ten pounds of white flour, four pounds of oats, and two pounds of buckwheat—a proper head start, I thought, on the anarchy and economic despair to come.

The door to Mrs. Vollstanger's apartment was open, and before I could knock, she invited me in. Mrs. Vollstanger had a big, well-lit, orderly apartment on the southwest corner, with a panoramic view of the bay and the Samoa pulp mill. You could predict with fair accuracy what the weather would be like by which way the smoke blew from the mill. Usually it was blowing in from the ocean, which meant fog and rain, but today the smoke flowed north, indicating fair weather.

"You've heard that the market slipped?" she said, handing me the envelope with the eviction notice for Annabelle Taft inside.

"'Slipped'?"

"Everything will be fine. We have a good man in office," she said, referring to then-President Ronald Reagan.

Mrs. Vollstanger rarely left the premises. Her groceries were delivered. She did not own a car. The tenants who curried her favor did her bidding, policed the unit, swept the lobby floors, ran errands, and maintained the laundry room. She spoke often in praise of the building's owner and of her responsibilities to his property, which, judging by its low rents and the number of liberties she was allowed with tenants, I could only imagine was some sort of tax shelter. Mrs. Vollstanger had raised four children, but I never saw any of them, and, given the way she shook with rage without warning and preyed like a trapdoor spider on the weaknesses of those in her confidence, I didn't wonder why.

From my own experience with tyrants, I had identified her tendencies early on and managed to stay in her good graces by paying my rent on time, keeping my distance, and doing her dirty work when called. Mrs. Vollstanger would've enjoyed serving the notices herself, I believe, but she had been attacked on one occasion and threatened on another, so the mission had been passed on to someone more expendable.

I doubted the legal soundness of most of these notices, which usually contained only thin basis for the eviction, such as suspected pets or, in the case of Annabelle, noise after 10 PM. But the job of a henchman is execution, not judgment, and I needed the money. Even when justified, I always felt bad about ousting people from their homes. I felt especially rotten in this case, since the market had just crashed and I was, for flimsy reasons, turning a young woman out on the street. I don't think Annabelle was any more than nineteen. She worked at my favorite bakery (the chewy chocolate-macadamia-nut cookies had no rival), and I knew from my few conversations with her in the hall that this was the first time she had ever lived on her own.

I knocked and thought I heard a noise inside, but there was no response. I figured she had spied me through the peephole and decided not to answer. Then I looked left and saw Annabelle coming down the hall with two stacked baskets of laundry. She wore shorts, and her lean swimmer's body was pale. Annabelle was from Montana, and by the drawings of surf and sun on the many letters that I saw posted downstairs for her friends and family back home, I'd deduced that she was proud of having landed on the mythological golden shore of California, even if it was cloudy, rainy, or foggy here in Eureka three hundred days out of the year.

I helped her with her baskets, then presented her with the envelope.

She squinted at it. "What is this?"

"It's, ah, an eviction notice."

"Why am I being evicted?"

"It's written there at the bottom. Noise after ten. It's in the lease....You never bothered me," I hastened to add. In fact, with no social life to speak of, I'd enjoyed the sounds of festivity that had come through her wall: giggling, clinking glasses, lovemaking. I knew it was the men who stayed overnight that had rankled Mrs. Vollstanger. My only complaint about Annabelle would've been that I was not one of the men.

She studied the paper without reading it, then shook it at me, her dark eyes so perplexed and hurt I felt like a villain in a Victorian novel. "Where am I supposed to go?"

"You have five days. There are a lot of vacancies downtown."

"You're a terrible person," she said, blowing a strand of hair out of her face.

"It's nothing personal. I'll help you move. I'm sorry about all of this."

"Get lost, and tell your—" Her voice broke, and she wiped at her eyes. "I thought you were nice."

Well, I was at one time, I thought, but by then she had slammed the door.

I hiked back up to Mrs. Vollstanger's and collected my fifteen-dollar fee. After Annabelle was gone, I would paint her apartment in exchange for a free month's rent.

Normally in the evenings I worked on my great Rabelaisian satirical novel about greed and voluptuous social dependence in an allegorical lunatic asylum inhabited by evil clowns (which seemed even more appropriate now that we were all going down the tubes), but I was distracted by Annabelle's distress, the dirtiness of the fifteen dollars in my pocket, and the fact that soon millions would be out of work and rioting in the streets.

I picked up a *Paris Review* and thumbed through it. All good art, according to my 1951 Greenwich Village Artist's Code, came out of tumult, revolution, and hardship. The moths fluttered about as if I were some magnificent symbol of decay. Hungry, I rummaged in my freezer, brought out a chunk of black bear, stared at it for a minute, then unwrapped it and set it in a pan on low heat with onions. The sun set behind the buildings. The bear was tough and greasy, but I finished it, imagining that through some pantheistic hoodoo I might incorporate the bear's spirit, at the same time pushing out of my mind the possibility that it was Mr. Vollstanger's liver.

In the morning I rose cautiously from my nest of blankets and peeked out the window to note that the world had not visibly changed. The smoke from the mill was still scurrying north. I made coffee and oatmeal with apples and then walked four blocks to the head-quarters of *The North Coast View,* where six months earlier I had answered an incredible ad that had read "Writers Wanted," and despite never having published a thing in my life, I'd been hired to write book reviews at twenty-five dollars apiece.

Two Irish-surnamed journalists in their late twenties owned and ran *The North Coast View,* a free, local, ad-heavy arts-and-culture monthly on newsprint that I had once heard referred to as an "innocuous street rag." I strolled into their office. Though I think it had helped me win the job, they regarded my 1951 Greenwich Village Artist's Code as quaint. Among writers the career path of quitting your job, selling your car, hustling like an old hooker with a toothache, and then eventually dying of syphilis or tuberculosis or shooting yourself in the stomach in a wheat field after you'd created a number of unrecognized masterpieces had been replaced by taking out a student loan and enrolling in the nearby university.

The joke was on them, however, for the Dark Ages were at hand, and only those who could ride the rails, roll their own ciga-rettes, and live on hand-sawn fish and black bear would survive.

"Are we still in business?" I asked point-blank as I came round the corner in my Goodwill Pendleton shirt, patched jeans, and wool watch cap.

"Until further notice" was the editor's complacent reply.

"You're not worried about the market crash?"

"We're not listed on the Dow Jones Industrial, last time I checked."

It was disconcerting to see everyone—Jim, Tarn McVie, Mrs. Vollstanger, the albacore fisherman, my two editors—take so mildly the greatest single-day point decline in Wall Street history.

"I'll get a book," I said.

"Take all you want."

In the back were hundreds of books publishers had sent hoping for reviews, the mass of them the sort of dreck that encouraged me about my own prospects of one day getting my novel published.

I selected a book about a group of oppressed women workers who cracked walnuts with their fists after their hammers had been taken away from them (at which point I personally would have quit cracking walnuts and headed home). As I strolled back to my apartment, the headlines in the newsstands trumpeted ominous declarations—"Bedlam on Wall Street"—though it was reassuring to see that they were still organized enough to turn a profit on calamity. I also noticed that the bakery I liked so much—the one where Annabelle Taft worked and which I would therefore have to avoid from now on—was busier than usual. Since Eureka was so far from the financial centers, I thought, the crash simply had not caught up to us yet, or it had somehow stimulated appetites for *krapfen* pastries and chewy chocolate-macadamia-nut cookies.

When I got home, I read the book about women cracking walnuts without hammers, took notes, drank so much cinnamon tea I fogged the windows, got the hiccups, had a sneezing fit so violent I felt like Hitler at the rostrum, passed back and forth through the clouds of moths, longed for a chewy chocolate-macadamia-nut cookie, and found that zebra, no matter how it is prepared, is best left on the zebra. My room grew dark, and, lit only by the streetlight, I lay in my nest of blankets and listened to the soft moaning of Annabelle Taft next door.

Annabelle moved out three days later with the help of a dozen friends in army jackets, ripped jeans, and fingerless gloves, who scowled and sniffed at me in the hall whenever possible. She did not collect her security deposit or clean her apartment. She left behind a nasty note, a broken umbrella, a tube of green lipstick, a one-piece bathing suit emblazoned "Bozeman Barracudas" (still wet in the bathtub), and a trash can full of *North Coast Views*.

Annabelle's apartment looked out over the rooftop, and I remembered how cute she'd been lying out there on her towel, trying to get a tan on rare and usually cool days of sun. I confess that "cute" does not accurately describe the many ways I had thought about her, none of which, because of my over-discipline and fear of intimacy, would ever amount to more than a fantasy. I also recalled how much fun it had been to talk to her about her California adventure, which brought to mind my first time out on my own: the exhilaration of shopping for groceries, acquiring furniture, preparing your own meals, having friends over, and staying up as late as you liked.

Normally I painted an apartment the size of Annabelle's in about four hours. The color, without exception, was oyster white, no trim. The apartments were painted so often that usually only one coat was needed. While I painted and moved my ladder about, I thought about women cracking walnuts with their fists and America coming down. I also thought about God, whom I had never believed in before, but now that I was trying to create flesh-and-blood characters so that my reader would feel something when I killed them off, I had begun to imagine that a higher being might have been doing this very thing on a much larger scale all along.

When I was done, I cleaned my brushes and rollers and put away the ladder, paint, and dropcloths. Tomorrow I would give Annabelle's keys back to Mrs. Vollstanger and get my receipt for one month's rent. I returned to my room and stood in the darkness for a while, looking out at the lights of ships on the bay. And I caught myself listening for the voice of Annabelle.

The next morning Jim was standing down the hall beside the open door of 214, an apartment I had painted six days before that had belonged to a woman who'd been evicted for having cats. Jim's wife, Hye, a school secretary, stood next to him, looking like someone who spent all her waking hours defusing bombs.

Jim called my name and strode over with a smile to shake my hand. He had a tremendous handshake, his forearm bulging.

"Howdy, neighbor," he said. "Guess you heard they voted me out?" He explained that, without his studio, he needed an apartment with better light so he could paint at home. This place had great light, he said. "And it's half the price of our place down on the waterfront. Hye likes it too," he added.

Hye was gone. The door downstairs was propped open, and she came trudging back up the steps with a boxful of books. In the dozens of times I had seen Hye with Jim, she had spoken a total of six words to me—cultural diffidence, I thought (she was Korean), or, more likely, she associated me with her husband's self-destruction.

Jim took a deep breath. "I've quit drinking."

Hye passed us, head down, as if we were strangers. I wondered how many times she'd heard Jim say this.

"Great news, Jim," I said. "Do you need any help moving?"

"Got most everything up," he said. "Now I need to lay some tarps. Come by later and check out my new studio."

"I'll bring you a pound of black-eyed peas for luck," I said.

Mrs. Vollstanger leaned over the rail above, pearls dangling, and smiled down at us in that chilly, maternal way of hers. "Do you have everything you need, Jim?" she asked sweetly.

On afternoons when the weather was tolerable, I liked to hang out in the park across the street from my apartment among the winos, unemployed lumberjacks, and a bearded man who sat cross-legged by the statue and offered to let you touch the "real Jesus" for only a quarter. Mrs. Vollstanger would be up there on the third floor doing telescope surveillance, and a few windows over and down Jim would be crouched before his easel, wool beret dipped over one eye, furiously trying to catch up on lost time.

I was trying to catch up on lost time too. My brain, floating in its amniotic chamber of inebriation for all those years, had gone to sludge. It was an effort to perceive things as they actually were and harder yet to render them clearly, which likely was the reason I clung to ready-made theories of art instead of developing my own. Following the example of my painter friends, I made daily "sketches" in my notebook: descriptions of my surroundings and the people as they passed, trying to retrain my eye in the hope that one day I would find my way to the book reviewers' pile, preferably in hardcover.

One afternoon the broad-shouldered Annabelle came along and sat down just a few feet from me. She wore pinstriped pants, knee-high rubber boots, and a windbreaker. A white band on her wrist read "Love is time." She opened her notebook and began to write.

Before I'd handed Annabelle her eviction notice, I had seen her outside the building no more than seven or eight times, but now I ran into her everywhere: in the galleries (where I could too often be found depicted in various unflattering attitudes), at the library and the co-op, coming out of that restaurant that sold spinach pies, or gabbing in the coffee shop with her friends. At each encounter, if she did not ignore me altogether, she pretended to have stumbled upon some large species of cockroach. It pickled my stomach to be so loathed (for I didn't need an artist's vision to see my role as a jerk in all of this), and it made me want to quit serving evictions, even if that meant the end of my free rent at the Totalitarian Hotel. Apology seemed a thin gesture, and so I fantasized about asking her out instead: I'd walk her through my situation so that she could understand the sacrifices one had to make for art, and then maybe we'd go to her place afterward, where a pastel nude of me with darts in my ass would hang from her wall.

"Hey, how are you?" I called out.

"Busy," she replied, nose in her book.

"Writing a letter?"

"A story."

"I have your bathing suit and green lipstick."

"You can keep them," she said.

"I wouldn't know what to do with them," I replied with a chuckle that stuck in my throat.

"I have a suggestion," she said, ripping the page from her notebook, tearing it to bits, and stalking away.

The stock market sputtered and bumped along. Black Monday merged into Black November and on without chromatic variation into December. The financial experts, like a pack of gloomy cheerleaders, kept up the rah-rah of the apocalypse even as the fishing boats continued sailing in and out, the bakery kept baking, new books and fresh newspapers kept arriving, and the street sweepers moved up and down the pavement undeterred by the mist and rain.

One night while typing, the windows sweating with the humidity of my inspiration, my cinnamon tea, and a pot of simmering pink beans and elephant, I heard Jim railing at the philistines below. I hurried over and knocked on his door. Hye let me in as if I were a country doctor making a midnight call.

Jim staggered from the open window, arms outstretched, cigarette in one hand and can of beer in the other. "I'm back, my boy!" he cried.

There were moths in the apartment, a situation I thought endemic to the building (since they were the exact same moths as mine) or possibly an affliction of artists who'd started too late.

"Jim," I said, "you can't shout. Mrs. Vollstanger will evict you."

"The *rentier!*" he shouted gallantly, waving an arm through a squadron of eye-winged moths. "The harridan! Have a drink, old friend. Hye, get him a drink. Come look at my painting. Come look at what I've done."

In the coming days Jim painted with his door open, jazz and cigarette smoke pouring into the hallway. Around four every afternoon, just before Hye got home from work, he'd knock off and make his sacred trek to the liquor store. In the evenings, well oiled, he'd come to visit me, bringing a paper sack full of beer, old *Esquire* magazines, Henry Miller novels, and perhaps half a buttered baguette from the bakery or a plate of creamed cauliflower that Hye had made. We'd laugh about the moths, which I'd discovered had hatched from my weevil-infested bag of black-eyed peas, since discarded. He'd show me his latest painting, and I'd read him passages from my evil-clown novel, to which he'd listen intently, all the while nodding and huffing and afterward announcing without fail how much he admired the rhythm.

At night, whenever Jim began to rave, I'd tense for the eviction summons of Mrs. Vollstanger, then go over and tell him to keep it down. Twice I overheard him and Hye arguing. Hye did most of the talking: Did Jim realize that he was spending more on paints, canvases, cigarettes, and booze than she was making? They no longer had enough to put a down payment on a house. He denied fiercely her charge that art for him was nothing more than an excuse to drink. Why, then, she wanted to know, did he not try to sell his paintings or at least show them in the local galleries?

"Because I can't *sell* things anymore," he said. "God damn it, Hye, no one is going to remember a *sales*man."

Hye began to cry.

"The market will come back, babe," he told her. "And when it does, we'll buy a house. The one you like in Trinidad with all the redwood trees in the backyard."

Each day I waited for America to snap from its strings and fall on its face like a broken marionette, but by January not only had the stock market recovered, it had begun to make gains. Many who, like Jim and Hye, had not sold off their investments were better off financially than before the soon-to-be-forgotten crash. The experts, reversing themselves like a school of parrotfish, predicted that the Dow might soar as high as four thousand points by the end of the year. Black Monday had had no real effect on anything but my imagination.

It rained most of January, and I slaved over my book about evil clowns. Each day, as its shortcomings became more evident, I approached the typewriter with less enthusiasm. Finally I sat on the floor and read my satirical harlequin folly front to back as if it were someone else's work. It was the sort of effort I would've panned as a reviewer: "With its too-easy targets, total absence of sympathetic characters, and overall lack of message, I see little reason to bother with such a cynical assessment of American society. It is perhaps harsh but also fair to say that, at an age when most novelists are producing their best work, this one is many years away from offering anything of value to a reader, much less revealing himself outside of posing naked on a wooden platform."

I banded and boxed the manuscript, lethargically paced the room, chuckled feebly to myself a few times, and thought about getting drunk. Finally I went to bed and slept for three days, getting up now and again for a slice of bloody red elk or a glass of water or to listen for Jim raging down the hail or Mrs. Vollstanger's unmistakable Gestapo knock on my door. I slept roughly, like a tree with all its bark burned off or a man buried in wet sand, but the dreams at least were good. In one I could paint with my mind, and in another everyone had a *u* in their last name.

When at last I got up to face the world again, the room was full of sunlight, and I had a strong craving for chewy chocolate-macadamia-nut cookies.

"You're the writer, aren't you?" asked the young woman behind the glass case at the bakery.

"How did you know?" I asked.

"We used to listen to you type. You know Annabelle moved back to Montana. She really loved your book reviews." Her hand dropped to her hip. "She's going to be an author someday too. You should write her."

Later that evening Jim stopped by and drove me nine miles north into the redwood forest to the rustic cabin he and Hye had just bought in Trinidad, a town with a population of only a few hundred. We stood on the balcony in the cool shadows of the massive trees. "Do you believe it?" he said. "Look at the light! Smell the air! You can hear the ocean!"

Two days later Mrs. Vollstanger lost her temper with me because I'd moved an electric stove to the wrong side of a room. We argued. I said some regrettable things, all of them true, and was relieved that my days at the Totalitarian Hotel were finally over. More depressed and confused than I would admit, I packed what I could carry, leaving behind my security deposit, a clean room, a succinct note, and a freezer full of wild meat.

I sneaked down the grand staircase and walked to the bus depot a few blocks away. There were only three other passengers on the bus, so I racked my bags and nestled in with two seats to myself. Before I dozed off somewhere around Petaluma, I watched the darkness roll past the windows and wondered how long I would have to go on knowing nothing about art, or women, or my country.

from **BOOMERANG**

Michael Lewis

WELCOME TO VALLEJO, CITY OF OPPORTUNITY, reads the sign on the way in, but the shops that remain open display signs that say, WE ACCEPT FOOD STAMPS. Weeds surround abandoned businesses, and all traffic lights are set to permanently blink, which is a formality as there are no longer any cops to police the streets. Vallejo is the one city in the Bay Area where you can park anywhere and not worry about getting a ticket, because there are no meter maids, either. The windows of city hall are dark but its front porch is a hive of activity. A young man in a backwards baseball cap, sunglasses, and a new pair of Nike sneakers stands on a low wall and calls out an address:

"Nine hundred Cambridge Drive," he says. "In Benicia."

The people in the crowd below instantly begin bidding. From 2006 to 2010 the value of Vallejo real estate fell 66 percent. One in sixteen homes in the city are in foreclosure. This is apparently the fire sale, but the characters involved are so shady and furtive that I can hardly believe it. I stop to ask what's going on, but the bidders don't want to talk. "Why would I tell you anything?" says a guy sitting in a Coleman folding chair. He obviously thinks he's shrewd, and perhaps he is.

The lobby of city hall is completely empty. There's a receptionist's desk but no receptionist. Instead, there's a sign: TO FORECLOSURE AUCTIONEERS AND FORECLOSURE BIDDERS: PLEASE DO NOT CONDUCT BUSINESS IN THE CITY HALL LOBBY.

On the third floor I find the offices of the new city manager, Phil Batchelor, but when I walk in there is no one in sight. It's just a collection of empty cubicles. At length a woman appears and leads me to Batchelor himself. He's in his sixties and, oddly enough, a published author. He's written one book on how to raise children and another on how to face death. Both deliver an overtly Christian message, but he doesn't come across as evangelical; he comes across as sensible, and a little weary. His day job, before he retired, was running cities with financial difficulties. He came out of retirement to take this job, but only after the city council had asked him a few times. "The more you say no, the more determined they are to get you," he says. His chief demand was not financial but social: he'd only take the job if the people on the city council ceased being nasty to one another and behaved civilly. He actually got that in writing, and they've kept their end of the bargain. "I've been in a lot of places that have been in a lot of trouble but I've never seen anything like this," he says. He then lays out what he finds unusual, beginning with the staffing levels. He's now running the city, and he has a staff of one: I just met her. "When she goes out to the bathroom she has to lock the door," he says, "because I'm in meetings, and we have no one else."

Back in 2008, unable to come to terms with its many creditors, Vallejo had declared bankruptcy. Eighty percent of the city's budget—and the lion's share of the claims that had thrown it into bankruptcy—were wrapped up in the pay and benefits of public safety workers. Relations between the police and the firefighters, on the one hand, and the citizens, on the other, were at historic lows. The public safety workers thought that the city was out to screw them on their contracts; the citizenry thought that the public safety workers were using fear as a tool to extort money from them. The local joke was that "P.D." stands for "Pay or Die." The city council meetings had become exercises in outrage: at one, a citizen arrived and tossed a severed pig's head onto the floor. "There's no good reason why Vallejo is as fucked up as it is," says a longtime resident named Marc Garman, who created a website to catalogue the civil war. "It's a boat ride to San Francisco. You throw a stone and you hit Napa." Since the bankruptcy, the police and fire departments had been cut in half; some number of the citizens who came to Phil Batchelor's office did so to say they no longer felt safe in their own homes. All other city services had been reduced effectively to zero. "Do you know that some cities actually pave their streets?" says Batchelor. "That's not here."

I notice on his shelf a copy of *Fortune* magazine, with Meredith Whitney on the cover. And as he talked about the bankrupting of Vallejo I realized that I had heard this story before, or a private-sector version of it. The people who had power in the society, and were charged with saving it from itself, had instead bled the society to death. The problem with police officers and firefighters isn't a public-sector problem; it isn't a problem with government; it's a problem with the entire society. It's what happened on Wall Street in the run-up to the subprime crisis. It's a problem of people taking what they can, just because they can, without regard to the larger social consequences. It's not just a coincidence that the debts of cities and states spun out of control at the same time as the debts of individual Americans. Alone in a dark room with a pile of money, Americans knew exactly what they wanted to do, from the top of the society to the bottom. They'd been conditioned to grab as much as they could, without thinking about the long-term consequences. Afterward, the people on Wall Street would privately bemoan the low morals of the American people who walked away from their subprime loans, and the American people would express outrage at the Wall Street people who paid themselves a fortune to design the bad loans.

Having failed to persuade its public safety workers that it could not afford to make them rich, the city of Vallejo, California, had hit bottom: it could fall no lower. "My approach has been I don't care who is to blame," Batchelor said. "We needed to change." When I met him, a few months after he had taken the job, he was still trying to resolve a narrow financial dispute: the city had 1,013 claimants with half a billion dollars in claims but only $6 million to dole out to them. They were survivors of a shipwreck on a life raft with limited provisions. His job, as he saw it, was to persuade them that the only chance of survival was to work together. He didn't view the city's main problem as financial: the financial problems were the symptom. The disease was the culture. Just a few weeks earlier, he had sent a memo to the remaining city staff—the city council, the mayor, the public safety workers. The central message was that if you want to fix this place you need to change how you behave, each and every one of you. "It's got to be about the people," he said. "Teach them respect for each other, integrity and how to strive for excellence. Cultures change. But people need to want to change. People convinced against their will are of the same opinion still."

"How do you change the culture of an entire city?" I asked him.

"First of all we look internally," he said.

The road out of Vallejo passes directly through the office of Dr. Peter Whybrow, a British neuroscientist at UCLA with a theory about American life. He thinks the dysfunction in America's society is a by-product of America's success. In academic papers and a popular book, *American Mania,* Whybrow argues, in effect, that human beings are neurologically ill-designed to be modern Americans. The human brain evolved over hundreds of thousands of years in an environment defined by scarcity. It was not designed, at least originally, for an environment of extreme abundance. "Human beings are wandering around with brains that are fabulously limited," he says cheerfully. "We've got the core of the average lizard." Wrapped around this reptilian core, he explains, is a mammalian layer (associated with maternal concern and social interaction), and around that is wrapped a third layer, which enables feats of memory and the capacity for abstract thought. "The only problem," he says, "is our passions are still driven by the lizard core. We are set up to acquire as much as we can of things we perceive as scarce, particularly sex, safety, and food." Even a person on a diet who sensibly avoids coming face-to-face with a piece of chocolate cake will find it hard to control himself if the chocolate cake somehow finds him. Every pastry chef in America understands this, and now neuroscience does, too. "When faced with abundance, the brain's ancient reward pathways are difficult to suppress," says Whybrow. "In that moment the value of eating the chocolate cake exceeds the value of the diet. We cannot think down the road when we are faced with the chocolate cake."

The richest society the world has ever seen has grown rich by devising better and better ways to give people what they want. The effect on the brain of lots of instant gratification is something like the effect on the right hand of cutting off the left: the more the lizard core is used the more dominant it becomes. "What we're doing is minimizing the use of the part of the brain that lizards don't have," says Whybrow. "We've created physiological dysfunction. We have lost the ability to self-regulate, at all levels of the society. The five million dollars you get paid at Goldman Sachs if you do whatever they ask you to do—that is the chocolate cake upgraded."

The succession of financial bubbles, and the amassing of personal and public debt, Whybrow views as simply an expression of the lizard-brained way of life. A color-coded map of American personal indebtedness could be laid on top of the Centers for Disease Control's color-coded map that illustrates the fantastic rise in rates of obesity across the United States since 1985 without disturbing the general pattern. The boom in trading activity in individual stock portfolios; the spread of legalized gambling; the rise of drug and alcohol addiction; it is all of a piece. Everywhere you turn you see Americans sacrifice their long-term interests for a short-term reward.

What happens when a society loses its ability to self-regulate, and insists on sacrificing its long-term self-interest for short-term rewards? How does the story end? "We could regulate ourselves if we chose to think about it," Whybrow says. "But it does not appear that is what we are going to do." Apart from that remote possibility, Whybrow imagines two possible outcomes. The first he illustrates with a true story, which might be called the parable of the pheasant. Last spring, on sabbatical at the University of Oxford, he was surprised to discover that he was able to rent an apartment inside Blenheim Palace, the Churchill family home. The previous winter at Blenheim had been harsh, and the pheasant hunters had been efficient; as a result, just a single pheasant had survived in the palace gardens. This bird had gained total control of a newly seeded field. Its intake of food, normally regulated by its environment, was now entirely unregulated: it could eat all it wanted, and it did. The pheasant grew so large that when other birds challenged it for seed, it would simply frighten them away. The fat pheasant became a tourist attraction and even acquired a name: Henry. "Henry was the biggest pheasant anyone had ever seen," says Whybrow. "Even after he got fat, he just ate and ate." It didn't take long before Henry was obese. He could still eat as much as he wanted, but he could no longer fly. Then one day he was gone: a fox ate him.

The other possible outcome was only slightly more hopeful: to hit bottom. To realize what has happened to us, because we have no other choice. "If we refuse to regulate ourselves, the only regulators are our environment," says Whybrow, "and the way that environment deprives us." For meaningful change to occur, in other words, we need the environment to administer the necessary level of pain.

In August 2011, the same week that Standard & Poor's downgraded the debt of the United States government, a judge approved the bankruptcy plan for Vallejo, California. Vallejo's creditors ended up with five cents on the dollar, public employees with something like twenty and thirty cents on the dollar. The city no longer received any rating at all from Moody's and Standard & Poor's. It would take years to build the track record needed to obtain a decent rating. The absence of a rating mattered little, as the last thing the city needed to do was to go out and borrow money from strangers.

More out of idle curiosity than with any clear purpose, I drove up again to Vallejo and paid a call on the fire department. In the decay of our sense of common purpose, the firefighters are a telling sign that we are approaching a new bottom. It isn't hard to imagine how a police department might wind up in conflict with the community it's hired to protect. A person who becomes a police officer enjoys the authority. He wants to stop the bad guys. He doesn't necessarily need to care for the people he polices. A person who becomes a firefighter wants to be a good guy. He wants to be *loved.*

The Vallejo firefighter I met with that morning was named Paige Meyer. He was forty-one years old. He had short salt-and-pepper hair and olive skin, with traces of burn marks on his cheeks. His natural expression was a smile. He wasn't particularly either religious or political. ("I'm not necessarily a God guy.") The closest thing he had to a religion, apart from his family, was his job. He was extremely proud of it, and of his colleagues. "I don't want this to sound arrogant at all," he said. "But many departments in nicer communities, they get a serious fire maybe once a year. We get them all the time." The Vallejo population is older and poorer than in many surrounding cities, and older still are the buildings it lives in. The typical Vallejo house is a charming, highly inflammable wooden Victorian. "In this town we fight fires," says Meyer. "This town *rips.*" The department was shaped by its environment: they were extremely aggressive firefighters. "When I came to this department you *rolled* to a fire," he said. "You were not going to see an exterior water stream from this department. We're going in. You have some knucklehead calling in with a sore throat—your giddyup is not so fast. But I'll tell you something about this department. They get a call that there's a baby choking or a ten-year-old not breathing, you better get out of the way, or you're going to get run over."

As a young man, to pay his way through college, Meyer had worked as a state beach lifeguard at lakes in central California. He assumed that there would be little drama in the work but people would turn up, get drunk, and attempt to drown. A few of the times he pulled people from the water, they were in bad enough shape that they needed paramedics; the fire department was there on the spot. He started talking to firefighters and found that "they all absolutely loved what they did. You get to go and *live* and create a second family. How can you not like that?" He came to Vallejo in 1998, at the age of twenty-eight. He had left a cushy job in Sunnyvale, outside San Jose, where there aren't many fires, precisely because he wanted to fight fires. "In other departments," he says, "I wasn't a firefighter. The first six months of the job here, I was out at two in the morning at a fire every other week. I couldn't believe it." The houses of Vallejo are mainly balloon-frame construction. The interior walls have no firebreaks: from bottom to top, all four walls carry fire as efficiently as a chimney. One of the rookie mistakes in Vallejo is to put the fire out on the ground floor, only to look up and see it roaring out of the roof. "When we get to a fire we say, 'Boom! Send someone up to the attic.' Because the fire is going right to the attic."

Meyer actually had made that rookie mistake. One day not long after he'd arrived, he'd jumped off the truck already breathing air from a tank and raced into what appeared to be a burning one-bedroom apartment. He knocked down the door and put the attack line on the fire and then wondered why the fire wasn't going out. "It should have been getting cooler, but it was getting hotter and hotter." Right in front of his face, on his plastic mask, lines trickled down, like rain on a windshield. The old-school firefighters left their ears exposed so they could feel the heat: the heat contained the critical information. Meyer could only see the heat: his helmet was melting. "If your helmet starts to shrivel up and melt, that's not cool," he says. A melting helmet, among the other problems it presents, is an indication that a room is about to flash. Flashing, he explains, "is when all combustible materials simultaneously ignite. You're a baked potato after that." He needed more water, or to get out; but his ego was invested in staying inside, and so he stayed inside. Moments later a backup arrived, with another, bigger hose.

Afterward, he understood his mistake: the building was three stories, built on a slope that disguised its size, and the fire had reached the attic. "I'm not saying that if the backup hadn't come when it did I'd be dead," he says, but that's exactly what he is saying. The scar on his face is from that fire. "I needed to learn to control my environment," he said. "I'd had this false sense of security."

When you take care of something you become attached to it, and he'd become attached to Vallejo. He was extremely uncomfortable with conflict between his union and the citizens, and had found himself in screaming matches with the union's negotiator. Meyer thought firefighters, who tended to be idealistic and trusting, were easily duped. He further thought the rank-and-file had been deceived both by the city, which lied to them repeatedly in negotiations, and by their own leadership, which harnessed the firefighters' outrage to make unreasonable demands in the union-negotiated contract with the city. What was lost at the bargaining table was the reason they did what they did for a living. "I'm telling you," Meyer says, "when I started, I didn't know what I was getting paid. I didn't care what I was getting paid. I didn't know about benefits. A lot of things that we're politicizing today were not even in my mind. I was just thinking of my dream job. Let me tell you something else:

nobody cared in 2007 how much I made. If I made six figures they said, 'Shit, man, you deserve it. You ran into a burning building.' Because everyone had a job. All they knew about our job is that it was dangerous. The minute the economy started to collapse, people started looking at each other."

Today the backup that may or may not have saved him is far less likely to arrive. When Vallejo entered bankruptcy, the fire department was cut from 121 to 67, for a city of 112,000 people. The department handles roughly 13,000 calls a year, extremely high for the population. When people feel threatened or worried by anything except other people, they call the fire department. Most of these calls are of the cat-in-the-tree variety—pointless. ("You never see the skeleton of a cat in a tree.") They get calls from people who have headaches. They get calls from people who have itches where they can't scratch. They have to answer every call. ("The best call I ever had was phantom leg pain in a guy with no legs.") To deal with these huge numbers of calls, they once had eight stations, eight three-person engine companies, a four-man truck company (used only for actual fires and rescue calls), one fireboat, one confined space rescue team, and a team to deal with hazardous materials. They now are down to four stations, four engines, and a truck.

This is particularly relevant to Paige Meyer because, two months ago, he became Vallejo's new fire chief. It surprised him: he hadn't even applied for the job. The city manager, Phil Batchelor, just called him to his office one day. "He didn't ever really ask me if I wanted the job," says Meyer. "He just asked how's the family, told me he was giving me the job, and asked if I had any problem with that."

He didn't, actually. He sat down and made a list of ways to improve the department. He faced a fresh challenge: how to deliver service that was the same as before, or even better than before, with half the resources. How to cope with an environment of scarcity. He began to measure things that hadn't been measured. The number one cause of death in firefighting was heart attacks. Number two was a truck crash. He was now in charge of a department that would be both overworked and in a hurry. Fewer people doing twice the work probably meant twice the number of injuries per firefighter. He'd decided to tailor fitness regimens to fit the job. With fewer fire stations and fewer firefighters in them, the response times were going to be slower. He'd need to find new ways to speed things up. A longer response time meant less room for error; a longer response time meant the fires they'd be fighting would be bigger. He had some thoughts about the most efficient way to fight these bigger fires. He began, in short, to rethink firefighting.

When people pile up debts they will find difficult and perhaps even impossible to repay, they are saying several things at once. They are obviously saying that they want more than they can immediately afford. They are saying, less obviously, that their present wants are so important that, to satisfy them, it is worth some future difficulty. But in making that bargain they are implying that when the future difficulty arrives, they'll figure it out. They don't always do that. But you can never rule out the possibility that they will. As idiotic as optimism can sometimes seem, it has a weird habit of paying off.

1965 TRIUMPH BONNEVILLE

Joseph Millar

WHICH I PAID FOR
with a loan from the bank
I skipped on four months later

and which I named Rosie
for its dark red frame,
its engine and twinkling spokes,

the transparent collage
faintly peach-colored
fiberglassed on its tank:

the zodiac and three faces
of Elvis, all four Beatles,
Fellini and Marx,

its dual concentric carburetors
impossible to keep synchronized,
its Rambler gas cap and Ceriani forks.

"Big English," which I rode through the hills,
the asphalt buzzing my hips and spine
outside Point Reyes where the fault line

runs straight down through Tomales Bay,
where the wind makes its sullen
unfathomable sounds.

Which I rode through the Mission
and through the Haight
which I rode by the sea in the rain

doing over a hundred half drunk
down Highway One
in a race with a Kawasaki.

Which was stolen in Golden Gate Park
while I made love in the rhododendrons
with a girl from Chicago named Vivian

who made me a velvet shirt
and probably saved my life
in those days before helmet laws

though she ended up moving to Santa Cruz
where she left me
for a Chinese surfer with an earring

and I hitchhiked back
through the country of Davenport
listening to the wind in the yellow grass,

the road unwinding silken, black,
the path alongside battered and dusty
under the bones of my feet.

GEOMETRY OF THE WINTER DESERT: FIELD AND HOME

Susan Straight

S TRETCHING AWAY FROM the narrow road exactly where Thermal turns into Oasis is the most beautiful confluence of mathematics and mapping you might ever find along one strip of asphalt: Strawberries are glistening red atop black raised rows, and silver water runs down the furrows in the distance, where date palms provide a solid backdrop. Nearby, table grapes are pruned and dormant, the vines twisted horizontally along their wires, just a few new gold leaves unfurling.

And behind the palms, mountain ranges on both sides of the Coachella Valley: the Santa Rosa Range and the Little San Bernardino

Photograph by Douglas McCulloh

Watermelon harvest near the Salton Sea. Photograph by Douglas McCulloh

Mountains, purple and red in the fading sun of late afternoon, crenellated as fabric folded a million times into deep shadows.

That's geologic movement. There will be a big quake here, maybe in the next few minutes, maybe in the next few years, maybe in the next three decades. Doug tells me this—his father is an eminent geologist—and then he points to the faultlines and the places where trees grow in the moisture pushed up by plate slippage.

But what is here now: grapefruit and oranges heavy on the trees as if each one were personally decorated by a citrus goddess; fields of cilantro and dill ready to harvest; seedlings of pepper and celery poking through holes in black plastic stretched tight over the sharp-edged rows; carrot-tops like tiny day-old ferns; those strawberries huge and dangling; and already, personal watermelons. This is the geometry of desire.

None of this would be in this long desert valley without two essentials brought from other places years ago, or months ago, or yesterday: water and workers.

In the canals that bisect the long flat valley, the water is sapphire. It comes via the Coachella Canal, from the Colorado River.

In the fields where men crouch and cut stems, where they throw white boxes of just-picked dill up onto moving trucks, the skin is brown. The people come from wherever they left behind when they needed work.

Maybe they left rivers behind. In Mecca, during the grape harvest of late summer, when the local population swells with migrant workers, I have seen men bathing in irrigation canals and washing their clothes in the pumps where the water flows out into the furrows.

Today, the winter temperature is 82. In August, it will be 120. I have seen people sleeping on flattened cardboard in parking lots, or in the beds of their pickup trucks.

We drive down long gray highways where people are just getting home from the day in the fields, or the restaurants, or the hotels, or the golf courses. We pass immense fields of new vegetables where white ropes of water are thrown across the rows like lariats. Here is a settlement, and another one. The names are hopeful. El Rancho. La Cienega. Desert Shores.

Geometry is everywhere here, too. The mobile homes and travel trailers are long and rectangular, spaced regularly on their square plots, with spiky agave in round buckets or bursting geraniums in coffee cans or green nopales cactus in ovals held high like fingerless mittens.

Kids are everpresent, playing in the dirt roads, looking up from tire swings like huge black Cheerios, kicking balls across the paths. Dogs are everywhere, meeting in groups that look like they gather at dusk to share stories as well. A companionable group of seven dogs waits at one entryway to a settlement. Women look up from doorways, linger on two cement porch steps talking to each other.

Trucks and vans arrive to leave off men, and men come out into yards to start grills, to visit. I ask one man in Spanish where Oasis ends and Thermal begins, and he smiles, and gestures in long arcs. Mecca is that way. Indio that way. Coachella that way. Oasis is right here, he says.

An oasis is a place of constant water in a dry desert, whether in North Africa or in Southern California. Palms grow in their damp hallways of silver and gray-green just next door to the clusters of trailers, with their metal sheds and white stones marking the boundaries of life.

Doug and I know college students whose parents and relatives come from here. One of my best senior writers this year at UC Riverside is Jennifer Valdez, whose aunt has managed a date garden for a long time; Valdez just organized future writing and arts programs for incarcerated and foster youth. Last year, on a photography workshop in the infamous community of Duroville just down the road, which was news due to the hazardous living conditions for the 4,000 mostly Native Mexican residents, Doug met Thania Espinoza-Sandoval. Her grandfather has spent 32 years working date gardens, climbing the palms to pollinate, paperbag and then harvest huge clusters of dates sent all over the world. He was born in Puruandiro, Michoacan, Mexico, and always told Thania, born in Indio, that he did this so she could go to a university. She is now a sophomore at UC Davis.

In the geometric precision of the rows, and the spirals of the flung water, men and women move with equal linear patience, collecting box after box of fruits and vegetables to feed the winter hunger of those who live in the cold. They might not be able to count the thousands of items they gather, but they know how many children they have. And California lifts each grape in two fingers, studying the sheen, where maybe one drop of moisture has dried in a ghostly circle.

WATER CYCLE

Chieun "Gloria" Kim

L AST SUMMER SHONE bright over the mobius strip
ribbons of red
you left in my hair.
The ends flickered
past my eyes
like strawberry fields bordering the highway,
slipping through and around this winded, heaving town.
Your calloused palms warm
in the soil beneath my feet,
I exhaled skies littered with swallows.

On the hottest day,
I wiped the sweat from your brown neck
with a liquor store bandana and shaded you with church lace.
Soil from beneath your fingernails
filled the crescent moon divots
dotted across my back.
I irrigated the pockmarked terrain by the river
and lay against your weathered slopes,
waiting to grow.

Then summer waned.
Roots punched through my pores
and seized my skeletal frame.
Ribs gnarled

into thickened root,
joints locked up
like twists of branch.
My bones
dried and cracked
without water,
vines twisted tighter
around my spine,
sinew and thirst contracted my limbs,
bolted me down until I
trembled
under the burden of flightless skies.

Rain pelts and hardens the bay to sheet metal.
In its surface,
I see the sun asphyxiate.
Roots swell
beneath flesh, my skeleton softens,
the surge of water
erodes me to marrow.
Cell by cell, run-off carries me downstream,
where rust-red, stone-faced abalone
swallow and spit me out
into the churning punch of green waves,
the freeway roar of currents.
I claw
at jagged handholds
in a deep-sea canyon that
squeezes me
through wrinkled lifelines
until I crash, winded and waterlogged,
back to shore.

Late tangerines wither to violets
above me.
Constellations project from dilated pupils,
the ditches you dug
into my back
fill with saltwater.
You cradle my head, pick strawberries
from the ribbons in my hair,
cover my eyes with velvet leaves.
Feed me
syrup stains of boardwalk grins,
heady mulches of the wetlands,
the cinnamon bruise of a kiss.

I am a fistful of earth on your coast again.

from *SUSHI AND BLACK-EYED PEAS*

Bill Hutchinson

YELLOW HOUSE, WHITE HOUSE

A STENCH FROM ALL corners of the cotton land is acrid, some lethal bug spray unleashed by a biplane that rattled our roofs yesterday. It emptied its batch on our front yards and over fifty acres of Pima planted on the east side of the crumbling road. Now it smells like squashed black ants. Roosters are still asleep on this nippy June morning of 1964, their tiny heads slumped under stylish crimson pompadours, their hens purring as if dreaming of exotic, free-range spas. The sun is right on time, playing peek-a-boo from behind the jagged spires of the Sierra, scaling Donner Pass with the audaciousness of a diva on a stage lift. Drowsily, I ride on the shoulders of a woman of slender stature and voluminous hair she's dyed Nice 'n Easy black. She has just gulped down three cups of freeze-dried coffee, a caffeinated chaser for an evolving mix of self-prescribed multivitamins, calcium tablets, shark-cartilage pills, at least four hundred milligrams of glucosamine and a teaspoon of Carlson's cod liver oil.

She is insisting I call her *"Mao-Mao."*

"O-o-o, say *Mao-Mao.* Say *Mao-Mao!"* she pleads in an accent as thick and peculiar as the tule fog that will blanket this redneck stretch of rural California come the longest days of winter. My mother speaks in rivulets of brainteasers and tongue twisters that would try Mahatma Gandhi's patience. She can make a Mexican

restaurant waiter want to stomp his sombrero. In a voice somewhere between alto and tenor, she'll order *inch-a-naddas* instead of *enchiladas,* and say *two-Wallies* for *tamales.*

She's the only mother I know who muffs the enunciation of *Momma,* making it sound as if she's stuttering the name of China's chairman. For a tyke still potty training, trying to form a word like *Momma* is tough enough. Attempting to form a mispronounced word like *Mao-Mao* produces mostly spit bubbles, and a risk of being pegged Communist. The best I can do is *Zsa Zsa*—as in the Budapest-born starlet whose ample curves and cleavage cause grown men to drool.

My vocabulary might consist of more than grunts and squeaks if I had a better wardrobe, something instilling confidence instead of confusion, more Marshal Matt Dillon and less Miss Kitty. As it is, my powder-blue cotton dress fits snug around the thighs, and the half-inch shoulder straps cut into my clavicles. One of a closetful of skirts and bloomers lovingly home-sewn when I was making the leap from egg to embryo, my garment bears the solar system, a planetary alignment of polyester crescents and rayon spheres. While I was waiting in her womb, *Zsa Zsa* was placing an all-or-nothing wager on the planets aligning to grant her pinkest of prenatal wishes. Lord knows she prayed long enough to deserve a daughter. She had two sons, three years apart, and waited seven years more for a chance at a girl. Her faith held firm until the moment Dr. Cyril H. Johnson slapped my flank and congratulated her on the birth of another boy.

I do not wish to embark on life as the lesser consequence of a go-bust bet, sanctioned to the role of dress-up doll for fading fantasies. I do not have to be her last chance. At age thirty-seven, her fallopian tubes are still functional. Nevertheless, my parents have made me the final drop in their murky genetic pool, even cinched it by christening me with my father's name. William D. Hutchinson Jr. is suitable for a clinch-jawed New York aristocrat in herringbone jacket and ascot, but the moniker doesn't fit the mug of a Japanese-Cherokee-Irish-African-American. There's a regal sound to William David or William Douglas, yet the authorities deprived me of a middle name. As a substitute, they bestowed a somber, meaningless letter puffing its little chest out as if envious of all surnames, about to trip over a dot. My brothers got middle names: Gary Stanley and Yukio Carlos. While customary for American fathers to brand their names to a firstborn son, mine did it *ass-jackwards*.

I wish they would take more solace in Dr. Johnson's accounting of all my fingers, toes and, most importantly, faculties. That's more important than the sex of a child. Plus, my two big brothers did not fare as well. Gary was born with a mental defect, one that caused him to mistake his art supplies for lunch on his first day of kindergarten at Lincoln Elementary School. "Your boy is mentally retarded!" his bespectacled, haughty teacher huffed during an emergency classroom conference, perhaps baffled by the cold shoulder she got from *Zsa Zsa* for suggesting Gary be committed to the state mental institution at Porterville.

Physicians have yet to find empirical evidence of glitches in Yukio's brain, but the eldest son of Sumiko Kinjo and William D. Hutchinson Sr. acts loonier than Gary. An adolescent with a growing thirst for alcohol and weed, my brother Yuki smokes a quarter-pack of cigarettes a day. He cannot walk past a window without throwing a rock through it, and he and his pals, the Oliver boys, are fond of blasting each other with BB guns. Walter, Ricky and Charlie Oliver resemble a trio of doo-wop desperadoes. Their gleaming white teeth flash like beacons against their charcoal-colored skin. They dress in matching ragged jeans and dirty T-shirts, and live in a wooden shack up the road that looks like it's about to cave in, and is overflowing with mangy mutts and angry sisters. Most of the time, they're sweet boys, polite around old folk and goofy around babies. However, Yukio can provoke the evil side of anybody. It's a wonder that, since befriending him, they haven't burned their shack down. They play with matches for sport, scoring points by igniting each other ablaze like gnomes gone mad in a fairy tale game. When they're not maiming each other, they're pushing a go-cart up and down the road, panting and yelling, *Choke the throttle, man!*

Boy or girl, I am my mother's last hope.

Goose bumps appear on my stubby bare legs as *Zsa Zsa* skips in front of a yellow stucco house she says is ours. She begins trotting like a Lipizzan stallion, one trained to dazzle a demanding crowd by using just its hind legs. I bounce with slumbering laughter as she gallops alongside a flowerbed sprouting pink sweet peas, red and white roses, and orange California poppies. Her feet grind to a shuffle on the gravel driveway of the single-story white house next door—an asphalt-shingled two-bedroom nearly identical to the yellow one. She hands me over to a stout woman wearing black horn-rimmed glasses. My father's mother styles her white hair in a baseball-size bun fastened to the crown of her head by a network of Sta-Rite bobby pins. She has a long, cheerful face, rubbery jowls, raw-umber eyes and abnormally floppy earlobes. Her skin is ten shades lighter than mine, but we share similar flat noses. She smells of talcum, denture cream and holy oil, yet she wears no makeup or perfume. Her ankle-length dress, another one of *Zsa Zsa*'s designs, bears a paisley pattern, resembling polliwogs swimming to the stash of hard peppermint candy in the pockets of a matching apron stained with bacon fat and Crisco. She wants me to call her "Grandmother Alice," but that is even more challenging than *Mao-Mao,* and produces a big burp when I try. The best I can do is *Caca.*

Caca and I wave goodbye to *Zsa Zsa,* who sets off to work in a burly '58 Chevy Biscayne. We stand in the driveway watching the taillights vanish in the blue tint of the hour, listening until snoring dogs and chirping crickets drown out the roar of the V-8.

It is only twenty grown-up steps between the two front porches, but it might as well be a transpacific journey. This daily driveway transfer, a routine handoff at an inconspicuous property line, is like the midpoint in the *It's a Small World* ride at Disneyland, where a little boat carries you from Tokyo to Texas in one bend of a narrow stream.

In the yellow house, *Zsa Zsa* always has a pot of sticky white rice steaming on her stove. Sometimes she spreads a scoop onto a sheet of dried seaweed she calls *nori*, then rolls it around slices of raw tuna. When deprived of tuna, she uses the canned mystery meat Spam. Either way, she calls the dish *sushi*. Using a pair of ten-inch-long sticks, she will dredge the round pieces in salty soy sauce spiked with green lumps of nostril-clearing wasabi. Stuffing a whole morsel in her mouth, she'll exclaim through bulging, happy cheeks and watery eyes, "Umm, umm, *oshie!*"

In the white house, *Caca* uses knives and forks and usually has a vat of black-eyed peas simmering on a burner and a pan of cornbread browning in the oven. When she tastes her own cooking, she says, "That's mighty fine, *praise da Lawd!*" She has a compulsion to begin nearly every sentence with the phrase *Lawd willin'*, and to punctuate nearly every sentence with the phrase *Praise da Lawd:*

"*Lawd willin'*, I'm gonna go to the store, *praise da Lawd.*"

"*Lawd willin'*, I'm gonna do some washin' and ironin', *praise da Lawd.*"

"*Lawd willin'*, I'm gonna get me a switch, *praise da Lawd.*"

In the yellow house, *Zsa Zsa* sings me tranquil Japanese lullabies she learned as a child growing up in Okinawa, a South Pacific island chain that could be mistaken for a band of mosquitoes joyriding on a spinning plastic globe. In the white house, *Caca* sings gospel hymns: *This little light of mine, I'm gonna let it shine…*resonates in her East Texas twang.

In the yellow house, I play with figurines *Zsa Zsa* calls *origami,* little cranes and boxes that magically appear when she folds pieces of paper. In the white house, I follow *Caca* from room to room trying to glimpse someone she keeps calling *Jesus.* The invisible man possesses superpowers to raise the dead and turn bass into bread. *Caca* is always asking Him to spare a life and save a soul.

I'm sprouting rapidly, probably faster than most of my peers. Yet *Caca* and *Zsa Zsa* are constantly egging me to *shake a leg.* I was a big baby from the get-go, eight pounds, eleven ounces. My body has ballooned three pounds a month since. At this rate, I should outgrow the largest of my dresses lickety split, and weigh three-sixty by the time I turn ten. I developed my first tooth at three months old, sat up on my own a month later, and stood up three months after that. My ability to walk coincided with the time President Kennedy butted nuclear warheads with Fidel Castro and nearly annihilated the planet. I was running by the day Walter Cronkite interrupted *As the World Turns* to break news of an assassin's sharp aim in Dallas, *Caca*'s hometown. Yet she and *Zsa Zsa* are forever griping: *Big boys don't put black-eyed peas up their nostrils; big boys don't throw their sushi across the table like mini Frisbees.* If I could, I'd tell them that unless they live in Scotland, only big boys of a certain persuasion dress like kiddy drag queens, *praise da Lawd.*

Stuck with the examples of my two brothers, who could fault my reluctance to be a big boy? A majority of toddlers would fold or ask for a better hand when faced with the dilemma of becoming a juvenile delinquent or a career special-education student. No one has yet convinced me that the toilet is far more efficient than my diaper. Given the chance, I'd extend my visa a few more years in this sloppy, lovely and unencumbered dawn of life. I am going to miss riding around on shoulders like an Egyptian prince. I've grown accustomed to serenades of both Gospel and Okinawan, of being ferried between the Far East and the Deep South, from the belly of Buddha to the Bible Belt.

I'm perfecting my walk on this driveway between the houses, falling and skinning my knees and elbows on the loose gravel. I'm getting comfortable planting my feet in two different time zones, so to speak. It's reassuring to know all I have to do is run a few paces to fetch help whenever, in either house, trouble is brewing.

-ALITY

I can run between our yellow house and my grandparents' white house now in seven seconds flat. My grandfather, Henry Hutchinson, timed me with the silver pocket watch he keeps in the breast pouch of his bib overalls. Not only fleet of foot, I'm adept at using forks, knives and chopsticks, and my favorite meal is sushi and black-eyed peas. While many of my second-grade classmates are fluent in English and Spanish, I am the only one who can sing *Silent Night* in Japanese. Friends are envious of my *origami*-making skills, awed at how I customize paper planes to do *kamikaze* dives.

"You best *gimme dat,*" my grandmother yells emphatically.

Halting a dash for the door, I unbuckle my tool belt.

Since becoming responsible for changing my underwear, I have found that plumbing captures my curiosity. I'm content whiling away my leisure time exploring the musty crawl spaces under our house. I feel useful searching for leaks in the maze of galvanized and copper conduits running from front porch to rear stoop. Here my back squirms across the wormy bare ground and the flickering beam of my flashlight points up at the roughhewn sides of our floorboards. I relish retrieving a pipe wrench from my tool belt to fix a loose bushing or fend off a black widow upset at me for crinkling her carefully spun cobwebs.

My tool belt is jerry-rigged from a leather cap-gun holster. The gun broke in half long ago and I've since lost both parts. I surrender it to *Caca* with the reluctance of a suspended Roto-Rooter man.

"Button the sleeves of ya shirt," my grandmother says.

This is one of the shirts my mother sewed. She lets us choose whatever material we want. The shirts she makes my grandfather are either blue denim or white. Henry doesn't go for fancy checkered ones like my brothers Yukio and Gary. My father prefers striped shirts. My shirts are Wild-West style, like the ones Hopalong Cassidy wears. Made of cotton and rayon, my buckaroo shirts feature spiffy pearl snaps, zigzag stitching, and breast pockets with yoke-shaped flaps that prevent my marbles from spilling out when I'm hanging upside down. In plaid, checks and stripes, the artisanal apparel present a variety for me to mix and match with store-bought blue jeans and corduroys, pointy-toed cowboy boots and Chuck Taylor All Stars. More durable and less confining than my old poodle skirts, the outfits accommodate the twisting currents of my cross-cultural roughhousing lifestyle.

"Go on, boy. Learn to be somebody, *praise da Lawd,*" says Alice, sending me striding aboard a yellow bus that takes me to Lincoln Elementary School.

With the exception of being white and wearing disposable latex gloves to better grip the wheel, my driver bears an uncanny resemblance to Alice's daughter-in-law, Bert. Her eyes look like potato bugs trapped in two whirlpools of milk, and her cheeks are as plump as a carnivorous cherub's. Her meaty arms waggle when she hits a pothole the way Aunty Bert's do when she's pounding the piano. We devious passengers secretly call our chauffeur *Puddin' Arms.* She offers Grandma a casual salute now, perhaps signaling she has not forgotten the crux of their very first conversation. The first time I went to catch this bus, Alice insisted on boarding, too. Nudging me through the unfolding double-doors, she kindly introduced me and, disregarding even the most cursory of background checks, deputized *Puddin'* to dole out corporal punishment as she saw fit. "If he don't mind on this bus and go to cuttin' up, you speak to 'im," Grandma implored. "If he don't hear ya, stop the bus and lay your fist right upside his head."

I make it to my destination once again without testing Puddin's latex-covered backhand. Lincoln School is on East Cedar Avenue where P Street—Tulare, California's version of Skid Row—dead-ends. As I get off the bus and wave goodbye to *Puddin'*, a handful of winos in a trash-strewn vacant lot across the street are stoking a fire in a rusted barrel with yesterday's *Advance-Register,* waiting for the P Street liquor store to open up. The houses in this predominantly black neighborhood have a tired appearance; some look downright slumped over with exhaustion. Every other front yard has two or three cars, as dilapidated as the houses, sitting on wooden blocks without tires or engines. My classroom is at the west end of a long single-story building of classrooms. It attracts the most vandals. At least once a month, we'll arrive on a Monday to find half our windows shattered. Our principal, Mrs. Rayburn, keeps threatening to put a tall fence topped with razor wire around the school to keep unwanted mischief-makers out and wanted mischief-makers in. The peeling paint on my classroom walls is off-white, the color of an old dog bone. The wooden tops of our desks are scrawled with graffiti, some of it dating back to when my brothers attended school here. The room smells faintly of ammonia. On the play-ground, the basketball courts have rusted chain-link nets hanging with the help of Duct tape. The merry-go-round is so wobbly it has been condemned. The books we attempt to read in class are Scotch-taped and missing pages.

There are about twenty-five kids in my class, all of us either black or brown. Miss Reynoso orders us to hush up and sit down. She hands out an official-looking form. The amount of paperwork we do is fourfold what we endured as first-graders. Back then, getting us to draw stick figures and memorize the alphabet comprised the extent of my teacher's curriculum. Now, she expects me to use my A, B, C's to spell out words and sentences, and to realize there's a difference between a clause and Santa Claus.

"Ah, Miss Reynoso, I just did my fingernails," Yolanda fibs, flinging a silky curtain of dark hair off her pale, bare shoulder, puffing on her red fingernails as if they are ablaze.

Yolanda has designated me to be her *"novio."* That's what she calls me. I didn't know it meant *boyfriend* until my Spanish-speaking classmates clued me in—some three days after I was drafted. I say *drafted* because I really have no choice in the matter. She is taller than I am and her voice is an octave lower, making her an intimidating foe. Her eyebrows are as thick as mine are, but meet in the middle like soul brothers shaking hands. The lettuce-sleeved sundresses she wears in spring are similar to those I wore in infancy. The bossy leader of a schoolyard clique, she is capable of unscrupulous behavior. I have remained on guard for her posse of diminutive disciples ever since they snatched me off the jungle gym and dragged me into the girls' restroom. At her command, they held me against a sink while she kissed me on the mouth, their giggles and her prolonged puckering echoing off the walls of the concrete chamber. Once freed, I spit and cursed the cooties.

"Ohhh, *pobrecita*," Miss Reynoso says, mocking Yolanda, making the Spanish-speaking kids laugh and leaving us English-only kids with blank stares.

Given the lengthy number of questions on this paper, Yolanda's fingers are likely to go numb. The questionnaire has something to do with a man who enters my classroom wearing a dark-blue, almost black, uniform. It does not seem fair that he can bring his holster to school and I have to leave mine at home. He's weighted down with a loaded revolver, extra bullets, a pair of handcuffs and a billy club. His strap hangs lopsided on his hips and he is adjusting it with both hands like a squeaky leather hula-hoop. A shiny shield on his chest reads Tulare Police. I'd like to ask if he's ever drawn his six-shooter in the line of duty, but Miss Reynoso shushes me, explaining she has invited the officer to gather our fingerprints and vital statistics.

"Ya gonna read us our rights like they do on *Dragnet?*" asks Biscuit Dawkins.

"Biscuit, you ain't got no TV. I saw your momma take it down to the pawn shop," hollers Bobo, the foul-mouthed boy sitting at the desk to my left.

"Yeah, Biscuit, closest you gonna get to a TV is pasting pictures to your transistor radio," adds the cross-eyed, clubfooted son of a Mexican caballero, José Calderon.

"You children are not suspects, you are potential victims," the cop says sternly.

"This is in case one of you is kidnapped," Miss Reynoso elaborates.

Like a Chicago wise guy, she whispers to the cop out the corner of her mouth, "...or you drive me so batty I mar your faces beyond recognition." She and the officer laugh. His teeth are a strange color, the color of dirty dishwater. He goes to the door to spit. A wad of chewing tobacco lands on the edge of the quad. The brown sphere tumbles and unravels on the grass like a time-lapse flower.

He is still snickering when he returns, wiping his empty mouth with the back of his hand, and wiping his hand on his pants. I think my teacher is only half joking. Kidnapping is not a subject she takes lightly. She is constantly cautioning us not to get into cars with strangers. No matter how far afield such crimes occur, she will read us the newspaper headlines with dramatic leaps and pitches dictated by the bold typeface:

PARIS PLAYGROUND PANIC

SINATRA'S SON SNATCHED

AUSSIE BEACH ABDUCTION

Since we live nearly two hundred miles east of the nearest beach, I feel safe. Yet the cop conveys that we have to be on guard everywhere, even in the sandbox. He is eager to know what we intend to do if attacked by a kidnapper. I am tempted to squeal on my captor Yolanda, but think better of it when she cocks her threatening unibrow in my direction. Unless restrained by all fours, I assure the officer I would kick the abductor in the most delicate part of his or her anatomy and scream at an octave that can crack a Coke bottle. I want to ask how three kicking and screaming kids could disappear in front of hundreds of Aussie sunbathers, but Miss Reynoso silences me again, telling us to print legibly and make it snappy.

The early questions are a breeze: whom to call in case of an emergency, parents' names, address and phone number, date of birth, height and weight. Suddenly, an unfamiliar word stumps me. My lips slowly sound out the syllables—*Na·tion·al·ity*.

Every morning we pledge allegiance to the United States of America. Standing straight and squared, right hands on our hearts, we tell the Star-Spangled Banner in the upper corner of our class-room that we are *one nation under God, indivisible, with liberty and justice for all*. One way to get Miss Reynoso perturbed is to say *invisible* instead of *indivisible*. I once told her that if President Johnson was invisible he could slip into meetings of the Viet Cong, hear all their secrets and finally see a way to end the war in Vietnam.

The *nation* part is understandable; *-ality* is what stymies me.

In my Central California town, where muddy pickup trucks rule the roads, cows outnumber people, and the fragrance of fresh manure hangs thick in the evening air, I sometimes wish I were invisible, or white like the cop, or just plain black or Mexican like the major-ity of kids in my school. Out here in the cotton fields surrounded by an uneasy number of Republicans and Am-Vet Post members, any solid color would be better than the hodgepodge I was born.

I am the only one in all of Lincoln School whom a single check-mark, or even two, cannot define. Except for my brothers, I have never encountered anyone like me. Our birth certificates say our mother is *Japanese* and our father is *Negro*, but it is more complicated than that. Momma sometimes calls herself Okinawan, while Dad never calls himself Negro or Black or African-American. Big Bill insists he is nearly full-blooded Cherokee, tells us there was an Irishman in the woodpile, and sometimes masquerades as Mexican. He wears the tattoo of a notorious Mexican street gang and speaks Spanish fairly well, having grown up in Texas when they did not care much about holes in the border.

Nervously chewing the pink eraser of my yellow No. 2 pencil, I turn to Bobo, whispering, "What you writin', Bo?"

"What ya think, *mutha'fucker?*" he hisses, acting all tough.

Sylvester "Bobo" James knows cursing bothers me. As a member of the House of Love Deliverance Church, I have learned that cussing is a sin—along with dancing to rock 'n' roll, gambling, fighting, stealing, boozing, smoking, taking drugs, being mean to old folks and stone-cold murder. Even going to the movies is a sacrilege unless the flick is *The Ten Commandments*. Still, all kinds of profanities spew from Bobo's mucky mouth, sometimes poetically:

Damn mutha'fucker, two-ball bitch;
Ya got a ring 'round ya collar and a polka-dotted dick...

I try not to curse aloud, especially since Alice busted me a few weeks back. My dopey neighbor started it by using my face as a target to try out a slingshot he devised from a Y-shaped eucalyptus branch, heavy rubber bands and a scrap of leather. I'm often the victim of Charlie Alvidrez's psychopathically rough play. He has shoved me off a swing, hit me in the head with a dirt clod, and even shot me in the jaw with a handcrafted bow and arrow. Once he chucked a spear through the front spokes of my bicycle and sent me flying over the handlebars, my head bouncing off the asphalt road. A short, wiry Spanish kid with a milky complexion and buck teeth, Charlie is a wild-eyed budding conman and would-be serial killer. Waiting at the bus stop one morning, he tells me of a live cat he threw into a barrel of burning garbage in our back yard. He said it matter-of-factly, like, *Oh, by the way, I threw a cat in your garbage can and set it ablaze. It should be nice and crispy by the time we get back.* I did not believe him until we got home that afternoon. We removed a blackened board blockading the top of the barrel and cautiously peered inside. Suddenly a pair of red eyes was lunging up at our faces, the mad, maimed stray wildly swinging its charred claws and shrieking. Screaming, we ducked and fell on the muddy ground as the feline scampered off smoldering, singed and mangy. Horrified, I looked over at Charlie, who was rolling around laughing like a hyena on *Mutual of Omaha's Wild Kingdom.* Like Marlin Perkins, I have concluded my partner is crazy for wanting to piss off feral animals.

"God damn you, sonofabitch!" I cried. I had good reason to cuss. The rock Charlie flung at me with his slingshot nearly hit me in the eye. A chill raced head to toe, immediately eclipsing the throbbing of my frontal lobe. Even as the foul words were escaping my lips, I knew my mistake was not looking before cussing. Instantly, I was reminded what a mixed blessing it is to live next door to God's top groupie.

"Boy! Get me a switch, *praise da Lawd!* God help ya!"

Tears began jumping from my eyes like Acapulco cliff divers on *Wide World of Sports.* My legs jangling fearfully, I turned to face Alice knowing I was doomed. Proverbs 13:24 is her favorite scripture: *He that spareth his rod hateth his son; but he that loveth him chasteneth him betimes.*

Alice grabbed a pair of pruning shears she keeps handy beside her porch, her eyes squinting with a determination to show me how much she *loveth* me. Finding me guilty of blasphemy, she imposed my sentence without a trial. She pointed a calloused finger to one of the twin sycamores in her front yard and ordered me to cut my own rod, threatening to burn my britches twice if I failed to find a satisfactory switch. I dragged the V-shaped pruning shears the way one would a divining rod weighing the size of a blacksmith's anvil, and shuddered as she vowed to beat the Devil out of me. Clipping a slender twig from the low branches, my spine stiffened to her raised voice: "That ain't a switch!" My chin quivered uncontrollably as I climbed higher on a wooden ladder to reach a leafy limb about three feet long. Sobbing apologies and promising to watch my mouth, I tried to delay the inevitable. She acted as if she did not hear me. I plucked the leaves as slowly as possible, hoping for a reprieve. As soon as it was clean as a fishing pole, she snatched the switch and swooshed it through the air a couple of times to test its flexibility. I shrieked like Charlie's smoldering cat before feeling the first of a dozen swats across my stinging butt. "Don't you ever let me hear ya cussin' and actin' ugly; *da Lawd* don't like ugliness," she scolded and swatted. Once she was through, we kneeled at her porch, praying and repenting for an hour.

Biscuit, who sits in front of me, isn't as foul-mouthed as Bobo. I tap his shoulder now and ask, "What you writin'?"

"Black and proud," he says, bobbing his egg-shaped head like one of my grandparents' backyard chickens. Biscuit is as bony as the malnourished children featured in the pages of *National Geographic*. We call him *Biscuit* because we once caught him eating one he fetched from a garbage can.

I shift to Isaac Vallejo behind me.

"I'm a *cholo, esa,*" says Isaac, who always wears baggy black pants and a plaid Pendleton buttoned to the top. A folded blue bandanna serves as his headband, its carefully creased lower edge furrowing his eyebrows. Biscuit, who can run a forty-yard dash in under six seconds, is the fastest in the class. Bobo—who is a foot taller and twenty pounds heavier than me—is the undisputed best athlete of the school, but Isaac is the only one of us who sports a goatee.

"*Whutz up, esa vato?*" says Isaac, rubbing his fuzzy chin and nodding at my incomplete form.

"There's no *cholo* on the form, Isaac," I say. The choices are Caucasian, Black, Hispanic and Oriental.

Our chatter catches Miss Reynoso's attention and she walks over asking if there is a problem. My heart is aflutter when she is so close. I love the way her teeth appear too big for her mouth. With her brunette hair cut in a bouncy bob, soft fair skin and ruby lips, she is the Latina version of Gidget. Some classmates like to call her *Miss Rhinoceros* behind her back, but I think she is the most beautiful teacher God has ever created. Miss Reynoso is the only teacher I have ever had. I liked her right from the start in kindergarten, fell in love with her in the first grade and, now in the second grade, my affection is even deeper. I want her to be my teacher forever.

Biscuit and I are pals because Miss Reynoso forced us to be. We started out as enemies fighting over a life-size pony I had cleverly constructed out of wooden blocks. Stepping away to fish for a compliment from Miss Reynoso, I turned to find Biscuit mounting my pony. Enraged, I pushed him from behind, knocking him off. He popped up as if the floor was a trampoline. His fingernails drew blood across the right side of my face before I could raise a fist. As I went to retaliate, Miss Reynoso intervened and sent me to the nurse. Then she made us stay after class, scolded us for fighting, and demanded we shake hands and make up. I was so sad about upsetting her I burst into tears. To cheer Biscuit and me up, Miss Reynoso treated us to cheeseburgers and milkshakes at the Bugle Café on South K Street. We sat in a booth next to the front window listening to The Monkees sing *I'm a Believer* on a miniature jukebox. Biscuit ate ravenously. Miss Reynoso, daintily.

I ate carefully, trying to keep ketchup and chocolate from staining the square white bandage covering my scratched cheek. Bobo, Biscuit, and Isaac have voted me the teacher's pet. If I am, my mother is to thank.

At a parent-teacher conference, Sumiko slipped Miss Reynoso a bribe—a stuffed Snoopy she rescued from the reject pile at work. She is a sewing-machine operator at the R. Dakin Toy Company in Lindsay, a town east of Tulare thick with orange groves but boasting the world's largest olive-canning company. When she has to clock in on Saturdays, I'll tag along to the sprawling factory in the middle of an olive orchard. Her machine is a gleaming contraption of chrome, chipped green metal and pushrods. Its needle moves so fast it becomes a silver blur. Momma sits in a row of hunched-over women, their faces illuminated by the overhead lamps of their machines. They wear surgical masks to protect their lungs from the blizzard of synthetic fibers and look like doctors stitching up patients. My mother sits next to her best friend and car-pool partner, Mary Reed. Born and reared in France, Mary lives on the left bank of an irrigation canal on the western edge of Tulare. She and my mother both survived World War II, but on the opposite sides of the world. She has a high-pitched accent that is thicker than Sumiko's brogue. Yet, they've formed a language of their own. I've witnessed them laughing and crying over family matters in each other's living rooms.

My mother genuinely enjoys finding homes for the cuddly castoffs she rescues from the factory junk heap. She has brought home one-eyed gorillas, three-legged dogs, frogs with crooked smiles and giraffes with stubby necks. Sometimes she fixes their flaws, but mostly she passes them off as one-of-a-kind gifts. Miss Reynoso's Snoopy had lopsided ears, but she did not seem to notice.

Another time, Miss Reynoso invited my mother to cook the class a traditional Japanese *sukiyaki*, a wintry stew of vegetables, thin noodles and sliced beef. I cannot recall anyone else's mom coming to class to cook after that.

"Now-wa we-a mick it all up-a an' koo-in POW," Sumiko instructed, drawing looks of bewilderment from my so-called friends. A tsunami of embarrassment buried me in my seat. I wished someone really would abduct me.

"She says she's going to mix it all up and cook it in a pot," I grudgingly interpreted.

Despite her tongue-tangled enunciations, my mother has become a formidable politician, recently winning election as vice president of the PTA. One of the key tactics she deployed was insisting constituents call her Sue instead of Sumiko, which voters tended to mispronounce as *Show-me-cow* or *Sue-me-now.* I still do not see how she was able to get her campaign message across so effectively considering I can barely understand her. She learned English by reading the Bible and praying with Alice, a combination that causes her to litter her speech with scriptural grammar. She says "thee" instead of "the" and "nay" for "no" and "thus" for "this." My playmates crack up laughing when they hear her yelling from our front porch, *"Beery, thus ye get in the house for dinraw, saith thy mother."*

Making matters worse, she is deaf in her left ear from accidentally puncturing her eardrum on a pointy metal dishtowel rack in our sunny yellow kitchen. Talking to her often goes like this:

"Ma...Ma...Maaa! What are we gonna have for dinner?"

"What? You wanna be sinner?"

"No! Dinner?"

"Who Linda?"

"No! What's...for...dinner?"

"Why you wanna beith thinner?"

As the designated teacher's pet, I raise my hand to ask Miss Reynoso what she would put down on the form for nationality. In her wispy, know-it-all voice, she tells us of her Latin heritage, how her parents are from Mexico, but her roots go back to Spain. She says she would proudly mark Hispanic.

"*Odelay, esa!* I'm a Hispanic *cholo,*" Isaac quips, marks his form and flashes several gang signs with his fingers that could mean he is a Latin King or desperately needs a bathroom break.

"You know there's the line marked *Other?*" Miss Reynoso mentions. But there is not enough room on the line marked *Other,* I tell her, to fully explain. She smiles, saying, "Do your best."

Confident, I cram in tiny letters: Japanese, Cherokee, Irish, Black and American.

"You ain't black, Billy!" Bobo says, peeking at my sheet and drawing erroneous conclusions from my straight hair, parted on the side and slicked back with dabs of Brylcreem. He is studying my skin, which is brown as maple syrup but will be as dark as the bottom of my grandmother's cornbread by the end of summer. He looks at my cowboy boots and buckaroo shirt, surmising, "You may be a Chinese cowboy, but you ain't black, mutha'fucker."

I tell him Grandma says it is not right to judge people by their color or clothes.

"My grandma says,'Ya never know when you are talking to Jesus,'" I tell Bobo.

"You ain't Jesus, and neither is you Irish," Biscuit butts in, explaining the Irish have red hair and green eyes. Since there are no other Irish kids in our class, my only reference point is an image of the dancing leprechaun on the Lucky Charms cereal box.

I do not know anyone who gets asked to prove his roots as much as me. I state my case like Perry Mason, explaining Alice's father was an Irishman named Charles Mink, who became a Texan after arriving in America as a stowaway on a boat from Belfast. Her mother was part Cherokee and part black, even though we called her Momma White. I go to a predominantly black holy-roller church, where my Uncle C.L. is the pastor and I sing and sometimes play the tambourine in a gospel choir. My favorite singer is Mahalia Jackson. Uncle C.L.'s wife, my Aunty Bert, directs the choir. She also has the distinguished honor of being the first black woman ever hired as a U.S. Postal carrier in Tulare.

"I guess you are a brother," Biscuit concedes.

I hand in the form. If the police are going to save me from a kidnapper, they had better know exactly who to look for.

At recess, Biscuit says I should learn the Black Power handshake. He also teaches me the accompanying rhyme:

> *Umgawa! Black Power!*
> *White boy—destroy!*
> *I said it; I meant it...*
> *I'm here to represent it...*
> *I'm black; I'm proud...*
> *I'm soul brother number nine...*
> *Sock it to me one more time!*

I try to put my own spin on the rap as we go through the five or six moves of the handshake. By the time I get to "Umgawa! Japanese-Cherokee-Irish-Black-American Power!" Biscuit's eyes start rolling. I vow to work on a better rhyme.

There are no holidays for boys like me, no Japanese-Cherokee-Irish-Black-American Day. While other kids have Cinco de Mayo and Columbus Day, I am mostly associated with Pearl Harbor Day. Kids call me "Jap" (which I dislike) and "Kato" from the *Green Hornet* (which I prefer). I do not mind the nickname "Geronimo" after the famed Apache warrior. However, don't call me "Hop Sing" from *Bonanza*—that's just geographically wrong. Mostly, I catch a lot of aggravation because of my sneaky, chopstick-using, karate-chopping, rice-eating people who ambushed the Pacific Fleet on a Sunday of all days. My brother, Yukio, is always begging Momma to let him skip classes the first week of December, when his history teacher reviews the events of the Day of Infamy.

"It's always Jap this and Jap that!" Yuki gripes. "They don't like Japs, they don't like *niggers;* they don't like nothin' about me."

On the bus ride home, I make the mistake of trying to be friendly to a pair of fat Mexican sisters, telling them about my father's eldest brother, Uncle Louis, who lives in Alaska.

"Uncle Louis says it's so cold there you'll freeze to death if you step foot outside with less than a bearskin on. He swears that in the winter it's night all the time. In the summer, it's just the reverse and people mow their lawns at two in the morning," I tell the sisters.

They crinkle their noses as if I broke wind. The older one calls me a name no one has called me before. "Eskimo," she says. The younger one smirks and calls me "Eskimo," too. Stretching their eyelids out with their index fingers, the pair has the whole bus laughing, causing my naturally squinty eyes to tear.

I am glad when my stop comes, relieved to get out and into my grandparents' white house. My grandpa Henry is napping in his easy chair under a portrait of Jesus Christ and a framed color print titled *The Rapture.* Examining the latter, one sees an overhead view of a small, rural town like ours. The picture depicts people flying out of cemetery graves, heading to the Savior, who is stretching out his welcoming arms against a cloudless, cerulean sky. Cars are crashing into trees as drivers float to heaven. People are ascending from houses, churches, schools, even out of a moving train. For every person headed to meet their maker, at least five remain on earth looking like they just swallowed the cat that swallowed the canary.

"Don't be one of them that gets left behind, Billy," my grandfather cautions, his eyes still closed.

Henry stretches his arms and yawns, pulling a pocket watch from the breast pouch of his overalls. As he is winding the silvery timepiece, I tell him about the form we had to fill out and how Miss

Reynoso directed me to the line marked *Other*. I do not tell him how the fat Mexican sisters made me cry. Still, when I ask what an Eskimo is, he senses my sadness. He says Eskimos are great hunters from way up north, close to the top of the world, tough people who can walk around in Bermuda shorts in subzero weather.

"As far as I know, there's not a drop of Eskimo in ya," he says. "Billy, you're like a square peg that if ya hammer long enough will eventually fit perfectly in a round hole."

I'd rather be an Eskimo.

I ask what he would mark on Miss Reynoso's form. He scratches his head of thick, wavy silver hair. Rubbing the round, wire-rim lenses of his glasses with a white handkerchief he also uses to blow his nose, he agrees it is not an easy question.

His birth certificate and documents bearing his family history burned in a blaze that destroyed the city hall of his Texas hometown. His mother, Momma Jo Hutchinson, told him he was born in 1892, raised around newly freed slaves who could not read the Emancipation Proclamation let alone understand it.

Like Alice's mother, Momma White, Momma Jo professed both Cherokee and black lineage, one of the so-called Freemen. In a worn, black-and-white photograph he has of his mother, she's the spitting image of Henry—except for her frilly, ankle-length dress. Tall and big busted, she posed like a linebacker in shoulder pads, staring uncomfortably into the camera, her dark leathery face framed by long, gray hair she wore loose.

At funerals and family reunions, I overhear kinfolk whispering about the mysteries Momma Jo masked behind her lips-sealed smile. "Poor child" and "taboo" are code words they use to respond to one of her deeper secrets. Speaking in hushed tones, they swap sketchy details gleaned from genealogical hearsay. Given Henry's caramel-colored skin tone and the waviness of his tresses, they peg my great-grandfather as a Cherokee slave owner from Oklahoma, who bought Momma Jo's mother and had his way with their daughter.

Born a slave, Momma Jo did not have a choice but to submit to her father's perverted wishes. My grandfather was the first of five children she bore her father.

This is disturbing news to my young ears. Even with my grammar-school education, I realize it's not normal for a mother and son to also be sister and brother. Henry must have grown up even more confused, not knowing whether to call his father Dad or Granddad. He insists he never heard his mother utter his father's name, or share a kind word about him. He gets perturbed when I probe more about his father. I drop the subject but cannot put it out of my mind given that medical research suggests the odds of being born deformed or with a mental disability like my brother, Gary, are drastically increased when a child is conceived as the result of incest.

Henry went through life without a last name until Momma Jo married John Hutchinson, a railroad worker as black as Texas crude. "Hutch" is what most folks called him. He and Momma Jo had five children of their own. They would have had more had a freak accident not cut his life short. How it happened remains unsolved, but somehow on the job one day a railroad spike slammed Hutch in the head with such force that it killed him instantly.

Now Henry points his finger at my shirt button and asks, "What's that?" When I look down, his digit races up my chest and thumps my nose. He throws his head back laughing hardily, saying, "I got ya again!" He says I have Momma Jo's nose, too.

"Remember them books your Momma bought?" he says, and I recall the World Books my mother purchased from a traveling salesman awhile back.

"Go look up your people from A to Z and that ought to clear up a few things," he says.

I'm a slow reader, but my brother, Gary, is even slower despite his seven years on me. Our mother tried to teach us how to read even though she can barely read herself. One day she gave up and bought us reading lessons to play on our record player. Housed in a handsome oak console with fake drawers, the turntable is slightly warped. As we follow the lessons in our little booklets, it is agonizingly tough for Gary to keep pace with the erudite instructor's undulating voice. Whenever he gets too far behind, we swing the needle back on the records. The vinyls have been so scratched they skip on every third phrase, which is fortunate because it allows Gary to catch up before we bump the Magnavox and keep going.

I have to dig through a mound of sour-smelling clothes to fetch the green-and-white-covered encyclopedias from a wooden bookcase in a corner of the bedroom I share with Yukio and Gary. Thinking of all the mental dossiers I have on relatives, I select volumes O for Okinawa, where my mother is from, and Oklahoma, where Momma Jo was reared; T for Texas, where Henry met Alice; C for Cherokee and I for Ireland, where my great-grandfather, Charlie Mink, once lived. I carry the books, two at a time, out the front door and pile them into Alice's wheelbarrow.

Henry and I sit on his back porch thumbing through the glossy pages. It doesn't take me long to realize he can't read very well either. We stumble and stutter, but I manage well enough to learn I am the byproduct of four defeated races.

"Ain't no defeat in survival," he says now when I voice this observation. "Defeat makes ya meek," he tells me, draping a heavy arm over my shoulder. "Psalms says, *'The meek will He guide in judgment; the meek will He teach his ways'*. It goes on to say, *His soul shall dwell at ease; and his seed shall inherit the earth.'*"

Grandpa's history lesson is too deep for my puny brain, yet it inspires me to develop my own race-based rhyme—a dirge as unique as Biscuit's, yet less offensive than the poetry of Bobo:

> *The American part of me nearly exterminated*
> *the Cherokee part of me.*

The American part of me sold into slavery
    the African part of me.
The American part of me A-bombed the
    Japanese part of me.
The American part of me scorned the Irish
    Irish immigrant in me.
"My country, 'tis of thee" is a lyric that
    best embodies me.

I hear my mother yelling it's supper.

"You better get," Henry says.

I load the encyclopedias into the wheelbarrow and head back across the driveway to the yellow house, pondering what my grandfather told me, making it stick to my long-term memory.

"'Ain't no defeat in survival,'" I repeat as I place the books back on the shelf.

RITES OF SPRING

David Mas Masumoto

SPRING ARRIVES WITH the first warm breezes and fogless morn-ings in our Valley. On our 80-acre organic farm south of Fresno, I disk our soil, breaking winter's crust. The peaches and nectarines awaken with blossoms, initially revealing their pink buds, then blooming into a glorious canopy. Millions of pink dots blanket the landscape. A new year has begun.

But harsh memories of a cold, bitter winter linger because it rarely rained. Welcome to a new climate age; massive swings in weather have become the rule.

Every spring, I plow the earth and something is plowed into me. Usually it's the spirit of the land, a sense of renewal, a bonding of family with the earth—and now it includes our daughter, who has come back home to work the farm.

But this year that something is a new realization: Change, especially with the weather, is the new normal.

The lack of rain troubles me the most. We'll get very little surface water due to a limited snowpack in the Sierra. I can pump from my wells, but water tables will quickly drop; wells can go dry. Most of the Central Valley has received less than half of normal rainfall. This may change with a late March miracle, but long-range forecasts are not optimistic.

Of course, what is normal? Typical weather models are based on 30-year increments, counted by decades. So if you were born in the 1960s or earlier, your weather memories don't count. (Lending credence to my claim that, as I get older, the weather just isn't what it used to be.)

Droughts are common, occurring in 1976–77, 1987–92 and recently in 2007–09. We farmers live with risk; a lack of rain has been fairly common in the last century. Old-timers remember the Great Depression, including California's decade-long drought from 1928–37.

But we have been spoiled—we're ending a century of abnormally consistent weather years. We developed farming systems built on a culture of expectation. When considering much longer timelines, the relatively wet periods in the 20th century have been the exception rather than the rule in California. Our few dry years have typically been followed by extremely wet seasons.

We're entering a new "weirding time." Much more volatility is to be expected, with extremes in weather part of the new norm. There's still debate concerning how much is a direct result from global warming, but it's clear: something is changing.

This past year, the U.S. Department of Agriculture updated its climate zone guide. Nationwide, a warming trend has advanced northward. Planting guides suggest gardeners can experiment with new plants typically grown in warmer regions. That doesn't mean I'll plant bananas and pineapples on my farm. It may simply mean spring comes sooner and lasts longer with more erratic weather.

I know change comes slow to a farm and farmers. But I do recognize a few years of severe drought demands immediate actions.

In San Diego, some farmers are stumping their avocado trees, cutting them in half to save water; they lose a few years of crop but try to keep their investment alive. Other farmers are switching from lower value row crops, like vegetables and other annuals, to higher value tree crops, hoping to earn more from their limited supply of water. These farmers will quickly learn a new reality: perennial crops mean they can't be uprooted and transplanted; you plant with a future expectation.

Even on our small farm, we've begun a gradual process of change. One of the best acts I did years ago was to fallow 15 acres, much to the chagrin of my father. He grew up with the premise you farm every precious acre you had.

I rationalized: why fight these swings of weather, not to mention poor prices (for raisins a decade ago)? With a new pioneer spirit, I pulled out old vines and, among other benefits, created a new avenue that splits the farm. What a joy every spring as I rediscover the new short-cut on the farm. Who wouldn't jump at such an opportunity in life?

Major shifts in weather point to a new challenge: Survival in agriculture will be based on the ability to change. I can imagine a two-tier strategy. One is based on the very large model: economies of scale benefiting the largest and most efficient operations. The other works for us small operators who are adept at the culture of change; we easily accept, adapt and adopt, finding our niche in the new food chain.

What I'm not so confident about is policy and technology. We don't have policies in place that are equipped to cope with the new normal. For example, we are still fighting over water as if we're clans locked in tribal warfare. We cling to a myopic sense of time: What happens when we have a 30-year drought?

Also, many believe that we can invent our way out of problems. Technology has created miracles; productivity increased, labor-saving machines were introduced and are now part of the landscape. But efficiencies can only reach a certain level before there's a decline on a return of investment. Have we begun to max out technological benefits?

I'm an optimist who has faith in a new creative human spirit that will foster hope on the farm. I believe in the art of farming. Great farmers will balance the forces of economics and productivity with the forces of nature, we will respond to weather as opposed to the fallacy of controlling nature. I don't seek solutions, thinking I have all the answers. Farming in the future is more like a mystery to live; I accept that I won't (and can't) farm the same way every year.

Recently, farm timelines have changed for me. Our daughter, Nikiko, has returned home after college and graduate school and is taking over the farm. I watch her struggle with learning curves and witness her response to new challenges. I also bite my tongue, knowing my way of doing things may not fit this new age of agriculture.

She's better equipped to handle change: She doesn't expect to, nor want to, do it all my way. She's young. She's naive. She's full of enthusiasm. All that's exactly required for future springs.

But perhaps this isn't much different from when I came back to farm after running away for college. Or when my father took a huge risk following World War II and the tragic uprooting and evacuation of Japanese Americans from the West Coast. He returned to the Valley, gambled and bought a farm, and planted family roots.

Likewise, is this any more dramatic than my grandparents who left Japan, sailed across an ocean to farm and work in a new, very foreign land? They struggled but stayed—a shared story by many whose ancestors came to California from other places.

Spring does this to me: I think a lot about what is and what is to be. At the same time, plowing the earth is an ancient rite, a renewal of the past, a ritual others have done for centuries and hopefully will do for many more. Like many, I'm reborn every spring.

CALIFORNIA WAS NEVER KANSAS

Tania Flores

I CAN'T TELL ANYMORE
where this valley ends and where my body begins

driving the length of california
I am shedding potentialities,
rejecting visions,
brushing off hallucinations from my lips and my waist.
not long until
skin ripping
from the contours of the buttes,
from this canyon like a womb

what they don't know is that
my body
is malleable, transplantable
and what they don't know is that
my body
absorbed this landscape,
acorn soup and antibodies,
poison oak immunity—
you would think I am native,
you would think I am what you are

they called me Mulan, asked if I am Puerto Rican,
but I am my mother's little brown Indian,

and I am told I can pass
even 6,000 miles away

our postman asked if I will be wearing only black.
the athletic goods store owner shouted that the problem is
    that all the Arabs have 10 children.
her husband told me the goddamn Arabs would never respect
    a Western woman.
he said, "You won't be in Kansas anymore, honey."

I cannot tell when I became from this place,
I cannot tell how many epithelial layers I share with these
    frightened men
who don't know that California was never Kansas.
these fearful men who don't know about sixteen years old and
"Wanna fuck?"
from a white man with a shaved head who thrust his penis at
    me and followed me in his car.
these threatened men who don't know about early June,
a grin and a hand on my upper thigh as I walked a street in
    Hollywood in shorts

these men who cannot know
the relief of remembering that
my body will be a secret, for once—
I will bring with me
sycamores in a dancer's arched back,
the branches of oaks in the angles of flamenco arms,
creek water in my veins

but the men on the street will see only a castle tumbling into
    the sand,
honey eyes
coffee and cream skin

in a hammam,
a Moroccan woman will scrub every inch of me,
the caked and damaged cells
will drift down the plumbing of Rabat.
I will be raw and new.
I will tell my hair, "Listen! You cannot speak in that tone
     to the air."
at night, we will whisper to each other
about the things we've seen while hidden
and the things we've heard while quiet

THE LAST MOJAVE INDIAN BARBIE

Natalie Diaz

WIRED TO HER display box were a pair of one-size-fits-all-Indians stiletto moccasins, faux turquoise earrings, a dream catcher, a copy of *Indian Country Today,* erasable markers for chin and forehead tattoos, and two six-packs of mini magic beer bottles—when tilted up, the bottles turned clear, when turned right-side-up, the bottles refilled. Mojave Barbie repeatedly drank Ken and Skipper under their pink plastic patio table sets. Skipper said she drank like a boy.

Mojave Barbie secretly hated the color of her new friends' apricot skins, how they burned after riding in Ken's convertible Camaro with the top down, hated how their micro hairbrushes tangled and knotted in her own thick, black hair, which they always wanted to braid. There wasn't any diet cola in their cute little ice chests, and worst of all, Mojave Barbie couldn't find a single soft spot on her body to inject her insulin. It had taken years of court cases, litigation, letters from tribal council members, testimonials from CHR nurses, and a few diabetic comas just to receive permission to buy the never-released hypodermic needle accessory kit—before that, she'd bought most on the Japanese black market—Mattel didn't like toying around with the possibility of a junkie Barbie.

Mojave Barbie had been banned from the horse stables and was no longer invited to dinner, not since she let it slip that when the cavalry came to Fort Mojave, the Mojaves ate a few horses. It had happened, and she only let it slip after Skipper tried to force her to admit the Mojave Creation was just a myth: *It's true. I'm from Spirit Mountain,* Mojave Barbie had said. *No, you're not,* Skipper had argued. *You came from Asia.* But Mojave Barbie wasn't missing much—they didn't have lazy man's bread or tortillas in the Barbie Stovetop to Tabletop Deluxe Kitchen. In fact, they only had a breakfast set, so they ate the same two sunny-side-up eggs and pancakes every meal.

Each night after dinner, Mojave Barbie sneaked from the guesthouse—next to the tennis courts and Hairtastic Salon—to rendezvous with Ken, sometimes in the collapsible Glamour Camper, but most often in the Dream Pool. She would *yenni* Ken all night long. *(Yenni* was the Mojave word for sex, explained a culturally informative booklet included in Mojave Barbie's box, along with an authentic frybread recipe, her Certificate of Indian Blood, a casino player's card, and a voided per capita check.) They took precautions to prevent waking others inside the Dream House—Mojave Barbie's tan webbed hand covering Ken's always-open mouth muffled his ejaculations.

One night, after drinking a pint of Black Velvet disguised as a bottle of suntan lotion, Ken felt especially playful. Ken was wild, wanted to sport his plastic Stetson and pleather holsters, wanted Mojave Barbie to wear her traditional outfit, still twist-tied to her box. She agreed and donned her mesquite-bark skirt and went shirtless except for strands of blue and white glass beads that hung down in coils around her neck. The single feather in her hair tickled Ken's fancy. He begged Mojave Barbie to wrap her wide, dark hips around him in the "Mojave Death Grip," an indigenous love maneuver that made him thankful for his double-jointed pelvis. (A Mojave Death Grip Graphic How-To Manual was once included in the culturally informative booklet, but a string of disjointed legs and a campaign by the Girl Scouts of America led to a recall.) Ken pointed his wooden six-shooter and chased her up the Dream Slide. The weight of the perfectly proportioned bodies sent the pool accessory crashing to the patio. Every light in every window painted itself on as the Dream House swung open from the middle, giving all inside a sneak peek at naked Ken's hard body and naked Mojave Barbie gripping his pistol, both mid-yenni and dripping wet.

Ken was punished by Mattel's higher-ups, had his tennis racket, tuxedo, Limited Edition Hummer, scuba and snorkel gear, aviator sunglasses, Harley, windjammer sailboard, his iPad and iPhone confiscated. Mojave Barbie had been caught red-handed and bare-breasted. She was being relocated—a job dealing blackjack at some California casino. On her way out the gate, she kicked the plastic cocker spaniel, which fell sideways but never pulled its tongue in or even barked—she felt an ache behind her 39 EE left breast for her rez dog, which had been discontinued long ago. Mojave Barbie tossed a trash bag filled with clothes and accessories into her primered Barbie Happy Family Volvo, which she'd bought at a yard sale. The car had hidden beneath a tarp in the Dream House driveway since she got there. She climbed through the passenger door over to the driver's seat, an explosion of ripped vinyl, towels, and duct tape. She pumped and pumped the gas pedal, clicked and clicked the ignition, until the jalopy fired up. Mojave Barbie rolled away, her mismatched hubcaps wobbling and rattling, a book of yellow WIC coupons rustling on the dash, and a Joy Harjo tape melted in the tape deck blaring, *I'm not afraid to be hungry. I'm not afraid to be full.*

Mom and Dad Barbie, Grandma Barbie, Skipper, and Ken stood on the Dream House balcony and watched Mojave Barbie go. Grandma Barbie tilted at the waist whispering to Mom Barbie, *They should've kept that one in the cupboard.* Dad Barbie piped in, *Yep, it's always a gamble with those people.* Mom Barbie was silent, hoping the purpling, bruise-like marks the size of mouths circling Ken's neck were not what she thought they were: hickies, or, as the culturally informative booklet explained, a "Mojave necklace." Skipper complained to Ken that Mojave Barbie had flipped them off as she drove out the wrought-iron gates, which, of course, locked behind her with a clang. Ken fingered the blue bead in his pocket and reassured Skipper, *Mojave Barbie was probably waving goodbye—with hands like that, you can never be sure.*

IT'S ALL PERFORMANCE

Carolyn Abram

R ACHEL MOBS A FEW hours after the driver has hauled her semiconscious body away, letting us all know that she's heading off to LiLo. LiLo's the expensive rehab place down in the Valley that all the parents send their kids to when they get caught in a bad way, like Rachel did. It doesn't matter much, except usually kids are better at not getting caught afterwards. "You learn tricks for hiding it, mostly," Emma Masterson told me once at a party.

Rachel also mobs me, *My mom says I need to apologize to your mom, so tell her I'm sorry. Also, you better fucking mob me while I'm gone.*

As the car pulled out of the drive, my mother told me she was *very* disappointed in me.

"I'm heartbroken," I said to her, and checked my mob for updates. Amy Xiang had spotted someone whose dress was totally see-through from behind. Marshall Nguyen was at the batting cages.

"When are you going to learn to take responsibility for your actions?" she asked me, looking to my father for support.

It's her ability to pretend they are still a team that pisses me off. "Sorry I shook your standing in the PTA," I said to her.

She turned a dark red, her eyebrows almost moving in anger, and stomped off. My dad trailed behind her like he does since she let him move back in. I wandered back into my room.

Without anything else to do, I mob into one of the porn channels. Everyone's been into the more hardcore stuff recently, the torture rooms and the orgies and the ones where there's this whole plotline of being in the middle of a police raid while you're fucking. Shit that really gets your blood pumping. I opt for something more sedate while my buzz is still wearing off. The entrance to the channel is a giant bedroom. I think it's supposed to be set in medieval times; there are all these fur skins draped over everything. A woman is on her knees, gripping a man's thighs in her hands as he fucks her mouth.

I shift my viewer to be in his line of sight, so I can look down at the top of the blonde's head. She looks up at us with coherent hunger; the mob sends careful flickers of pleasure from my wrist up through my spine. I take a deep breath and pull at myself.

We grab the blonde's head and press it deep against our pelvis. She coughs against us and gags. A tear slides down her cheek. Her eyes pop open in surprise as we explode into her.

There are maybe fifteen seconds where I feel nothing but good. That's it. Then I start thinking about Rachel. It's more fun when she's there too, when the porn and reality get all tangled and at this point it turns out I'm wrapped in her legs and pulling strands of her hair off my chest.

Donald Pfeidels mobs a photo of Emma Masterson asleep in his shirt, completely unguarded, drooling on her own mob as she sleeps against her hands. Marshall Nguyen has beaten level thirty in *Lord of War X*. Cathy Stewart is tweezing her eyebrows.

I feel both restless and exhausted. I know I won't be able to sleep. There's an itch in the back of my mind, something unfinished. The way you feel in class when the teacher's blacked out your mob and you just know all the messages and updates are building up, waiting to be read. The show is the most boring thing I've ever watched in my life and somehow I need to see it through.

It was Rachel's idea to begin with. She muscled herself up from where she was lying on my bed, the TociMox making her gaze at me unfocused. "We should watch the show," she said. "Your parents' show."

"Shut up," I said. I synced her to the mob board so I could flick through her music.

"You brought it up in class today," she pointed out.

I shook my head. "What are you talking about?"

"I bet I know why she picked him."

I grunted, trying to get her to leave the topic behind.

"He was probably a monster in bed. Like you."

I didn't say anything, just kept messing with her playlists.

"I bet he still is. I'd fuck him in a second."

A wave of anger stabbed through me and I turned to face her. "Are you serious?"

She smiled. Her pupils got even bigger and she bit down on her lip. She leaned forward until she was on all fours and started crawling toward me. "You know Freddy said he wanted to try going mono with me."

I looked out the window. The view of the hedges wobbled slightly. I wondered how long it would take me to hack through them to the neighbors' yard. Rachel's hand pawed clumsily at my face. I snorted and twitched away.

When I was little, they used to show me the scene of my dad proposing, on the last episode of the show. They watched it on their anniversary, and I used to beg to watch it all the time, when I was home sick or when I couldn't sleep. They are in Tahiti, in the sunset. My mom is in a golden ball gown and my dad's in a suit. I'd be lying to you if I said that image of my dad twirling her around doesn't sometimes still float through my head when I wake up from a nightmare and try to calm myself down.

Rachel tried to stabilize herself on the bed with just her knees and failed, tumbling to the floor while trying to pull off her T-shirt. She landed with one arm wrapped in the soft cotton, and got the giggles.

She was so pathetic and cute sitting there, hair all over her face, trying to untangle herself. I forgot that I was angry and kneeled to help her.

I worked on removing her top, while Rachel worked on mobbing a sexy photo of me removing her top.

"Stop," I told her, and kissed her hard until her hand curled naturally around my shoulder instead of fumbling at her wrist. But then her mouth went slack and she pushed me away.

"I told you, I'm mono now," she whined.

I let go of her and sat up straight, getting a head rush in the process. She pawed at me again, snapping my attention back. She was too high to be fun. And I wasn't high enough to think it was all funny. I just felt tired and kind of annoyed.

She rolled to her side, her breasts spilling together. She has the biggest and darkest nipples I've ever seen. The first time I took off her top it really freaked me out, deep purple discs the size of hamburgers. She caught me staring. "How come you never wanted to be mono?"

"Fuck off," I said, forcing myself to stand against the growing weight of the air and stumbling over to my desk chair. The walls blurred together as I spun around. It occurred to me that my room was a circle.

That was when I heard her crying.

"Stop moving so fast," she begged.

I stopped the chair.

"Don't look at me," she said, contorting toward the floor.

I sighed; she was coming apart. When Rachel was high she usually wanted to do stuff: let's go swimming, let's find people and make a bonfire, let's drive up into the hills, let's fuck, let's mob a movie we've never seen. But when she had these off days, when she got sad, it usually turned into anger, and I didn't particularly want to deal with that.

I stood over her and pulled her up, maneuvered her back to the bed. Smoothed her hair back, even with her hands covering her eyes. When she finally let go of her head her eyes were red and swollen, her nose covered in snot. I tried to wipe away the tears, but they kept coming, hot against her cheek.

"I should just die. No one cares if I live or die." She wailed, gasping for air. "I should just die."

"I like you a lot, Rachel, you know that." I tried to make my voice soft, but it was echoing and rebounding against the walls in such a way that I couldn't tell if I was doing it right.

"You hate me," she insisted. "Freddy's always mad at me. No girls even like me."

"That's because all of us want you," I said. "Especially Freddy. Even me. Girls get jealous."

She looked at me and for a second I thought I had cheered her up, but then her face fell, and whatever words she said got lost in her sobs.

I tried to shush her. My mother was bound to hear eventually if she kept this up. I wrapped her in a hug, which steadied her a bit. "Hey, you wanted to watch the show? With my parents?"

She hiccupped, nodded.

The first episode started and I could barely pay attention. I don't know how people watched this sort of television. I kept switching over to other people's mob activity, but Rachel kept asking for me to bring it back. It hadn't been remastered for the mob, so it was just a flat view, a bunch of talking heads in the frame. You couldn't change the angle of view or interact with the set at all, couldn't explore. There were no mob-pulses to make you feel angry or sad or happy with the characters. The walls of the background were all about to fall down; the backdrops they put behind my mom when she talked were just cheap sheets in different colors. They had practically hosed her down with makeup.

NEW CALIFORNIA WRITING 2013

NEW CALIFORNIA WRITING 2013

"The house, is, just, like amazing," a blond guy with tiny white teeth said to the camera. "Like, have you ever been someplace this fancy?" His name and age were at the bottom of the screen: Jesse, 32. "And Holly," he continued. "Wow. I mean. Wow."

I realized why it all looked so familiar. It wasn't that different from our house now. With the big gold-plated fixtures and the formal sitting rooms.

"Ohhh," Rachel sighed when my mom appeared in a backless black dress. She sniffled and burrowed against my chest.

My mom was so young. When I look at photos of her, I always think how good her plastic surgeon is; she looks so similar. But watching her move around and really *be* was bizarre. One by one guys got out of limos and introduced themselves. It took a while to get to my dad. He hugged her hello and said *It's a pleasure to meet you* in Spanish. But this was before my mom learned Spanish, so she smiled and told him how embarrassed she was that she didn't understand. He promised to translate inside. She turned to watch him go and just for a second made eye contact with the camera. Inhaled sharply.

"Caliente," Rachel mumbled. "Jump his bones."

"There's something about Rodrigo," my mom said to the camera. "I just love a guy who can be so confident, you know?"

The other guys were like Jesse. White and blond. Lots of Southern accents. Too much hair gel. And no one could beat my dad's self-satisfied smile. When the other guys are ribbing each other, my dad just sips from his drink. What an asshole. My dad looked so dark compared to them. *Swarthy,* that was the word Amanda Breckenridge used to describe me when we were hanging out. She was a brain, not nearly as pretty as Rachel, but she was tutoring me and clearly wanted it, so I felt kind of obligated.

At the end of the episode the guys line up for cuts, or whatever they call it, where my mom hands out rose boutonnieres to the ones she picked to stick around. The rejected ones leave the house and give little speeches about how bummed they are that they didn't get the chance to know her better.

"How can she be so mean to them?" Rachel asked, wiping tears from her eyes. "It's just so sad."

I brushed her hair out of her face. I decided it was good there were no mob-pulses; they would only make her mood swings worse.

The next episode was the first of the "dates." My mom goes out with some guy with spiky frosted hair. They hike out to the Hollywood sign, sit just underneath it, and he puts his hand on the side of her face and leans in to kiss her. I looked over at Rachel, asleep. When I turned back they were still kissing. She was so young. The way she hopped over the rocks on the trail, the sound of her voice. Her hair was even different. Softer and more bouncy. The music swelled and rose. I couldn't place what I was feeling, but I didn't like it.

Mercer Atkins was racing up into the hills on his motorcycle; a girl who wasn't from school clung to his back and shrieked in delight, her hair flying out from under her helmet. Archie Porter was toking with Melanie Elmsworth. There were reporters outside Amy Xiang's house, hoping her mother would emerge. Emma Masterson broadcast Donald Pfeidels in his briefs, asleep by a pool.

My mom takes ten guys on a "group date," where they film a music video together. Rachel pulled her head up suddenly in the middle of this, the part where the scene is my mom in bed with one of the guys, his shirt off and his chest smooth as resin. "What is she *doing?*" Rachel nearly screamed. "Doesn't she know she's making it too easy?"

Maya Montoya and Leila Porter had gotten colored eyelash extensions. Melanie Elmsworth blew smoke rings. Donald Pfeidels was awake now; Emma mobbed them making out.

Another rose ceremony, another three guys gone.

"I just know if she'd gotten to know me, the real me, and not listened to those phonies in there, we could have had something really special," Adam, 28, tells the camera.

I kept going, transfixed. Every episode the scene recreated itself, my mom leaning her head to the side and smiling, whichever guy she was with reaching his hand out toward her. She would get giggly when she drank. The dates are all weird activities—with my dad they walked on a tightrope between two buildings—and they all end with my mother's tongue down someone else's throat. Back at the house there are all these little wars between the guys, all of them telling my mom different versions of the same story, trying to get the ones they don't like thrown off the show.

Then there was the briefest of knocks on my door as my dad walked in.

In history today, Mr. Stevens told this story: A researcher studying in Africa had a pygmy youth named Kenji as his guide and companion. He had gone trekking with Kenji and they got to the edge of the forest. There, they got into a car and began driving toward the distant, snow-capped hills, which the pygmy had never seen before. At one break in the trip, Kenji looked out over the plains and saw a herd of buffalo in the distance. He asked the researcher what sort of bug the buffalo were.

When the researcher tells him that they are buffalo, the pygmy laughs and tells the researcher not to be so dumb. So they get in the car and the researcher drives him toward the buffalo.

"So what do you think happens as they drive toward the buffalo?" Mr. Stevens had asked.

"The car explodes and they die," Freddy said. The class laughed. It was a relieved laugh, like Mr. Stevens was getting too serious, like we were all too intrigued by the story.

In the chemistry lab next door Adelaide Powers had snapped a perfect photo of a fireball leaping out of the gas jet. It had to have taken more than one try to get such a good shot; I wondered how they had distracted Dr. Misra. Rachel had mobbed me a photo of her underwear, glowing neon green beneath the blue tent of her skirt. It's ballsy to take a photo like that in the middle of class. I was red-faced and distracted.

"Mr. Lopez-White," Mr. Stevens called me out. "Do I need to mob you to get a response?"

I tried to focus on him. "What?"

He sighed. "If they were driving toward the buffalo, what do you think happened to the *appearance* of the buffalo?"

"They got bigger?" I tried.

The buffalo get bigger and bigger. Kenji wants to know what sort of witchcraft the researcher is using to make the bugs grow. When they get to the herd, Kenji finally agrees that they are, in fact, buffalo, but he wants to know how they grew so fast.

"Now, Mr. Kellerman, why do you think I'm telling you this story during social awareness week?"

Freddy glanced up from his wrist. "Um." He squirmed in his seat, leaned forward and coughed.

I glanced back at Rachel; her hands were in her lap.

That was when Mr. Stevens blacked us out, shutting our mobs down for the remainder of class. "So, let's talk about ways you guys are like the pygmy in that story," Mr. Stevens said.

We stared. He started to pace. "Okay, for starters, do you think that outside of L.A., heck, outside of this zip code, everyone has a brand new waterproof mobile attached to their wrist?"

This sounded like a trick question, so I waited before I shook my head *no,* joining everyone else.

"Right. In other parts of the country, kids your age might not even have a mob. Or they might have a really old one. Any other examples?"

Slowly people started saying things. It was sunny here, someone said. In some parts of the world, people go hungry. People can't afford homes, but a lot of our families have two homes. People don't go to private school and wear uniforms.

"People recognize our parents," I offered.

Freddy snorted, "Who recognizes *your* parents? Only old freaks."

Rachel raised her hand.

"Yes, Ms. Beauvoir?" He leered a little at the smile she gives to teachers and parents.

"I don't get it," she said. "Isn't the researcher being just as 'socially unaware' as Kenji is?"

He looked at her thoughtfully, his lips resting against his index finger. "That's a valid point. But for the purposes of our discussion, it's one and the same. Can you think of some way your life view is limited by your surroundings?"

"Well, obviously not," she said. "No one ever lets us leave here."

My dad was talking but basically stopped midsentence as he saw me and Rachel. I jerked up and closed down the viewer, which startled Rachel awake.

"David, Jesus," he said.

"Jesus, David," Rachel mimicked. She blinked a few times at my dad and smiled. Even high, I've seen Rachel coherently tell parents about her school projects. Today all she could muster was, "Mr. Lopez, you are sooo beautiful."

My dad dropped his eyes and looked away from her, turning to face the door.

"What did you give her?" my dad asked. He turned to Rachel. "Honey, can you put on some clothing?"

"Nothing," I said.

"I'm not an idiot."

"Well, I don't know. She was like this when she got here." I tried to hand her a T-shirt. "Rachel, can you put this on?"

"Screw you," she said, dropping back onto the bed so everything jiggled. "Mmm, screw me."

"Get off the bed," my dad said. "You're lucky I came to get you, not your mother."

"Fuck off," I said, sliding off and standing up.

He ignored me. "You mean to tell me she showed up here half naked just passed out on the bed?"

I shrugged.

"Your mom is expecting us all to have dinner together."

"Well, I wouldn't want to disappoint Mom, would I?"

"Do you want me to get her or not?"

The floor rolled when I stood on it. I sat into my chair, hitting the armrest on my way down. "So we'll go have dinner and she'll be better when we get back."

"You can't leave someone alone when they're like this."

My heartbeat had returned to normal. He hadn't noticed that I was watching the show. Or that I was still a little buzzed myself. "Then tell Mom I'm not coming down to dinner. Tell her I'm doing homework or something."

He gave me a skeptical look.

"I said something."

It was too late. I heard my mom's quick footsteps coming down the hall and I was just grateful that at least I wasn't in bed with Rachel anymore.

"What happened to you guys?" She strode into the room and her mouth opened a little. "Oh my god. Oh my god. What are you doing?"

"Nothing," I said. "She's a little messed up. I figured she'd be safer here than wandering around. It'll wear off."

She sat down over Rachel, pulling her up. "Rachel, honey, Rachel." She jiggled her, snapped her fingers, called Rachel's name louder and louder.

I had that odd feeling I'd had when I was eight and I went over to Jonah Clarke's house and his older brother showed us how to get into the private channels through our mobs. Technically private channels don't have to be porn—that's what we all share on so our parents can't see what's happening—but that was what Jonah's brother showed us. When I got home, I felt a little sick, worried that I was acting weird and somehow my parents would be able to *tell*. That was how I felt now, looking at my mom. Like I could see this other version of her, the version that used to exist, almost like a ghost moving within her body. I checked myself: it was just the high wearing off, making everything more intense. I just needed to stay within the realm of normal and they wouldn't notice. Or care.

Rachel finally opened her eyes. "Stop," she moaned. Then it turned into a shriek. "Stop it." She jerked away from my mother's hands. "You shouldn't be leading him on like that, slut!"

My mother didn't even flinch. "Honey, you need to tell me what you took."

"Leave me alone."

"Nope, can't do that. I'm going to call your parents."

Rachel started to scream and cry, "No, you can't. You can't. Stop it." Her voice got louder.

My mom let her drop back to the bed and opened the contact list on her mob. "Look up Rachel Beauvoir's mother."

"I hate you," Rachel screamed. "You don't deserve him. I hate you all." She called her a bitch, a cunt, every curse she knew spewing out of her lips.

"Oh, honey," my mom said, looking at her with pity. "I have been called far worse things in my time."

My dad stepped forward. I realized we had both been waiting for my mom to issue instructions. He grabbed one of my sweatshirts off the floor and placed it over Rachel's chest, like he was tucking a blanket around her. He sat down where my mom had been, beside Rachel. My mom was already talking to someone. Already apologizing. My dad lowered his voice, pushed Rachel's hair down behind her ear. "Rachel, it's going to be okay. I promise you."

She stopped screaming and made eye contact with him. Nodded and swallowed. I left the room.

As I start the show back up again, Rachel's comments about my dad, about all the guys on the show, string through my brain. There are fewer guys now. You start to know them. The sensitive one, always needing my mom to reassure him that she actually likes him. The all-American guy, tongue too thick for his mouth. I could pull these guys out of history class.

My mom is, and I'm just being honest here, kind of a slut. She's all over them. Not just all over my dad. All of them. It's tame, compared to the other stuff I watch, but still, it's my mom. A few of the guys are more reserved, talk very sincerely to the camera about wanting to take things slow and build a friendship first. They don't seem to realize that every other guy on the show has managed to corner my mother's tonsils. It's late and I know across the house my parents are in bed together. It all feels like a lie. I've been watching too long; it's blurring together with all the porn; I stop looking away when she has yet another fireside make-out session. I'm almost fascinated. That's really what she was like.

Scandal in episode ten: one of the guys has a girlfriend back home. My mom confronts him in front of everyone else, then chases him down when he tries to run away from the conversation. She's furious.

And here's the thing. My mom is slutty and she's angry and I like her more than I like her now. I like that she's putting this guy in his place. She's alive and all her face muscles move, expressing a whole host of emotions.

She and my dad, they can't keep their hands off each other when they're together. They're being tourists and seeing all these places and I've heard them talk about going there, but all they do is make out. Sit on a tour bus making out. Go to a castle and make out. It makes me sad in my stomach, if that makes sense. I've never seen them like that. I've seen them happy together, sure. Even now, I see them trying to be affectionate with each other. Trying to fix whatever it is that's broken, but when I look at them together in the past, I can't help but think that the woman my dad slept with wasn't the one who broke them. Something else happened to them. Something irreparable and inevitable.

There are only a few episodes left, so even though it's already two in the morning, I decide to finish the whole thing, get it out of my system. Parts are a little familiar. I realize they showed me the section where Mom meets Dad's parents, where he meets hers. Now I'm starting to feel bad for the other guys. It's down to three. The third one decides to leave, has some sort of realization that he wants to get back together with his ex-girlfriend back home. My mom bursts into tears when he tells her, her face puffing against its sunburn. "Is there something wrong with me?" she asks the camera.

She goes out on a date with my dad and the other guy. Halfway through the date she hands each a card to the hotel room they'll share that night. The music builds as she crawls into a big fluffy bed with each of them. I wonder how similar the scenes would look if you played them side by side. I am oddly disappointed when the camera fades to black.

Finally we are at the last episode. My mom and dad go swimming in the rain together, make out on the beach. Then she breaks up with the other guy. He has this look of pure devotion when he opens the door for her, and you know she's about to break his heart. She starts babbling, finally says, "I'm in love with someone else," and he nods, blinks slowly.

The next day is the proposal, just as I remember it. Though this time I notice how sweaty my dad is. How my mom's hair has been teased up beyond belief. I think about the other guy, wonder how he felt when he watched this. Did he think she made a mistake? Or that he'd gotten lucky this time; he didn't wind up with her and that was right? I wonder if that guy went home and married his girlfriend. If they had any kids together. I wonder if my mom wonders these things too.

Four months ago, it was a day kind of like today. Rachel and I had just started hanging out, and since my mom was traveling a lot for work it was probably one of the first few times Rachel and I had even fucked.

It was her idea to go swimming. We were lying in bed, mobbing photos of us cuddling, when she just got up and said she was going for a swim. Melody Barnes was at a party at a new nightclub, surrounded by beefy bodyguards. Donald Pfeidels, Mercer Atkins, and Marshall Nguyen were at a bonfire on the beach, light so bright it bleached out their faces. Rachel got up and wrapped herself in my towel and just walked out toward the pool without a word. I threw on my shorts. It was late, maybe midnight. My parents don't like it when girls stay over. My dad turns a blind eye but feels obligated to have Serious Talks about it when it's all blatant.

"Rachel," I whisper-called to her down the hall. Even with my parents' room on the opposite side of the house, I thought I should be careful.

I could see her at the other end of the hallway, backlit. I snapped a photo, mobbed it out. "Come on, don't wake up my dad," I said to her.

She turned and just grinned at me, then kept walking into the main room. I followed her, the tiles cool against my feet. I wouldn't say it anymore, but that night I think I loved her.

She left the door open for me and when I got outside she was already in the water. She hooked her arms on the edge of the pool. "The water's warmer than the air," she said.

I sat down and dangled my legs into the water. She was right.

"Come on," she whispered. In the water her knees scraped against my ankles and I flexed my feet to support her. I could hear the quiet splashes and ripples her body made as she moved. Leila Porter was at a wedding of some sort, posing with the bride. Maya Montoya was at the mall with her sister. Rachel leaned out of the pool and undid the button of my shorts, peeling open the zipper. "I'm naked; you have to be too."

I leaned back on my hands and she tugged my shorts off of me, letting them float away in the pool. I thought, briefly and transiently, that I should remember to go get those before we went inside. But the tile ledge of the pool was cold against my ass and Rachel's warm body tugged insistently against mine. I was hard, again, and she ran her tongue up and around the curve of my cock. I turned my head to the side, where the master suite opens up to the pool. No lights, no movement. I was all set to enjoy myself when Rachel stopped and pushed herself off from the wall, floating away from the side.

"Cocktease," I called. She giggled and slipped underwater with a squelch.

I jumped off the side into the water and pulled myself over to her. She smiled and wiped her hair out of her face. I jumped on top of her and dunked her in the water. She went under with a yelp and kicked frantically to get away from me.

"What the fuck?" she asked when she surfaced, pushing me. She was spitting water and her hair was tangled across her brow.

"Shhh," I warned, smiling. I mobbed another photo of her. She gasped in horror when she saw it on her own mob.

We floated there for a while, just talking. Mostly about stuff we remembered from when we were kids. I told her about going out for milkshakes with my dad after baseball games when I was little.

"He used to play in the minor leagues, you know, so if he thought I played well, that was pretty cool," I said. "Now, though..." I ran a wet hand through my hair. Rachel's hair floated away from her like jellyfish tentacles. "It's like he expects me to be better. All I get is lectures about how to grip a bat, you know?"

We talked about our favorite birthday parties and our nannies. Rachel told me about her little sister, about her grandma who lived with them until she couldn't remember their names.

"All that she did at the place they moved her into was watch soap operas on TV. Old-fashioned TV with the stations and everything. She thought she was watching home videos, for some reason. We'd go visit her and she'd tell us about the scrapes her children had gotten into with their evil twin, and she couldn't even remember who we were, or why we were there." Rachel's voice, usually so confident, wavered. I wanted to touch her. Obviously I could have. But this time I was afraid to for some reason. I couldn't figure out *where* to touch her.

I was trying to solve this problem, and Rachel wasn't saying anything, wasn't even looking at me, when I heard a door click shut in my house.

I splashed onto my stomach and squinted as the house lit up. My dad was just coming home. It didn't make any sense. He looked down the hall toward my room and then turned behind him. A woman in a tight pink dress stepped in gingerly, holding her heels in her hand.

Melanie Elmsworth was making out with Emma Masterson. Cathy Stewart was studying for the SATs. Amy Xiang was leaving a premiere party with her boyfriend.

"Oh fuck," Rachel hissed behind me.

I looked back at her, feeling so stupid for following her out here, for even letting her into my house. I was terrified of her. She was going to mob a photo of this out. It was too good. It would get too much attention. More than any of us would ever want to pass up.

But Rachel didn't laugh or smile or mob anything. She just swam over to me and sort of draped herself over my back. Her body was slick, like some sort of phantom mermaid. This is why I'll always let her come over and get high, let her hook up with anyone she wants and come to me later that night just to sleep. Because that night when I couldn't figure out the right way to touch her at all, she fucking *held* me.

I didn't get out of the water. I watched the woman smile at my dad. He grinned and stuck his hands in his pockets. They stared at each other for a minute. I wondered if they were saying anything. Then, he put out his hand like in the old movies when men asked women to dance. She put her hand in his and they walked into the hall toward his room.

It felt like I was watching something someone had mobbed. Like every few seconds I had to remind myself that I wasn't watching someone else's broadcast. It was my dad, and he didn't want anyone to know.

My whole life everyone told me I was just like my dad. We looked the same. We both were athletic, both kept to ourselves about our feelings, both were protective of the people we loved. And I couldn't avoid the reflection of the two of us that night, each of us with a smuggled girl.

I've broadcast almost nothing since that night. Rachel or my other friends will mob photos or videos of me, but that's it. All I want is to stop feeling like I'm my dad, being watched through the windows of my house as I destroy every good thing anyone ever said about me.

I still can't sleep. The show lasted a lot longer than I had thought it would. It's five in the morning. I'm not tired at all, but I'm hungry. I go down to the kitchen and rest my forehead against the cool door of the fridge.

"David?" my mom says, from her hall. I jump a little. Her face is sleepy and distorted, and her glasses are askew. Normally she wears contacts, so I forget what she looks like when they aren't in. She's wearing an old T-shirt of my dad's.

"Sorry, I was hungry," I say.

She nods. "I was going to get up soon anyhow." She yawns and sits at one of the chairs. "Need any help?"

I shake my head.

"There's leftover meat from dinner in the right."

I find it and stick it in the microwave. When it's ready I sit down next to her. "Rachel said to tell you she's sorry," I say.

She rests her head on her hand. "That girl's got a mouth on her, doesn't she?"

I smile, chew my food.

She reaches out and puts her hand on the back of my neck. "I can't believe you're so big," she says.

It's so comforting, her hand there, but I shrug her off anyhow. "Can I ask you a question?" I say. Something about the twilight, about the gray light already beginning to dawn in the kitchen, makes me feel like we are not in our real home. Normally she would be yelling at me about Rachel. Lecturing me about something. I would be taking my food to my room alone, trying to avoid her questions and her affection. We've been transported somewhere else, somewhere where it's only us.

"Yeah, baby, of course."

"Why'd you choose Dad?"

She turns to look at me. "Why do you ask that?"

I keep staring down at the hunk of meat on my plate. "You could have been with any number of guys, right? That's how it worked, isn't it?"

She yawns again, stretches. "I loved him, David."

"Would you do it again?"

"What do you mean?"

The willful forgetting of what he did pisses me off the most, but in this light I feel like I can handle it.

"He cheated on you, Mom. Would you pick him again, even knowing he was going to do that?"

She leans her head from one side to the other, stretching her neck. "I love *you*, David. I would never want to be without you."

I think about this. "I don't forgive him," I say. "You shouldn't have, either."

"Oh, David." She puts her hand on my arm and I don't shake her off of me.

"I watched the show," I say. "You could have been with anyone."

"The show?" she asks, then chuckles a little. "Honey, that show, I mean, it's crazy that it worked out at all."

I take another bite of the food.

She leans back a little in the chair. "You know how those shows worked, right? The producers, during those interviews, they'd ask these specific questions, then cut and paste your answers until you'd said what they wanted you to say."

"So it's just cut and paste that made you and Dad get married?"

"No, not like that."

I stare down at my empty plate. She stands up and clears it to the sink. Rinses it and puts it into the dishwasher. She unbends, reaches her fist toward the sky, and put her other hand to the small of her back, stretching. I can see it again, the ghost of my mom's young self, fighting to break out from behind the brittle skin. She's limber and practically vibrating with energy. She's crawling over every guy she can get her legs around.

She looks out the window at the paling light. You can see the fog over the water. That was why my mom got this place, she always said, for the view. She grins as much as she's able and turns to me.

"Did you know I was on a show before the one where I met your dad? It was the other way around. I was one of twenty women. A guy was going to pick one of us."

I shake my head a little. It makes some of the things she said make more sense, about coming back this time, being ready *this time* to find love.

"So, back then, everyone got a story line. You probably saw it on my season too. There's the bad boy. The crazy one. The one with a heartbreaking past."

"Yeah."

"So my story line was that I was the one who chose work. I left on my own, because my boss said if I didn't come back I'd get fired. I really thought I was in love with the guy, but it was too scary to leave my job." She looks out the window again, tilts her head a little. "Anyhow, that's all old news. The point is Dad and I had the same story as anyone else. I thought I was going to be with someone else, but it wasn't meant to be. I was meant to meet Dad."

"So Dad was meant to cheat on you?"

Her shoulders slump a little. "It's not that simple, David."

"Really?" I ask. "It seems pretty simple. He fucked someone else. He spent all this time being a liar."

"David, stop." Her voice is tiny. It catches like she might start to cry. I lay my hands flat on the countertops, feel the heat condense on the arch of my palm.

"Sorry," I say.

"It's okay." She turns her whole body to lean on the counter, wipes at the resin with her palm, as if wiping away a fleck of dirt. "You're so much like him. He was so angry at me when he watched the whole show."

"I'm not," I try to explain.

"People shouldn't see their parents like that. It's weird."

When I was little, I remember these women who would stop my dad when I was out with him. They'd come up to him and tell him how lucky my mom was. They'd squeeze his shoulder and he'd smile kindly and pull away. If my mom was with him, he'd put his arm around her. And you could see that my mom felt so pleased that he did that. That he put her first. I could feel the satisfaction just waft off of her. It made me feel safe.

I want to get up and hug my mom. She looks so lonely. Then the sun pokes up and illuminates the room with an alien glow and the night is lost. She's just my mom, tired and old. I hear a door close and realize my dad is coming out, too. I get up and head down the hallway to my room, then turn and peek back into the kitchen. My mom stiffens when he puts a hand on her back. Then she turns around and tugs at his shirt, bringing him to her. She kisses him and his hands release her for a second, then grab her tighter. He leans back, pulling her toes off the floor. It's all performance. I stay.

SARDINE LAKE 1992

Vincent Guerra

MY FATHER WANDERED and found them
   rose quartz, amethyst, obsidian

a dandelion's ghosted globe

and a stupid paper chart
for lost alone in the woods

in our sarcophagi sleeping bags
and our arms in our shirts

      each starry animal
the major and minor

and the glacier's pale belly
upon the rocks

in the tilted valley where we camped

my brother, younger, unknowing
this will end

My father held the flashlight

crowded by pines, his bristled face
his smell

I knew then I didn't care
about stars
       but what was close

wouldn't last

       *

Swings and graveyards
       double-shifts

never feeling quite himself

his clay torso in the shed
beneath a sheet of plastic

life piled on life

For what?—

the thoughts
that sometimes come

we don't write down

The years commuted

in his silver Tercel with half a million miles
the melatonin, felt curtains

earplugs in order
to sleep through the day

       *

In the monochrome
     of the macula, the either/or
of the eye

the Sierras under sheets
of snow, an unused room

I sat awake in

a rehearsal of birds
Venus

indian paintbrush mixing its pigments

till my eyes adjust

And in the morning we'd switch-back

toward the lookout

the metal stairway like a carnival ride
     in which the ride is
        standing and looking

across airy mountains

where one can see from miles
the fires

We gnashed our jerky
     and on the sunny metal

slipped off our packs

seemed to float

THE RIVER IN MY CITY

Stephen D. Gutiérrez

T HE RIVER IN my city is a mean river, a stingy river hesitant to give any lifesaving waters when you need them. When you desire all that the river has to offer, crave its life-affirming qualities with a desperate yearning, the river holds back, asks "More, more, more!" from you than you want to give. It wants all, so you turn away in disgust and fear, dejected and sad.

This is the awful truth. The river is no plaything but an ugly force.

I would like to take a moment, then, to describe the river.

The river runs through my city, the City of Commerce in L.A., and makes itself felt day and night with its turbulent roar. It runs behind the houses on Bartmus Street, just a regular river to the outside viewer but full of enchantment to us, the denizens of this small, tidy neighborhood not known for its natural wonders but indeed marked by its presence.

"Roar, roar, roar," goes the river all night, and when you stand aghast at its power it pays no attention to you but just keeps on going.

So it has always been, so it is.

So it was then.

"Stay away from the river, it's dangerous!" they warned us as kids, those good people our parents guiding us well. "Don't climb that damn ivy hill so you can watch the trucks pass! You're going to get killed!"

They knew little about the barges that, entering the river, floated unsteadily side to side before straightening up and, the captain catching sight of us, saluting us with a crazily appropriate toot, a fog-cutting blast.

"You've got no business up there!" they said. But that was long ago.

Now we watched the river from afar. On an island within view of it, we gauged its mystery. There, in a hut marked Recreation Hall, I played ping-pong with my friends, or past the brambles smoked pot with these same jokers in a clearing or, finding a secluded spot to puff on a joint after the elemental warning, caution, approval and recommendation all rolled up in one (ha ha!), "This is some really good shit, man, check it out!" I enjoyed the slow burn alone, without company, and later joined them. We walked across the fields in adolescent funk or pleasantly high. With my friends, I explored what I already knew so well.

We gathered early at a safe spot and commenced our routine with little formality. "Hey, dude."

"Hey, dude."

From our vantage point, the river could barely be seen on the other side of the island without effort. We needed to stand on a table, climb a tree, squint hard and bring it into focus, into fleeting sight, the river. But weren't we too old for that? Yes, we were, so we pretended silliness, and took ribbing as the price. "What are you doing up in that fucking tree?"

"Nothing. Getting all cosmic."

"I got your cosmic. Get down from there before I haul your ass down, you monkey dick." But when I caught sight of it, I didn't care what the fools thought of me.

"It's cool, man."

"What?"

"The river."

"What the fuck you talking about?"

"The river in our city." It roared and it bubbled. Even from far away, I could sense its power and frothy surge, its white-streaked flow and reddened backwash.

"You guys ought to check it out, it's real."

And so on the island we passed our time, and lived, and grew older, and laughed, and shared secrets escaping our hearts with a little too much booze washing down whatever grief we swallowed hard and tried to forget.

We all came from spots that marked us in different ways, nobody knowing the extent of those markings till later, sometimes not even the nature of them. So Ray's dad, who we always thought Native American because of the ruddiness of his face, turned out to drink hard. Dennis' mom, so nice and generous, nursed a deeper problem of bitterness and hate. Unemployment plagued a family because of sloth and no other reason. Not because of the goddamned economy and the fucking Japs taking over, as Mr. Jimenez claimed, burping, every time you bumped into him in his garage, sitting on a high stool, nursing a tall one at the work bench littered with empties.

A cheap radio tinned out dispiriting *rancheras*. "You boys get the hell out of here, okay? I'm thinking."

He was thinking. Everybody was thinking.

But the river went on its way without a care in the world, as my mother might say. It did its work.

She was tied down on the bank, struggling, gasping, at the first sign of flooding. She was unbearably soaked.

She was a sad strange creature beset by problems, she was, with deep-brown, penetrating eyes full of intelligence and hurt, and sternness setting her lips in desperate survival mode during these years that I am talking about here.

She kept a watch over me.

"Are you going to the park?"

"I am!"

"Come home early! Dad needs you!"

"For what?"

"Just come home early! You live at the damn place!"

"Better than here!"

"Get out! Get out of my hair!" She screamed out the last word.

She set me loose and free, propelled me out the door. Into the night I went. It was my special time to be, and live, the night.

I walked on solemnly.

"Okay, so I'm going now. I won't tell anybody you're a witch," muttered to myself. But I didn't mean it.

I didn't mean it at all. It was just the thing to say.

Everybody bore a burden. Everybody kept a secret or two, tucked safely away in a pocket he didn't know disallowed complete concealment, like a soiled handkerchief sticking out of a breast pocket unaware to the wearer strutting about so confidently.

But no matter! These personal histories marking us so definitely, these incomprehensible trials, so tenderly alluded to here, and so awful for us all didn't consume us yet. They could be left behind at the island, with the river's help. We didn't know, though, that the river was bringing us more troubles even as it washed away our old ones.

We didn't know, we didn't know. How could we know?

We were mere babes in—excuse the phrase—the woods. At the island!

And the woods were dark and mysterious and haunting, but without terror yet, because we had each other, clinging fast, no matter how coolly we played it off. No matter how ignorant we chose to be.

"Hey, Steve, how's it going?"

"Great! How about you?"

"Great!"

Most of the time, I'm saying, this is the way it went. This is the tone we set.

And then we got into it, lost ourselves, and became kids again. We gamboled on the island till the sheltering lights dimmed, one by one, and we, traipsing along still or sitting in the bleachers of the baseball field impressing ourselves with grand tales now or caught in a game of basketball at the other end by the railroad tracks so rusty and defunct they led to nowhere, remarked the sudden darkness and got ready to leave.

"Let's split, man."

"All right."

When we gathered up to go home the river was cold and uninviting. Crossing the shallow tributaries that fed it, we knew death in the air. Around the banks of the waterways, animals scurried in the bushes and night turned still.

It was lonely walking home, parting at the water's edge.

"Okay, man, see you later!"

"Okay."

"How's your dad, man?" somebody might ask, a final parting.

"He's okay, man."

The friend might pause for me, but, getting nothing, go on.

And so we split up, each of us taking his separate trail, sometimes accompanying one another as far as a lighted shack, a glowing cabin in the night. Then we said goodbye.

"See you later, man."

"Later."

And we went into our homes.

In our homes whatever was happening was news to us.

So the river reached into our lives regardless of any wall meant to keep it out. It was too powerful and mighty to be contained. Part of a vast system of tributaries and creeks, smaller rivers and assorted waterways, it was, one way or another, The River, all of it.

It defined our neighborhood by its presence. "The Santa Ana. The 5." It was so important a river, so vital a waterway it couldn't be avoided as a landmark worthy of recognition. It was a concrete signature spelling us out for the rest of the city, of the nation, of the world!

The river runs right through Commerce! It traffics in commerce through Commerce! Big, grinding, roaring barges keep it busy all day! It surges with the day's traffic!

It's kind of dangerous, too, so loud and noisy and grim.

But to hear the river at night was a joy. Under cover of darkness, wide-eyed, alone in bed with an old rag dog retrieved from the garage recently, I tuned in, and, unashamed now in my solitude, in my room, opened myself to everything comforting. Gruffy the Puppy whispered things to me. "Listen to the river," he said. "Listen, and don't be afraid."

The river roared, a constant rush, an edifying current, a drowning-out solace. "Listen to the river," he said. "Sink into it and die."

Then I turned to my brother in his bed.

"Albert."

"What?"

"Are you awake?"

"Yeah."

"What's wrong with Dad?"

"He's getting worse."

"At least he's quiet tonight."

"Yeah."

We paused in the night.

"Go to sleep, dude. It's late."

One night, coming home from the island, I encountered chaos. The river had overflowed its embankment and wanted to drown everything. Flooding the house, the river had soaked carpets, walls, knocked over furniture bobbing in a topsy-turvy dance in the kitchen.

"What happened?" I asked.

"Nothing. Mom hit Dad. Get in the car," my sister said.

Then the keys were thrust into my hand.

On the way out I saw my father sunk into his wheelchair, ankles wet, sulking with the glowering rage of the trapped. His arm was bruised with a purple blot and his face showed signs of the raked.

I splashed through the living room and out the front door.

In the driveway, my mother was ready. She stood timorously alert by the car. As if the river had bested her, she looked frenzied and beaten, frazzled and alive. She clung to a small life preserver, pressing it to her chest unawares.

"Mom, let's go."

I eased her into the car and got in after my sister took her place behind the driver's seat. I drove along the main tributary getting us out of our city. From a certain point, I could loop onto the river beneath it.

It flowed beneath a bridge, constantly sparkling, constantly inviting. In my river-ready barge, I could take her away. We could escape the inferno of the house, free ourselves from the upended, dismal mess back there, the hot-breathed locus of the river's boiling heart.

It wanted us now, inside her. It wanted us for some time now.

"Come, come, come to me," it sang.

My father's slide into the river's maw cost us terribly. What he suffered from, only the river knew for sure. In those days, such obviously damning, never-heard-before words made little sense.

"Early Alzheimer's." "Huntington's." "Mid-life dementia."

We knew of this frightful thing from family lore, but not of its real self, its unholy, dreadful incarnation. We balked at its demands. We caved. Not quite surrendered prematurely, but suffered from the onset with terror and panic. From its horrible beginnings, we descended into a hellish family life I don't wish to re-enter any more than I have to.

Now my mother sat next to me, stone-faced and fervent, her eyes alive, her hands tightly clenched in her lap.

"Where are we going?" she asked.

"I don't know. Where do you want to go?"

"Grandma's," she said. "Take me to my mother's."

"Okay."

So that would mean another route. But already we had reached the apex of the bridge's arch. Below us the river roared, the car stopped at a red light. Outside the windows the cascade of shiny white droplets streaming in one direction curved against the cascade of shiny red droplets streaming in the other, all of it attended by the roar, the roar of the river.

My mom made a quick move. "Mom!" I jammed the car into Park and followed her out.

On the bridge overlooking the river flowing beneath us, a gleaming, broad expanse of turbulence and beauty, I caught her. She had reached the rail and was throwing herself over, one leg—who could imagine such strength in her?—lifted high and her body aimed in the opposite direction, down below, directly at the river. She presented herself to it, and it said, "Yes, yes, jump, jump!"

I pulled her back with force. I got her in the car.

My sister got in on the other side of her, trapping her between us, and we drove away, away, away from the river behind us, its terrible beauty still a mystery.

THE MYTHSCAPES OF POINT REYES

Sylvia Linsteadt

EDITH HAS FOLLOWED hares with brightly lit tails, like street-lamps, out into scrub, into warrens that somehow shift to accommodate her bulk. The warrens are lit by tallow candles and lead through blackberry bushes deep into the earth, into sets of animal bone, human bone. A smell of rot. Old women with heron feet and gopher bones in their hair sit in these caverns, singing in high, high voices while heating animal fat in iron pots. Long cotton wicks are dipped into the fat, then hung on a series of bone racks, then dipped again, again, until the racks are heavy with candles that smell of oil and meat. The room is lit with a thousand candles, along the ceiling, like hard constellations. Edith is led by many black-tailed hares, or sometimes by coyotes that croon and howl tales of death, heroism, mischief. Unlike the hares, they never wait to lead Edith back out again, so she is left with the singing old women and their tallow and stink of meat.

Tonight, she decides to ask the women for a candle. She has only one left, taken from the abandoned grocery store in downtown Point Reyes Station. Now the shelves and cases are all empty. The old barns at Pierce Point Ranch, musty and mottled with lichen, creak and groan in the windy nights. She needs a little flush of candlelight to beat away panic, to singe the edges of solitude.

It had all happened in a single morning, the fog receding as usual around 9:30, coffee dripping, newspaper out of its blue plastic bag, home from college with her parents. Everything just stopped working—cell phone, Internet, car. It was like a great collapse of dust fell on Point Reyes Station. She heard a crack like a tree and nothing would turn on. The weeks passed. Panic, anger, not enough candlesticks or matches in the town, because after one shipment ran out, no more could be sent for, not even by post, because the mail trucks wouldn't start. Strange beings began to walk in, from the forest, from creek beds, from the salt marsh—women with gopher bones and crow eggs in their hair, bird talons for feet; great creamy elk with blue eyes and antlers like knives; jackrabbits and ravens and coyotes; a few black bears, with shifting human shadows. These creatures took up residence in abandoned Priuses, Volvos, pickup trucks, in basements or parks.

Fathers, grocers, mailmen and farmers, librarians, wives and infants left, rolling suitcases or dragging duffel bags, on bicycles wheeling heavy carts full of their things, to the city, where they hoped this uneasy plague of wildness hadn't come. Mourning doves and rats and gray foxes were meanwhile nesting in roofs, closets, laundry rooms, unafraid. Wherever they could find an opening, they snuck in, as if claiming territory, saying *this was never yours.* Old crones with bones in their hair. White egrets that sometimes became beautiful, pale naked women. Young men with fire in their eyes who smoked impossibly long pipes in the town square and sang in tongues that sounded like trees swaying, birds waking. Girls chewing gum in tight jeans followed them into dark corners, followed the flourishes of their long, long pipes. Abandoned houses filled with the old women, egrets, and lithe young men, where they lived with the birds and rats and foxes. Egret women snuggled under down comforters with the long-piped men, and left smudges of forest on the sheets. Or ripped them open in bursts of white, wove the feathers into skirts and wandered the night bare breasted and drifting.

And then Mount Tamalpais, her form like a sleeping woman, moved—like she was sitting up and yawning. Houses collapsed like take-out food containers, and people died. Edith's family died. She survived, and some others, who lived in the forest, making do scavenging from houses, stores, relearning the rest. The mountain moved, and the boundaries of Point Reyes moved too, and now it was no longer of the world it once was from. Like passing through a waterfall, or through time, out the other side and no way back. Nowhere to go, as if the place now had impermeable, ever-shifting walls. San Francisco was no longer across a red bridge and the gray thrash of bay waters.

Tonight, she waits just beyond the schoolhouse, with its dark-green chalkboard still scrawled with cursive, from the 1930s, with the names of fruits. The gloaming rises up from the sea to her left and the bay to her right. It edges between the crisped oat grass, the stand of Monterey cypress trees. It tugs at the tail feathers of wrentits and white-crowned sparrows that chitter their last songs from yellow bush lupine. It sweeps down into the burrows of mountain beavers and pocket gophers, sighs blue dusk into the soil, into their little dens.

Tonight, it is Bright-neck who leads her. A gray fox. The black tip of his tail glows like sun on obsidian. He waits, waving the black light of his tail, until she sees him, then darts into the coyote brush. She follows the tail, the silver-black slip of his body, the glow of red fur at the backs of his ears, now used to this running and jumping over rocks, around bushes, avoiding gopher holes and poison oak. Down steep, steep hillsides, the western slopes of the point, the sea breaking white and salt-cold far below. Once, Edith tumbles, turns her right ankle in a gopher hole that collapses under her weight. Thorns of cobweb thistle scrape her hands. Bright-neck stops, comes back for her. He stands an arm's length away, the flush of orange fur around his face glowing too, like embers. For a moment she thinks she can see a Douglas fir tree forming in the hairs, then a boat. Then nothing. His eyes are dark. He snaps his teeth around a large cricket, the legs kicking out under his molars. Edith dusts herself, pulls a thistle out of her palm, rotates her ankle a few times, and stands. The fox is off again. He sweeps the glowing black of his tail through the evening, leaving bands of light in the air behind him.

A dusky-footed wood rat lodge, tucked under twisted coyote brush with leaves so thick they don't release any soft juice under Edith's fingernails. Bright-neck waves the black tip of his tail, pushes his nose into the opening, between dense piled sticks. The lodge is five generations old. Each wood rat adds a little, chews away the rot. Lives in solitude, except to mate.

Edith and Bright-neck enter, and the lodge fits them, dark and smelling of wet grass. Then animal fat, up through the tunnels. Through brush and into the earth, opening wide, tallow candles dripping light against the walls. The sound of heron-bone flutes and kitchen knives cleaving. Edith follows the gray fox. Underground air wet and cold on her skin.

Normally, she only watches from the doorway, staying in the shadows. She knows they see her, but they never say anything. She watches the old women with gopher bones in their hair as they stand over iron pots and stir the fat. They sing in voices that smell of placenta and earthworms and *Amanita muscaria,* those fungi of flight and vision. They smell of cow shit and sour milk, of gold flakes and sedge banks and rotting elk. They smell of the newborn fur of mammals, sexual fluids, the small green leaves of yerba buena. She can never remember the sounds, only the smells that they fill her with. And some nights, it is only the smell of orange poppies. Or the soft feathers of heron chicks. Sometimes semen. Sometimes human excrement. She can't remember their faces either. Only the deep lines in them. Like the lines made in the earth by coyote-ghosts who limp and drag heavy foothold traps. The tallow light makes the lines even deeper with shadow. So deep Edith thinks she can see their white bones, their eyes dark like handfuls of the richest dirt. Wide hips and large breasts. One wears a dress dyed purple with mushrooms. Another, with yellow eyes and coyote claws, wears the green of malachite. All wear aprons of cowhide. The aprons are streaked with dry brown blood.

Tonight, Edith steps into their cavern. Seven women over iron pots. Their song smells like salmon and the tart skins of huckleberries. She can almost taste it. But it slows to a stop when they see her standing in the entrance, the roots of a Monterey cypress dripping water into her hair. Her fingers shake, and the water caressing her scalp makes her shiver.

"Sorry to interrupt, I didn't mean—"

A woman called Gull-foot makes a beckoning motion with her hand. Her apron is painted with blood in the shapes of city skyscrapers and church spires.

"Come over here and help me stir. My arms are getting sore."

Edith walks toward her so fast she trips on the uneven ground. She looks down and sees bones under her feet. The thick femurs of cows and elk and mountain lions.

"Slowly," says Gull-foot. Edith tiptoes over the bones and stands beside her. Smells salmon and huckleberries and the metal of blood. The woman's skin, up close, looks like the brown cracks and plateaus of Douglas fir bark.

"Thank you, I hope I didn't disturb the bones." Gull-foot doesn't reply. She guides Edith's hands to the handle of a metal ladle. It's almost too hot to hold.

"I was wondering—I mean, I don't really know how these things work, but. I need a candle. Or how to make a candle. I'm all alone and at night I don't have any light, I used it all up, and I'm afraid."

"Hold onto the ladle, and stir this for me."

The skin on Edith's palms turns pink within seconds. She stirs, and leaves the very top layer of her skin stuck to the ladle. It drops into the vat. Tears are on her cheeks from pain. Sweat beads from standing over the steam. The oils tuck into her pores. A second layer of skin falls into the iron pot.

"Good."

The women begin to sing again. Edith smells wet acorns and the bodies of lambs, just as they are born, still sticky.

ARTEMIS IN THE BARNYARD

Zara Raab

(1940)

SHE DIDN'T HEAR the gate in the flurry
of hens, squalling, stretching out their necks,
checking for foxes one second, the next
pecking nuggets of millet and barley
hidden in the wood shavings, then stiffening
their plumes again in fright. She didn't hear
the gate's click, the man slipping in, daring
to gaze on her—the oval of her face,
the halo of ruddy hair, her legs splayed,
her axe raised high over the waist-high stump.
But just as her axe reached the pinnacle
of its arc, she felt his presence; as he
turned to go, her wedge finished its arc, she
severed the neck of the Plymouth Rock—
white plumes going Mars red on bloodied oak.

She had scared him off; he wouldn't return.
She turned to the work at hand and when
that was done, still thinking of him, she went
down to the barn where the millet was stored.
Lifting up her yellow apron as if
to rescue overripe plums from their tree,
she bent over the millet bin and scooped

an apron of seed with her thoughts of him.
These she scattered to the Plymouth Rocks.
The rest she sowed; it prospered in her fields.
In the hills and river banks of Branscomb,
she grew famous for her hens whose eggs she
sold in the General Store on Branscomb Road.
Even now, standing in her fields under
a rising moon, she hears someone sighing.

BOHEMIAN GROVE

Geoffrey G. O'Brien

G RAB OUR MISSING spears and begin
  to think the Bohemian Grove, trees,
theatricals, songs that hold exquisite
filterings of sunlight down to the boys
were women there in the powerful glades,
in the 20s, there's nothing like it, to have
loins for the first time running around
in leaves, in the 70s I sang a song of we
became ourselves again as women, specifically
houris, the "leaves of love" falling
by chopper and could see the security cordon
of leaves running around excited to be
playing a part in the hush of the woods
Donald called me "songbird" and to be fit
for the world one must periodically leave it,
affectionately, for the age and straightness of trees
in the 80s, whispering at the clearing's edge
about how to keep both houses, no one hurt
when respect is earned by singing a short theme
in the 40s, at the tree line, theatricals, excited
to be putting on a helmet and running around
in the dark, on my knees in the sun
being told as a group what to do about
how soft I was, the pillows in my chamber

with choppers landing and a glow through the trees
spread uncomfortably around the clearing
till there's nothing like it, going missing
and the distance you begin to think, respect
hushing the woods with a part to play
blacked out in the secret authority
of choosing a heavy gold dress to wear
over on the other side of the clearing
songs hold the men like houris
for the first time leaving the world
affectionately at play in choppers and leaves
no one is hurt at the edge of themselves
running from the news of sunlight
into heavy dresses the warriors wore
for a production of the 50s, absence of birdsong
there in the powerful soil.

CUSTODIO Y LOS DARDOS DEL SUEÑO

Juan Velasco Moreno

EN CALIFORNIA los meses me disparan dardos de sueño,
Los hoteles más jovenes se suicidan de un sólo
Salto, se estrangulan con sus lenguas de hielo.

En California el cáliz sabe a ciénaga,
El crujido del cristal y la palmera te persigue.
El silencio te invade cada gesto,
Los cuchillos se hacen tus amantes.

Los meses huyen a California en sigilo:
"¿No te quedas aquí para siempre,
Donde nació el fuego? ¿No te quedas
Donde se descompone la sangre?"
Trozos del horror me besan,
Se sacrifican para que me quede en California.
Cuando los nombres ya se han ido,
Sólo queda el reflejo de una madre de cristal.

CUSTODIO AND THE DREAM DARTS

THE CALIFORNIA MONTHS shoot me with dream darts,
The youngest motels end it all in one fell swoop—
Suicide strangulation on their tongues of ice.

In California the chalice smacks of slime,
Pursued by palm trees and crackling glass
The silence invades your every gesture,
Razors and knives become secret lovers.

The months flee to California in secrecy: "Won't you stay
Here forever, in the cradle of fire? Won't you stay
Where blood rots away?" Shards of horror
Kiss me, sacrificing themselves just so
I will stay in California. When their names
Have all flown away, what remains is only the reflection
Of a crystalline mother.

POINT REYES: RENEWED BY FIRE

David Rains Wallace

W HEN I STARTED visiting Point Reyes in the 1970s, the landscape from Limantour Beach up to the crest of Inverness Ridge had a special appeal. I had spent my early childhood in the New England countryside in the 1940s, so vestiges of the pre-Seashore ranching days made me nostalgic—homestead sites, dammed lakes, fence lines, timothy hay growing in old fields. On the other hand, watching the wild ecosystem come back, with its brush rabbits, jackrabbits, quail, hawks, and bobcats, was endlessly fascinating.

Yet I wasn't too clear about what that wild ecosystem was. I knew that north central Point Reyes supported a forest of bishop pine, *Pinus muricata,* a species confined to areas of relatively dry and nutrient-poor soils along the Pacific coast. Granitic bedrock and proximity to the ocean (where the trees benefit from fog drip) make the Limantour area a good place for it. Like its close relative, Monterey pine, it is a closed cone species, the firmly attached asymmetrical cones remaining on the branches instead of opening to release their seeds and then falling off as with most pine species. Named for San Luis Obispo ("obispo" being Spanish for "bishop"), where it was first identified, bishop pine now occurs in scattered stands from Santa Barbara to Humboldt County, with an isolated population in Baja California. Fossils show that its ancestors were more widespread during drier times over the past two to five million years.

Hiking the Limantour area back in the 1970s, I saw plenty of bishop pines. Yet the pines on the crest and west slopes of Inverness Ridge seemed a little too peripheral and vestigial to be considered a "bishop pine ecosystem." Point Reyes' main bishop pine forest occurred on the ridge's east slopes, down to Tomales Bay. I knew places along the Inverness Ridge Trail where bishop pines were large for a species that seldom grows over 50 feet tall or lives more than a century, but few young pines grew in the understory of huckleberry and other shrubs. Although hot weather or gray squirrels can open some cones, those factors don't release enough seeds to regenerate a pine forest, and bishop pine seedlings compete poorly with other tree species in their parents' shade. Saplings of hardwoods like bay laurel, wax myrtle, madrone, and oak mainly grew there, and the largest pines seemed senescent.

There were places on the ridge's west slopes where small pines predominated, but these spots were shallow-soiled granitic out-crops and the little pines were dwarfs, older than they looked, growing where few other woody plants could survive. On deeper-soiled sites, Douglas fir saplings poked up here and there among grass and brush. Although the landscape changed little from year to year, the overall plant succession seemed headed toward the mixed hardwood and Douglas fir forest that grows on the sandstone and shale bedrock to the south in Point Reyes.

Then came the wildfire of October 1995, which consumed the vegetation from Mount Vision west to Limantour Beach with astounding thoroughness, partly because the pines burned so readily. The fire burned more patchily in the Douglas fir and hardwood forest south of Kelham Beach. Standing on a headland a few weeks after the fire and seeing almost nothing but blackened earth in every direction, I felt less inclined than before to take plants for granted. And the astounding speed with which the plants reclaimed the area over the next few years made me take them even *less* for granted.

They began to seem less vegetative and more dynamic—almost animated. Bracken fern and coyote bush sprouted from charred bases days after the fire. Grasses and forbs like trefoil, lupine, clover, and rush-rose covered the soil by the summer. Shrubs and vines—blueblossom ceanothus, huckleberry, manroot, blackberry—shaded out many of the herbs by the summer after that. Some patches of blueblossom grew six feet tall in that time.

No plant species in the post-fire Limantour area seemed more dynamic, however, than *Pinus muricata*. The fire killed almost all the existing pines in the burn area. Yet its heat freed countless seeds—which can stay viable for decades within their sealed cones—by melting the resin of the cones, thus opening the scales. Fiery updrafts sent the winged seeds showering onto the westward slopes and headlands, including many places where pines had not occurred. Pine seedlings started appearing a few months after the fire and a year later formed large, irregular patches in sites where grass, brush, or Douglas fir had seemed the permanent vegetation.

Those seedlings seemed different from the bishop pines I'd known before. The pre-fire trees had a lot of character, both the picturesque, umbrella-shaped large specimens and the gnarled, persistent little ones. But they were a bit drab—their needles plain green; their trunks, branches and cones grayish. The post-fire bishop pines had an electric quality, as though some plugged-in current was emanating from them, making bark and needles glow.

A phenomenon in the soil may have contributed to this impression of enhanced vitality. Mycologists found that the fire stimulated a population explosion of fungi that live symbiotically on the roots of young bishop pines, which helps them absorb mineral nutrients in return for photosynthesis-produced food. Uncommon before the fire (when other fungi species performed this function for the mature trees), the young fungi—*Rhizopogon* and *Tuber*—grew abundantly from spores that probably had been resting in the soil for decades.

Looking east from Limantour Beach toward Inverness Ridge in 1997, I saw few of the farmland vestiges that had made me nostalgic before the fire. The burned landscape reminded me more of Yellowstone National Park. The headlands and slopes now had a similar shaggy look, like a landscape for elk rather than cattle, and in 1998 the park service did indeed introduce some tule elk here from the Tomales Point preserve.

Although flames temporarily decimated vulnerable species like the mountain beaver (not a beaver but a uniquely primitive rodent species with a race endemic to Point Reyes), the post-fire landscape seemed to attract and stimulate wildlife. Butterflies and other insects thronged the burned area even before the wildflowers bloomed, as though anticipating the feast to come. One insect species, a small black moth, proved new to science. Soon after the fire, I had my first and only sighting of a golden eagle—listed as rare at Point Reyes—at the park. Near Limantour I saw the only long-tailed weasel I've ever encountered in the park, although that may just have been due to the enhanced visibility post-fire. Meadow voles underwent one of their periodic population explosions, probably encouraged by the wealth of leguminous forbs.

There was no doubt after the Vision Fire that the Limantour area is a bishop pine ecosystem, just as there was no doubt after its 1987 fires that most of Yellowstone is a lodgepole pine ecosystem, also dependent on fire for renewal. I understood now how *Pinus muricata*'s ancestor dominated a prehistoric landscape that included mammoths, sabertooths, and ground sloths as well as the surviving elk, deer, and mountain lions.

As the last ranching era vestiges have vanished, roads revegetated, dammed lakes and hay fields reverted to marshes and riparian woodland, I've sometimes missed my pre-fire nostalgia, but not that much. Bishop pine forest seems right for the place, although the wildfire on which it depends for renewal can be catastrophic. Still, whether started by an illegal campfire like the Vision Fire or by more natural factors, wildfires are inevitable, like earthquakes. We have to adapt to nature's perils in the end, like all the other organisms. The thousands of teenaged bishop pines now growing from Limantour Beach up to the Inverness Ridge Trail are vivid reminders of that fact, although the landscape doesn't look quite as shaggy now as it did in 1997. In fact, some of it resembles a 1950s Weyerhauser tree farm ad, as the carpet of even-aged pines gives the slopes an almost industrial look. Some hikers find the close-growing young forest a bit claustrophobic and monotonous compared to the sweeping panoramas that the Bucklin and Drakes View trails offered before the fire. But time will open the forest as weaker trees die, and diversity will increase as young ferns, shrubs, and hardwoods creep into the understory, exploiting patches of sunlight that already penetrate the canopy.

Above, where their needles endlessly sing in the wind, the little pines' two-foot-long, silver and amber terminal shoots still seem to glow from within. Female cones in various stages of development—bright green new ones, year-old orange ones, weathered gray ones—ring the trunks and branches, patiently awaiting the next wildfire.

from **S H A R D S**

Ismet Prcic

Y OU KNOW YOU'RE dreaming, because you've seen this sneaker moving like this before. The movement you're seeing is not voluntary. There's an outside force. Something else is moving the foot and with it the sneaker. A hog.

The sneaker is a Reebok, white and baby blue, reasonably clean, its laces tied neatly. It bobs up and down several times, then comes to a gradual, bouncy stop for a few moments of pregnant immobility, then goes through a few sideways moves that make one of the lace loops sway like a noose, after which there's another wicked stretch of time in which the sneaker is not moving because the hog is chewing. You can't see the hog but you know it's chewing, because you've seen the sneaker move and then not move like this before. You've seen it so many times it's boring, like the back of your own hand, like your own dick. Bosnian Muslims don't eat pigs but pigs have no problem eating Bosnian Muslims. Or anybody else. They have no problem eating dead meat. It's all very boring. And before the close-up of the moving sneaker widens enough to show a whole human leg and the hog munching on its thigh, stopping to chew, then digging in again, making the lace loop sway, you come to on a sofa in someone's house in the Valley.

Yesterday, after work, your coworkers said there was a party, that you should come. You took a ride with them because you didn't want to drive, because Jason gave you speed and pot and you felt keyed up and groggy at the same time. They promised to drive you back to your car but here you are still in the Valley on a Saturday, sweating all over someone's couch.

The sofa sags like clammy old tits. The ceiling has a cellulite problem and from a poster on the wall a white man and a black man are pointing their guns at you, about to blow you away. On the coffee table there's an array of remote controls, some smut magazines, mounds of pistachio shells, and a soldier's helmet half-full of peanut M&M's. You swing your feet to the carpet and sit up. The air around you is yeasty with half-drunk, abandoned beers. You try to remember whose place this is but can't picture any faces. It scares you, this inability. What if they don't remember you, either? What if, after coming across you lying on their sofa, glistening, they decide to call the cops on you? You stand up, trying to make no noise.

On top of the paranoia you feel like shit. You feel like someone went through your intestinal tubing with a blowtorch. You're buzzing with this unreachable, untreatable pain. You're vibrating with it. You pick up a long-dead beer from underneath the table and pound it.

There's a short, plosive sound somewhere, a door closing or a collision of two things, then a screech of metal against metal as a shower curtain is pulled open, and a gush of water against bathtub enamel. You set the bottle silently on the table and locate the front door. The next moment you're outside, running across the grass, past parked SUVs and mailboxes and driveway hoops, everywhere underneath the scorching California sun that sits smack in the middle of the merciless blue void.

The Valley is a hellhole with palm trees, a perpetual quasi suburbia. You walk briskly for about fifteen minutes and wouldn't be able to find your way back even if you wanted to. Neighborhood-watch signs make you queasy. You think you see curtains move in the windows. There's a brawny bald fellow tinkering inside the gaping crocodile mouth of an El Camino in a driveway, and you dash across the street to avoid him.

You need a ride. You need a ride or a way to call for a ride, probably a phone. It's a long way back to Thousand Oaks from here. You check your pockets and find a guitar pick, some bitten-off nails, a rolled-up Sav-on Pharmacy receipt, and no coins. Your wallet has your driver's license, an ATM card, your Bosnian ID card, some business cards with chicken scratches on the backs of them, names and numbers, idiotic ideas, makeshift maps, book titles, band names, bullshit. There's no money, which means you'll have to find an ATM, get out a twenty, take it to a store somewhere to break it, then find a pay phone. You think if you just follow a major street you'll eventually hit a minimall.

Mostly there aren't any sidewalks. Walking is discouraged in the Valley. Motorists at red lights gawk at you or avoid your eyes and lock their doors.

You've seen pigs eat dead villagers: big, pink, fleshy hogs feeding on gray, wet, dead people. You've seen other things, too: chopped-off heads near makeshift goalposts, human-ear necklaces, dickless, toothless, breastless, scrotumless, noseless, eyeless, fingerless, armless, headless, legless, pissed-on, shat-on, came-on, carved-up, stabbed-through, burned-up, bludgeoned, fucked-with bodies of men and women you knew. You've seen all this and yet the images that come back to you now, night after night, nap after nap, are from the TV footage you saw toward the beginning of the war: a close-up of a sneaker, moving, then stopping, then moving again until a slow pan reveals the hog.

Memory is bullshit.

Stop it.

You make yourself look around. Corner of Somewhere and Someplace. The crosswalk signal is red. Cars are zooming by: an Asian lady in white, a fat redhead smoking a cigarette, a man with

NEW CALIFORNIA WRITING 2013

a thin mustache, a hippie stereotype in a tie-dyed VW van, a police cruiser. You can't stand standing there.

There's a song in your head, something accordiony from back home. You think about firing bullets into unsuspecting bodies, rib cages ripping open, heads caving, oozing stuff. The music in your head gets louder and you realize that it's not exclusively in your head.

A man wearing black slacks and a wife-beater stumbles out of a beige house and opens a tall door to the backyard, where apparently someone is playing a song you know on an accordion. He's yelling into his cell phone and it takes a surreal moment for you to realize that he's speaking Bosnian.

"...park it on the grass, then, I guess—fuck it!" he says, then waves to someone behind you.

You turn around and find a burgundy minivan there, its driver with one hand on the wheel and the other holding a cell phone to his ear, waiting for you to get out of the way. As soon as you hop aside he has the minivan slanted up the gentle slope of the lawn, its fender kissing a rosebush. You look up and down the street. There isn't a parking spot in sight for miles. It's another party. With Bosnians this time.

Out of the van comes a gaggle of boys and girls, all of them screeching in English. The wife-beater man makes them all high-five him before he lets them squeeze by and fuck off into the backyard.

"Domaćine," says the driver, locking the van with one of those key remotes. *Be-beep!* Both men raise their arms like they haven't seen each other for years, step into a hearty hug, then smack kisses on each other's cheeks, three apiece.

"Come on in, come in!"

"Did you start without me?"

"Shit yeah, we started last night."

"I heard, I heard!"

The driver walks toward the door, then realizes that the man in the wife-beater hasn't moved.

"Are you coming?"

"Yeah, I just want to smoke a cigarette in peace. Go get yourself a beer."

"Hurry up."

You watch all this like it's a play; it isn't until the man in the wife-beater gives you a look that you realize you're just standing there, staring at him lighting up. He's thick and meaty, older than you, with thinning black hair held up and against his skull with what must be bucketfuls of gel, all of it painstakingly combed to give the whole head a ribbed texture, like in Mafia pictures.

"You want one?" he says to you in English.

You don't usually like talking to Bosnians in America. You feel like they stand in the way of your complete assimilation. You don't like the doubling of words in your head, things coming out in Bonglish. But then you remember you still need to make a phone call.

"All right, give me one," you say to the man in Bosnian, watching his eyes pop open, bloodshot and blue, almost teary.

"Are you here for the thing?" he asks, lighting your cigarette, a menthol, nodding back toward the house. You get a whiff of his breath and for a second you're back with your dad and his slivovitz-drinking friends, yelling at the soccer game on TV, clapping yourself on the forehead when they just miss it by an inch, watching them swear and say stuff like "My aunt Devleta would put that in" or "Fuck his mother, he's got two left legs."

"No, man—I was just walking by and heard the music."

"Where are you from?"

"Tuzla. You?"

"The whole of Tuzla a single goat did milk, and then keeps on bragging that it feeds on cheese." It's an old song about your town, and he's smiling like he's proud he remembers it after all these years. "I've been there a million times. My ex-girlfriend studied there. Jasna Babić. You knew her?"

"I don't think."

"Kind of shortish, blonde hair?"

"I don't think so."

"Tits up to here?"

"I don't think so, man."

"Man, she fucked like a pike."

He takes a drag, a sad toke of nicotine fumes and nostalgia, looking glassily away. You try to emulate him.

"She got blown up by our own shell," he says, and smokes. You don't know what to tell him, so you just ape his mannerisms. You read in *How to Make Friends* that it puts strangers at ease.

"I told her a million times to fuckin' get out," he continues, but then stops himself. Something like anger blows across his face. His eyes change. "Oh, fuck her. Her fuckin' choice." He smokes some more and then says, in English, "There's plenty of pussy in the sea," and laughs, smacking you on the back so hard it uproots you. His cigarette is almost to the filter now, and you still have to ask about the phone.

"Listen—" you start.

"When did you get here? To the States."

"Uh...end of ninety-five."

"How'd you get out?"

"Got wounded in battle. They let me go."

"Wait a minute, you were a soldier?"

He's suddenly very close to you, looking into your eyes like a lover or a nemesis. You nod, leaning backward. You swear to God he starts to cry a little, embraces you like he did the driver earlier, and kisses you on both cheeks.

"You have to come in and party," he manages through his genuinely shrinking throat, then hugs you some more. Clamping your neck, he maneuvers you toward his house. "I won't take no for an answer. Not even in theory."

"I should—"

"My pops would love to meet you," he says, ushering you past a line of color-coded garbage bins. "He still can't forgive himself for not going back to fight when you guys needed it the most." Most of the backyard, you see, is taken over by a long, white tent. Underneath it forty or fifty people are packed around a long table, fanning themselves with paper plates, gulping down beers, yelling, laughing, standing up to make announcements. Little kids run in and out of the house with sticks in their hands, marshmallows stuck on their tips. Their mothers run after them, screaming for them not to run. They scream in Bosnian and the kids answer in whiny English, complaining that so-and-so's mother is letting so-and-so do what he likes, look. In the yard's far corner there's a kidney-shaped hole in the grass, the beginnings of a pool, in which a hairy man with a T-shirt tied around his head is using the shallow end to spit-roast a pig. Something is a little off.

"Here," says the wife-beater man, handing you a Beck's. "Let's find you a spot at the table."

As you follow him you figure it out. Next to the tent there's a three-colored flag with a yellow symbol in the middle, an Orthodox Christian cross and a Cyrillic *S* in each of its quadrants, four *S*'s you've seen before. They stand for *Samo sloga Srbina spašava,* your enemy's creed from the war you fought in and survived: Only Unity Saves a Serb.

You look for the easiest way to get the fuck out of there. Through the house, maybe? Or across the pool, onto that bench, and over the wall into someone else's yard? Definitely not the way you came. Too many bodies to go through. You're mad at yourself. You should have realized something earlier: three kisses for the Holy Trinity, not to mention the pig in the pool. Shit. You sidestep timidly toward the house.

The wife -beater man has made it to the head of the table now, and he leans in and speaks directly to someone sitting there whose face you cannot see because there's an enormous blond hairdo in your line of vision, like a clown's Afro. You don't see him until he stands up, wobbly on his feet, this perfervid patriarch dressed in Chetnik war paraphernalia, *šajkača, kokarda,* greasy gray beard down to his bellybutton, a pistol grip protruding from his pants.

"Where is this soldier man?" he yells, looking around while his son tries to keep him standing. He speaks in a patchy Serbian dialect with a rural Bosnian lilt, only a Bosnian Serb, a wannabe. You're six feet from the back door when his hammered eyes finally find your own. The man smiles and waves you over.

Running right now would not be a good thing. A calm voice from within tells you to do what you're told. You raise your bottle to the man and take a royal swig to buy yourself some time, then saunter over. Some of the people around the table pat your back. Those that can't reach you raise their glasses in your honor, then go back to their conversations.

"Make some room for the war hero," snarls the patriarch at the clown-fro lady, who has a face full of deviled egg.

"I'm done anyway," she blurts, spraying egg bits out of her mouth as she stands. The wife-beater man and his pops shepherd you into her seat. Up close you can see that the old man has an elaborate tattoo on his shriveling forearm, a black shield with a red and blue border. In its center floats a two-headed eagle with two yellow swords held crossed beneath a human skull. Cyrillic letters are inked above and below it: FOR KING AND FATHERLAND. FREEDOM OR DEATH.

In 1993, your unit crawled through a sticky minefield to take out a machine-gun nest as prep work for the early-morning offensive. The Claw, the leader of the unit and a truly insane individual, crept into the nest without his boots on and stabbed the last Chetnik in the back. He came out with a souvenir, a banner with an identical skull-and-swords design. A pirate flag, he called it.

The patriarch claps your back and squeezes your arm, telling you how his dad was a Chetnik in the Second World War under the direct command of General Dragoljub "Draža" Mihailović and so were both of his brothers, and how he, the youngest, was too young to fight back then and how his father liked him the least because of that, and sent him to "Čemerika" without a dinar to carve a place for himself in the world. As he talks you start thinking of a different way to get out of here. Plum brandy.

"We should have a toast for staying alive despite everything," you say, and swig your beer again.

"Wait for us," the son says, looking around for his beverage.

"You're gonna toast with beer?" You turn to the old man. "We need something stronger for this, right?"

"He's right," the father says. "Miloš, go get the *rakija.*"

An effete, shuddering fan trained on the back of the old man's head putters to a stop. He swears, leans down to the grass, and fumbles with its cord until, resuscitated, it starts to twirl again, halfheartedly.

"Connection," the old man explains.

You clink your beer against his and you both drink. He starts to talk again.

"See, both of my brothers were savagely killed. Dragiša, God save his soul, was caught and executed by the partisans in 1942 or 1943, we are not sure exactly when. His body was never found. Zdravko, God save his soul, was axed to death by the Zeleni Kadar in northeastern Bosnia. Fucking Turks. They chopped him up into pieces like a birch log. He came back to us in four burlap sacks."

He slams his fist on the table like he's in a bad play. Deviled eggs jiggle on his plate. His eyes well up. You hold his gaze while tightening your lips and shake your head in your best approximation of commiseration.

"After that my father hated me, said that if I'd been with my brothers to watch their backs they wouldn't be dead now. But I was only twelve years old."

Miloš comes back with a plastic Fanta bottle full of yellowy liquid and a tray of clashing shot glasses. As he passes by her a woman in black stands up from the table.

"What do you want that for?" she booms at him. She has a mouthful of gleaming golden teeth.

"To drink."

"You want to kill your father?"

"He told me to get it for a toast."

"It's the middle of the day and he's drunk already. You'll give him a heart attack in this heat."

"Raki thins the blood, Mother," he says, and puts a shot glass in front of his father and another in front of you. He fills them all the way to the lip and then pours himself one as well.

"To survival, despite the enemy's best efforts at achieving otherwise," you say, and raise your glass. Miloš and his father follow.

"Whiny Turkish cunts!"

"Fuck their mothers on their shitty prayer rugs!"

You hold up yours until everyone at the table who wants to join in has a beverage in their hand, then slam it to the back of your throat, feeling like someone napalmed your stomach ulcer. It takes a conscious effort to suppress your urge to vomit. It's not the brandy making you sick.

Your mother's body flashes in your mind's eye, a skeletal figure too brittle and head-shy to hug after her stint at the camp. You shake your head to get it off your mind. In her stead emerge fallen trench-mates, their faces rigid and pale like papier-mâché masks. And before the floodgates are open all the way you slap yourself, hard.

More toasts are shouted from all around the table: toasts to dead relatives, to dead relatives' saints, to the personal saints of the host's family members (his name is Jovan Cvetković, you hear), to slogans like Serbia-to-Tokyo, to President Milošević, etc. Every time a shot goes down Jovan's gullet he tries to stand up, pull out his weapon, and fire into the air, but Miloš and some younger cousins step in and dissuade him. They remind him that he's in the Valley, in America. In response Jovan drops back into his chair and moans. You're livid, but the sight of that Zastava sticking out of the old man's pants keeps you from doing anything stupid.

Meanwhile the food's been served, and now everyone's plowing through it: soups, stuffed squash, stuffed peppers, savory pastry coils. There's an accordion player, a fat person in a green felt hat with a crow's feather stuck in the band and a mustache of the sort that vandals draw on posters. He plays and sings with varying degrees of success. Every once in a while he gets a clutch of people to get up and dance kolo. They wave you over every time, and eventually you tell them the shrapnel in your leg cuts off your circulation when you sit for too long and Jovan yells at them not to bother you. Really there's no shrapnel, just nausea and cloying memories, confusion.

At some point they unload the pig, head and all, placing it on the table so it faces you with one eye closed and the other agape and forlorn. They pull the spit out of its ass and put half a lemon in its mouth. They pour beer over it and laugh and smack their lips and ask for cutlery. They're all really happy.

You're ripping apart. You see your mother climbing through an open window in Tuzla and your arms grab for her in the Valley. Your muscles remember how they had to hold on to her when she bucked and shrieked that day, trying to end it. *Let me go,* you hear her say, and the people around you dig into the pig. Your arms are rigid, holding on to nothing. Your stomach climbs into your chest. The sneaker moves in your mind, then doesn't. You want to run away or cry or start swinging.

In your heart you don't know what you want.

When some woman serves you a big, glistening piece of flesh, you throw up all over it, all over the plate, the side of the table, your lap. Somebody tilts your chair and you hit the grass, still vomiting.

"Lightweight," you hear Miloš say. You kneel there.

The woman, the clown head, helps you up. She walks you through the back door and into the house, shielding your head with her hand when you pass below a chandelier, and puts you in front of the bathroom door. She knocks.

"Hold your horses," says a female voice from inside.

She raises your head.

"Are you all right?"

You grunt.

"Are you sure?"

You nod.

"Okay. Wait until she's done and use the bathroom."

"Thank you," you manage, covering your mouth for her benefit.

"Don't puke on my carpet now," she says, smiling. Then she's gone.

You look around the hallway. Pictures everywhere, collages: Jovan in a Chetnik uniform, Jovan in a suit, younger Jovan with seventies lamb chops and a mustache, his wife in a floral-patterned dress, hugging a baby to her chest. A family portrait with a head count of more than a hundred. Miloš as a child on a donkey at a beach somewhere, Miloš on prom night with a blonde date, Miloš at the wheel of a red Camaro. A huge portrait of General "Draža" Mihailović with his round little glasses and the puff around his eyes and a beard to match Jovan's, only blacker. Next to it, framed in thin wood, is a photograph of a purplish medal. You get closer to see the caption. It reads:

General Dragoljub Mihailović distinguished himself in
an outstanding manner as commander in chief of the

*Yugoslavian Armed Forces and later as minister of war by
organizing and leading important resistance forces against
the enemy, which occupied Yugoslavia from December
1941 to December 1944. Through the undaunted efforts
of his troops, many United States airmen were rescued and
returned safely to friendly control. General Mihailović
and his forces, although lacking adequate supplies and
fighting under extreme hardship, contributed materially
to the Allied cause and were materially instrumental in
obtaining a final Allied Victory.*

—LEGION OF MERIT AWARD CITATION GIVEN BY HARRY S.
TRUMAN, PRESIDENT, THE WHITE HOUSE, MARCH 29, 1948

Underneath, in Cyrillic longhand, someone has written:

*The highest award the U.S. government can bestow upon
a foreign national.*

Your whole life, since you were six years old, your teachers
have told you that "Draža" Mihailović was a bad man, a quisling,
someone who fought with the Nazis against the Yugoslav Army and
ordered the slaughter of thousands of Yugoslavs who were not of
his faith. But here he is, an ordained American hero. You stagger
away in rage. In fear.

No one's come out of the bathroom yet. You go farther down
the corridor, into a bedroom, and find a phone. You dial your
apartment and after two rings your roommate picks up.

"Hello."

"Eric, I need a ride from you, dude. I'm in a pickle."

"Where are you?"

"In the Valley."

"Still at that party?"

"No, I'm in the house of a psycho and need to get the fuck
outta here, pronto."

"Can it wait? I'm making ramen."

"You should be in the car right now, dude."

As you say "dude" there are four pistol shots in rapid succession: *BANGBANGBANGBANG!* You look around and notice an envelope on the bed stand addressed to some other Cvetković. The mother.

"Are those gunshots?"

Ignoring the question, you read the address into the phone twice. You're pleading now. "Come get me, man."

You hear some commotion out in the corridor, and turn around in time to catch a glimpse of Miloš and his mother hurrying down the hall, arguing about where to hide the pistol, fussing.

You remember a cataclysmic night on the front line, when the snow was the color of bone in the close-to-full moonlight and the branches were spread above you like blood vessels on the anemic belly of the night sky and the bullets dove from nowhere, crashing into soft things and bouncing off hard things, and the enemy mortars smashed everything into powder. You remember the story the Claw told you that night, the one about how, some time ago, he was given orders to crawl up a hill and rendezvous with another squad of guys who were crawling up from the other side. He was supposed to wear a white band around his left arm to distinguish himself from the enemy, since otherwise their uniforms were virtually identical. He told you about how he reached the top and lizarded his way into a trench full of guys with white armbands on their left arms, squatting there, shooting the shit, until finally he realized that they were actually Chetniks, that by some strange twist of fate they'd decided on the same white armband to set themselves apart. You see the Claw keeping his cool, creeping backward, silently cocking his Kalashnikov, and killing them all from behind.

The bathroom's open now and you lock yourself in, determined to wait it out. The little room is decorated in belabored beige: beige tiles, beige shower curtain, red and beige towels, your own beige face in the mirror. You splash water on yourself, take some into your mouth, spit it out, take it in, and spit it out. Through the small, pebbled window you can see the accordion player typing an intricate melody on two keyboards simultaneously, acting like no shots were fired at all. You sit on the beige toilet lid, put your head into your beige hands, and stare at the tile grid on the floor, at a wastebasket, at the grid again. You think of death and Mother. You try to figure out what's right.

The wastebasket is small, wicker, and lined with plastic. You push at the base of it with the edge of your foot and the wads of tissue tumble and rearrange themselves, exposing a dull glint beneath. You reach in and retrieve Jovan's gun.

Your hand knows what to do with it; your index finger turns inward. The grip feels good. You sniff the barrel and it smells of youth, of Bosnia. You switch the safety off and stand up. You cock. In the mirror you look like the Claw, standing there against the beige. You lean closer. Your eyes are all pain.

Police sirens start off low and grow higher until they shut up the accordion player and silence the clamoring Serbs. There are conversations you can't really hear. Questions are asked. Things are blamed on the kids, fireworks. Apologies are given and warnings issued. You realize you're standing there with a gun in your hand. Where is Eric? How long does it take to get here from Thousand Oaks in an Oldsmobile?

You pace the bathroom. You hide the gun. You pick it up again. Hide it. Pick it up. You lift the tank lid, toss the gun in. You close the tank.

Half an hour later a car horn sounds and you know it's your ride. There's a party going on in the backyard again. You focus on what you need to do, take a deep breath, and get out of the bathroom and down the hallway. There are kids sitting around the table in the kitchen, laughing. You make your way across the living room. The white front door is the only thing you see. You can feel it, this elation in your chest, this glee in the muscles of your face. Your lips curl. You reach for the doorknob and wrap your fist around it.

"Soldier!" Jovan yells from behind you. "Where are you going?"

He stumbles toward you, pushing himself off the walls, almost falls but doesn't. He makes it to the back of the giant armchair and, with fifteen or so feet ahead of him without anything to balance himself on, stops there and leans on it with both hands.

"Stay a while longer."

"I have to go, sir. I didn't mean to stay this long. I have some things I have to do."

He grunts. "Eh, okay. Okay, but come over here before you go so I can thank you for what you've done for us."

He raises his arms, stumbles forward, and catches himself just before he hits the back of the chair with his face. The car horn sounds again. You can see the brown Delta 88 right in front of the house.

"That's my ride," you tell him, and start to step out the door.

"Tell me one thing."

You wait. You turn to him.

"How many of them did you—," he stops, dragging his left forefinger across his neck, "—with your own hand?"

You look at him, this son of a bitch. His eyes smirk. You want to say, *I'm Mustafa Nalić,* but you can't. You want to forgive him. In your heart you want to hug him but you're afraid you'd break his spine. You want to shake his hand but you're afraid you'd pull his whole arm out of its socket. You want to kiss his cheek and spit upon it.

"One night I infiltrated an enemy trench and killed six with one clip. They thought I was one of them. They were joking around. I just mowed them all down."

He smiles and nods his head.

"Good for you," he says.

from **"COLLAGE/BRICOLAGE:
OR FRAGMENTS OF TRUTH"**

Claire Kageyama-Ramakrishnan

III. NIGHT OF ELLIPSES

NOTHING IS ABSOLUTE. Not this—
My father wakes in a barrack, blinded by
sand blasting winds. His ears ache from the sounds

of firecrackers. He wipes his eyes free of debris
and thinks about his lunch, the sandwich

that wasn't a sandwich, just bread
with nothing between. Near midnight,

my father's ears ache from the gun fire
he mistakes for firecrackers. He wipes

his eyes free of debris behind walls
that should have protected him, but

never muffle the shouts and sobs
in the desert. Sage brushes the wood walls...

The moon moves swiftly...December 5th 1942—
     The searchlight is the moon,

the guards commanding the searchlights
     aim their rifles at the Manzanar rioters...

IV. OUR NEIGHBOR RALPH BRANDT, 1973–1983

1.

He scaled the wall and pissed in our yard.

2.

Poisoned our four Chihuahuas.

3.

Sat on his roof and gave us the finger.

4.

Tied kite string to pillars on our porch, left a note
for my mother—*I hope your Jap husband
trips on this.*

5.

Shouted at us when the police arrived—
I shot down Kamikazes with Japs like you!

6.

Hitchhiked home
from the Veteran's Hospital.

7.

Spray painted our driveway—
Japs Go Away.

8.

Crawled under our house, knocked at
the floorboards of the bathroom
for two nights.

9.

Launched a Fourth of July rocket—
almost hit my brother.

10.

Offered coffee when my father
stood at his door
with a rifle.

MARIA EVANGELISTE

Greg Sarris

HER NAME WAS MARIA, which was what the priest at St. Rose Church called all the Indian girls, even this girl Maria Evangeliste, who ironed his vestments and each Sunday played the violin so beautifully as the communicants marched to the altar to receive the sacraments that Jesus was said to smile down from the rafters at the dispensation of his body and blood. That was why on a Friday when she hadn't returned by nightfall, and still no sign of her at mass on Sunday, the priest worried as much as her family, and after mass notified the sheriff. The flatbed wagon that she had been driving was found by an apple farmer outside his stable, as if the pale gray old gelding was waiting to be unhitched and led to a stall inside. The two cherrywood chairs she'd purchased on the priest's behalf stood upright, still on the wagon bed, wedged between bales of straw. The priest had contracted the chairs for his rectory from a carpenter in Bodega, and Maria, needing any small amount of compensation, offered to drive the old gelding nearly a ten-mile trip west and then back. Still, she should have returned before nightfall for she left at dawn, the priest's money for the carpenter secure in her coat pocket.

A number of things could've happened to her. The horse might've spooked, jerking the wagon so that if she wasn't paying close attention she would've been tossed to the ground—she might be lying on the roadside someplace, knocked unconscious, a broken back,

God forbid a broken neck. She could've been raped, left in the brush somewhere even. At the time, in 1903, American Indians had not yet been granted US citizenship and therefore had no recourse in a US court. A lone Coast Miwok girl in Sonoma County was easy prey for marauding American men and boys who roamed the back roads, as the old Indians used to say, like packs of dogs.

But wouldn't they have hesitated, considering the possibility that Maria Evangeliste was a US citizen of Mexican descent, a guise many Indians used? Surely, approaching the wagon they would have seen the wooden cross hanging from her neck. If that didn't stop them, she had the ultimate defense, an embroidered crimson sash the priest wore at mass and had given her that morning as proof of protection from the church, which she'd kept folded in her other pocket, ready in the event someone should assault her, even if only to search her pockets to steal the priest's money for the carpenter. But none of these things happened.

As she rounded a hilly curve on the dirt road, which is now paved and called Occidental Road, she spotted two women. They were Indian women in long nineteenth-century dresses, scarves covering their heads and tied under the chin, and Maria Evangeliste recognized them immediately. They were twin sisters, childless elderly southern Pomo women from the outskirts of Sebastopol just a couple miles up the road. They did not resemble one another, one twin short and stout, the other taller, much darker, the color of oak bark. But, at that moment, hardly would Maria Evangeliste have remarked at their appearance, or the fact that, side by side, they stood in the middle of the road halting her passage, or even that she was in the vicinity of the rumored secret cave old people talked about in revered whispers. She understood what was happening without thinking, knew all at once. So when the taller of the two women commanded her off the wagon with only a nod of the chin, she knew she had no choice but to get down and follow them. And, it is told, that was how it started, how the twin sisters took Maria Evangeliste to train her as a Human Bear.

Why Maria Evangeliste was traveling on Occidental Road is a mystery. The usual route from Santa Rosa to the coastal town of Bodega was, and still is, the road west across the lagoon to the town of Sebastopol and then more or less straight to the coast. Returning from Bodega, she would have had to venture north along one of two or three narrow roads, wide paths really, to reach what is now Occidental Road—which would have been a longer, circuitous way to go, not to mention more dangerous given that she would be more isolated in the event she was assaulted. There was also greater risk of the old horse stumbling, some kind of accident with the wagon, on an unreliable road. Did she not want to pass through the town of Sebastopol because it was Friday, late in the day, and gangs of men off work from the sawmill and nearby orchards would already be gathered around the pubs, men who were drinking and might catch sight of her alone? There was an encampment of Indians where Occidental Road emptied onto the Santa Rosa plain—had she a friend she wanted to visit? Winter rain flooded, and still floods, the lagoon—was she traveling at a time when the water was high, when she needed to cross the northern bridge over the lagoon rather than the bridge in Sebastopol?

Following an ancient story of how the Human Bear cult started, where a lone boy picking blackberries was kidnapped by grizzly bears and afforded their secrets and indomitable physical prowess, it is said that most initiates to the cult were likewise kidnapped. Human Bears might watch a young person carefully for some time, months or even years, regarding the young person's suitability for induction. Stories are told of Human Bears traveling far distances to study a potential initiate, often in the guise of wanting only to see an old friend or to trade. They might even warn chosen individuals of their impending abduction, reminding them that they had no choice henceforth but to acquiesce and keep silent. Had Maria Evangeliste made arrangements beforehand, driven the priest's wagon north to fulfill her obligation?

Four days later, on a Tuesday morning, she returned. She lived with her family and a changing assembly of relatives forever in search of work in a clapboard house west of town. The small house, said to be owned by a dairy rancher for whom her father worked, sat above Santa Rosa creek. Behind the house, lining the creek, was a stand of willow trees. A relative of my grandmother's, who first told me the story, said Maria Evangeliste appeared from behind the trees. Later, another older relative pointed to a bald hillside while we were driving on Occidental Road and mentioned the story, claiming that Maria Evangeliste was first discovered standing in front of her house, not behind in the willows, and that in the faint morning light she was still as stone. Both versions posit that she was unharmed, returned as she had left, groomed, unsullied.

She could not tell where she had been. Did she lie, perhaps say that she lost control of the wagon after the horse spooked? Did she say as much in order to lead others to believe she'd run off with a young man? What was the sheriff told? The priest? However the case was resolved in the minds of the sheriff and the priest—whether from whatever story the girl might've relayed or from whatever either of them surmised themselves about what happened—the Indians were not so easily satisfied. For the Indians, enough of them to pass on a story anyway, the girl's answers were suspect and pointed only to one possible outcome: the two old twins in Sebastopol had found a successor.

I visited the bald hillside a couple of weeks ago, parked my car on Occidental Road, then crawled under a barbed wire fence and hiked through brush and looming redwood trees, dark shade. Where would the secret cave be—this side of the hill, below the steep face of naked rock, or around the backside? Would such a cave exist still? Might not loggers or farmers have destroyed it long ago? Unable to see past a thicket of blackberry bramble, I could no longer look back and see the road. The outcropping of rock, exposed above the curtain of treetops, was a face with crater formations and crevices, as if the hill, like an enormous and uninhibited animal, was observing my approach. I became agitated. The story filled me. Oh, these are modern times, I told myself. What's a story these days? If anything, I should be worrying about trespassing on private property. Nonetheless, I stopped. Looking over the blackberry bramble to the trees, I attempted to regain my bearings, again trying to gauge my distance from the road.

In 1903, when the twin sisters abducted Maria Evangeliste, loggers had leveled the trees a second time—or were about to. The magnificent original redwoods, reaching down from the Oregon border to present-day Monterey County, were for the most part cleared between 1830 and 1870. The trees before me, a third growth of redwoods, were about a hundred years old, and a hundred feet tall. In 1903, the gigantic original trees that once sheltered the grizzly bears were gone, and, whether or not the second stand of trees still stood, the grizzly was extinct in the region, killed decades before by Mexican vaqueros and American settlers. The Human Bear cult, like the grizzly bear, was dependent on the trees and on an open landscape, unencumbered by fences and ranchers protective of livestock. Stories abound—even among local non-Indians—of ranchers felling a bear only to find when they went to retrieve the carcass an empty hide. The twin sisters, how did they instruct their last recruit? Did they show Maria Evangeliste a route that was still safe to travel under a moonless nighttime sky? Did they have only memories to offer, power songs unsung outside the old cave?

Secret societies, such as the Human Bear cult, both perpetu-
ated and reflected Pomo and Coast Miwok worldview, where every
human, just as every aspect of the landscape, possessed special—and
secret—powers. Cult members with their special power and connection with the living world played an integral role in the well-being
of the village. Human Bears, assuming the grizzly's strength and
extraordinary sense of smell, could locate and retrieve food from
far distances. They possessed "protection," often songs, that caused
illness, sometimes death, to anyone who might attempt to harm
them—or some feature of the landscape they might use, such as
a cave. You would thus think twice about harming anyone. Same
with a bird, a tree, any tiny stone. Respect becomes the only guar-
antee of survival. This respect is predicated on remembering that,
even with unique power, you are not alone, absolute. As renowned
late Pomo Indian doctor Mabel McKay told me, "Be careful when
someone [or something] catches your attention. You don't know
what spirit it is. Be thoughtful." The Kashaya Pomo elders refer
to Europeans as *pala-cha,* miracles: instead of being punished for
killing people and animals, chopping down trees, damming and
dredging the waterways, the Europeans kept coming.

There were numerous secret cults. Many were associated with
animals, bobcat, grizzly bear, even birds and snakes. Others were
associated with a particular place, a meadow, a canyon, an underwater cave where the spirit of the place empowered its respective
cult members. Cults were often gender based: women's Bear cults
were considered among the most powerful. In all cases, cult initiates endured long periods of training, not only learning about the
essentials of their animal powers, for instance, but simultaneously
of the larger environment as well.

Sonoma County, about an hour north of San Francisco, was
at the time of European contact one of the most geographically
complex and biologically diverse places on earth. Below arid hills,

covered with only bunchgrass and the occasional copse of oak and bay laurel, were rich wetlands, inland bays, lakes, a meandering lagoon, a substantial river, and numerous creeks where hundreds of species of waterfowl flew up so thick as to obliterate the sun for hours at a time. Immense herds of elk, pronghorn, and black-tailed deer grazed along these waterways on any number of clovers and sedges. West, lining the coastal hills, were redwoods so thick that several yards into a forest all was dark as night. The shifting shoreline, steep cliffs dropping to the water then to broad sandy beaches, was rich too, rife with edible sea kelps, dozens of species of clams, mussels, abalone, and fish, salmon the most prized. Despite these distinct environments—arid hills, lush plains and wetlands, redwood forest—the landscape was usually inconsistent, tricky even. Amidst the arid hills below Sonoma Mountain were numerous lakes and spring-fed marshes. Meadows, prairie-like, appeared unexpectedly in the otherwise dense and dark redwood forests. A narrow creek might empty into a wide and deep perch-filled pond just on the other side of a small, barren-looking knoll. Traveling through an expanse of marshy plain you might discover, stepping from waist-high sedges, a carpet of rock a mile wide and several miles long, habitat for snakes and lizards that would otherwise be found in the drier foothills. Nothing appeared quite what it seemed. The landscape, complex in design and texture, demanded reflection, study. The culture that grew out of a ten-thousand-year relationship with the place became like it, not just in thought but in deed. Pomo and Coast Miwok art—the most complicated and intricate basketry found among indigenous people anywhere—tells the story.

Human Bears learned the details of the landscape: where a fish-ripe lake hid behind a bend, where a thicket of blackberries loaded with fruit sat tucked below a hillside. At the same time, regardless of their unique ability to travel great distances and seek out food sources for the village, they could not disrespect the hidden lake or thicket of berries, needing always to know the requirements for taking the fish or fruit. The lake had a special—and potentially dangerous—spirit, just as the Human Bear, so too the blackberry thicket. Developing a heightened sense of the Human Bear's unique power necessitated a heightened sense of the land. Ultimately, the Human Bear cult didn't play an integral role only in the well-being of the village but, more precisely, in the well-being of the village with the larger world.

By 1903 most of the landscape was transformed. Gone were the vast wetlands. The water table throughout the region had dropped an average of two hundred feet: creeks went dry in summer. The big trees were gone. Many of the great animals were extinct in the region, not just the grizzly bears, but the herds of elk and pronghorn, and the mighty condors gliding the thermals with their fourteen-foot wingspans. Regarding these remarkable ancestral birds, *Tsupu,* my great-great-great-grandmother, sitting atop a wagon toward the end of the nineteenth century, gazed up at the empty sky and asked, "How are the people going to dance without feathers?" If there was a route safe for Maria Evangeliste to travel as a Human Bear in 1903, would there still exist a familiar bountiful blackberry thicket? An ocean cove where she might collect a hundred pounds of clams?

Just as the landscape was transformed, increasingly so too the eons-old way of thinking about it. Catholic missionaries put in the minds of Coast Miwok and Pomo villagers the notion of an eternal and spiritual life that was elsewhere, that could not be derived and experienced from the land. The God of an elsewhere kingdom over-ruled, in fact, deemed as evil, anything on the earth that might be considered equally powerful, worthy of reverence and awe. While Christianity was forced upon the Natives, usually under conditions of duress and enslavement, the new religion might have made sense. After European contact, Coast Miwok and Pomo no doubt looked upon the transformed landscape and found that they recognized

NEW CALIFORNIA WRITING 2013

the place less and less, that, in essence, they were no longer home. Indeed miraculous, the new people could kill animals, level a hill, without retribution. Couldn't their one almighty God from another world stop a Human Bear? Yes—seen once as necessary to life and land, a protector of the village, the Human Bear—anyone who would participate in such things—was now more and more an enemy of our well-being, dangerous at best, evil.

Did Maria Evangeliste know what stories people told about her? If, secretly, she left a cache of ripe fruit or clams outside her home as Human Bears once did in the villages, might she not implicate herself, reveal her secret life in a world hostile to that life? Wouldn't relatives deem the food devil's work and toss it out? She was the last Human Bear, they say. When did she stop visiting the cave? When was it over?

The morning she returned she said that she had lost control of the wagon. Or she said she visited a friend and hadn't tied the old gelding well enough. Or she said she met a man. In any event, she went that afternoon with the priest and retrieved the wagon with its still upright rectory chairs from the apple farmer. And that was how, before sunset, she came back to town, driving the wagon as if nothing was unusual, four days had not passed at all. She continued to play violin in the church. She was still entrusted with work for the priest. Sometime later she married a Mexican immigrant. They had eleven children, all of whom lived to adulthood. A great-granddaughter sat next to me in catechism class. The last time I saw her, Maria Evangeliste that is, was sometime in the early 1970s, about ten years before she died at the age of ninety. I was at a funeral in St. Rose Church. She was in the crowd of mourners, a small Indian woman in a dark dress. She wore a veil, respectfully.

I left town sometime then and did not return for thirty years, until only recently. I visited, seeing family. And for the past eighteen years,

I have served as chairman of my tribe, which brought me back to Sonoma County at least once a month. But I wasn't really back— I wasn't home—which I hadn't realized, much less understood for some time. I wrote about Sonoma County—stories, essays, plays— from memory. In fact, I'd hardly written about anyplace else. But what was I remembering? What did I understand?

Sonoma County had changed dramatically. From the center of once small-town Santa Rosa, strip malls and housing developments spread over the vast plain, covering irrigated clover and vetch pastures, fruit orchards and strawberry fields. Gone, the black-and-white spotted Holstein cows. Gone, rows of prune and pear trees; the apple orchards north and east of Sebastopol, almost each and every one routed by grapes, pinot noir, cabernet. The arid foothills are now also covered in grapes: gone, the copses of oak and bay laurel there. Visiting, I noticed these changes; coming home for good, I saw how thorough they were, how far-reaching. Where was my home?

I bought a house on Sonoma Mountain. Bay laurel trees, live oaks, and white oaks surround the house, and, past the trees, there is an expansive view west over vineyard-covered hills and the urban sprawl below, to the Pacific Ocean, which is where at night the web of streetlights stops—and where on a very clear night the full moon lights the sea. That light—that path of moon on the water—was how the dead found their way to the next world, or so our ancestors said. And those same ancestors gathered pepper nuts from the six-hundred-year-old bay tree outside my gate. But I was like that—suspended between the old bay tree and the far horizon—as I negotiated what it meant to be home. I hadn't lived on the mountain before. I grew up below, in Santa Rosa.

Then the place remembered me. Stories beckoned. The dead rose, collected with the living, so that more and more the landscape became a meeting hall of raucous voices. I knew the faces. Not merely my tribal members, as if I was convening a tribal meeting, but the land itself—mountain and plain, oak trees and city lights, birds and animals, Indians and non-Indians, Mexicans, Italians, Blacks, Filipinos, Jews—whomever and whatever I'd known, whomever and whatever I knew, was before me, beckoning. Yes, the dead and the living—how could anything die this way? History, it's no less tangible, palpable than that grandmother under whose care you found yourself. In a kitchen you have known all your life with its familiar smells and colors, this grandmother sets a plate of warm tortillas on the table with a bowl of chicken soup and says eat.

Driving here and there, to the university, to the laundromat, the market, here and there with no worry of catching an airplane, seeing this relative or that friend before I left again, I had time, the idleness that accompanies routine, and the old lady with the tortillas and soup was able to catch my attention. Driving over a bridge west of town—west of Santa Rosa—I glance down and see the riverbank and willows: a bonfire lights a moonless night and Filipino men are gathered around the fire there, and my grandmother, a seventeen-year-old Coast Miwok girl, eyes my grandfather for the first time, a *pinoy* dandy in his pin-striped suit, the big gold watch chain dangling from his breast pocket reflecting firelight, and the bloodletting fighting cocks clashing midair, their tiny silhouettes jumping in his watch glass like a pair of enchanted dancers performing a wild tango my grandmother already wants to learn. From behind the townhouses on Coffey Lane, Holstein cows emerge one by one, full udders swaying, and collect in front of the 7-11, where Mrs. Andreoli, forty and soon to be a widow, opens the wooden gate to her milk barn. And Old Undle, old Pomo medicine man— "don't say his real name"—he's on a bench uptown in Courthouse Square, suspenders and Stetson hat, or he's in his garden behind the fairgrounds where two hours ago he built a fire below the tall corn stalks and thick gourd vines, witnesses as he holds now an ember in the palm of his hand and sees and hears in the orange-red ash "all manner of things": people and animals, songs, old earth rules. Isn't this how some folks saw Maria Evangeliste when she returned on foot after four days to her parents' house? And years later, when they found themselves next to her, scooping rice in the market or picking prunes in the heat dusty orchards, didn't they still think and remember?

Here I am not a stranger. Looking back, I see how I'd been a stranger, a newcomer at best, wherever else I had lived. I drove back and forth to the university, to the market, in Los Angeles. I did errands in Manhattan. But it wasn't the same. No stories. No old earth rules. Or, put it this way, I had to learn the stories, listen to the rules as a newcomer, and, like that, as mindful as I could be, make a home. Still, Fifth Avenue midday remained less busy for me than a remote redwood grove in Sonoma County. I could be alone in Yellowstone. Or the Grand Canyon. These latter places in particular, beautiful yes. And solitude. But then what is solitude, however blissful? Can it be experienced except by disengagement from the land's stories, spirits? Wilderness. The old people said the land became wild after we became separated from it, when there was no longer enough of us to hear its demands and tend to it accordingly. Could Thoreau and Muir experience the landscape as pristine and know solitude in it as such, if they knew its stories? If that old woman was there, tortillas and chicken soup in hand, would the land be silent?

Two weeks ago last Saturday at a tribal General Council meeting, I saw Maria Evangeliste's great-granddaughter, the same girl I knew in catechism class. Approaching sixty, a heavyset woman now with a shock of dyed black hair, she sat amidst the sea of faces listening to questions and answers regarding the status of our casino. She looked disgruntled, arms crossed over her chest, face puckered in a scowl, and walked out before the meeting was over, leaving me wondering if she was mad at me or someone else on the Council or life in general. Her life, from what I'd heard, hadn't been easy. Five children. Two were in prison. One was dead. Ten grandchildren, five of whom she was raising. Where was the soft-faced, flat-limbed teenager who listened with me as Sister Agnes Claire attempted to explain the Holy Ghost? Some tribal members say I've been away too long, that I've gotten "too white." Did she feel that way about me, that I didn't know my people well enough any longer? Her husband, the father of her five children, was a Mexican immigrant. Did she know that her great-grandfather was a Mexican immigrant also? Had she heard the stories about Maria Evangeliste? Did she care? Perhaps I write for no other reason than to leave a record for her or anyone besides me who might care, a set of tracks, however faint, down the mountain into the plain and back, connecting to those infinite other pathways that take us and keep us in the land and its life here. But this is what I'm thinking now, as I consider what it means to be a writer here. It wasn't what I was thinking during the meeting, seeing Maria Evangeliste's great-granddaughter.

I went to the cave. Driving on Occidental Road, I was quite certain of the spot my cousin had pointed to years before—the bald hillside—if for no other reason than that a hippie commune was there at the time, a settlement of teepees past the redwoods, which I mentioned, prompting from my cousin her story of Maria Evangeliste.

The road curved under a canopy of oak trees and tall pines, four o'clock in the afternoon, autumn, the land was already in shadow, the road lead gray like the occasional patch of sky above. Human Bears traveled only at night in the pitch black; they did not set out from their villages in human form for their caves until late at night either. Secrecy was the initiate's first rule. Mabel McKay once told me of a father up in Lake County who, curious about his daughter's whereabouts at night, unwittingly followed her to a Human Bear cave, whereupon her cult sisters gruesomely murdered him right before her eyes. "Ain't supposed to be seeing them things," Mabel said. "Respect." With this story in mind and a darkening landscape, it's no wonder that past the barbed wire fence and into the trees, I was agitated, so much so that when I looked back and couldn't see the road, I stopped. Respect? Was I disrespecting? These are modern times, I kept telling myself. What's a story these days? Wasn't I curious just to see the cave as a landmark, an outpost of memory? Yes, nothing more. I would leave something, a dollar bill, my handkerchief, out of respect. A lone jay shrieked from somewhere on the other side of the blackberry bramble. I looked up, above the line of trees, to the outcropping of rock, enormous and still watchful, then I left.

It was enough, I told myself. Enough. But I kept thinking of Maria Evangeliste. In the car, driving back to town, my excitement only grew. Past the overreaching branches and thick brush on either side of the road, I saw how a uniform gray light enveloped the land, a color such that everything I could see seemed made from it. I had never seen the light in such a way at that time of day, and, I thought that though Maria Evangeliste, after her first four nights with the twin sisters, emerged and came back to town at dawn, the light and land must have looked this way, new, as she had never seen it before. Then I rounded a curve, and, coming down the hill, I saw the broad plain clear to the mountain. City lights shone like tiny flags in the gathering darkness. I pulled over, stopped the car. No, I thought then. After Maria Evangeliste first came out of the cave, it was like this: stories, places—an entire land—that she knew day or night, light or no light, not as if for the first time, but better.

Author's note: Evangeliste was not the actual name.

THE DISPATCHER

Jess Row

FOR THE MOST PART, during my imprisonment, I was left alone. This was after the first seventeen days—the period some commander on high had decided was the longest any prisoner's information could be considered useful or accurate. In that time I was plunged headfirst into icy baths; I was hung by the ankles until I felt I'd turned into an obscene pendant around God's sweating neck. Electric charges were applied to my fingertips, my scrotum, the webbing between my toes. Fortunately my home village was far away in the mountains, a ten-hour drive over terrible roads, and so there was no way for them to verify anything I said, other than by sending a helicopter. And I wasn't *that* valuable a prisoner. So I concocted an elaborate fantasy in which my late uncle M— commanded a squadron of rebels, shipping arms over the border. I was his assistant, I told them; I operated a ham radio to keep him in touch with headquarters.

I'd never seen such a radio, but remembered a reference to one in an American children's book my English teacher once lent me.

They believed me, or else were so mystified that before long my seventeen days had passed and they were forced to lock me into the proverbial dungeon and throw away the key. The crackdown was entering its busiest phase, and the prison had yet to be expanded, so for the time being I was deposited in a room that formerly had been their sleeping quarters. Wonder of wonders, I was afforded a stained, lice-infested mattress instead of a concrete floor. I had my very own poster of our country's most famous singer, half-undressed, fixed with surgical tape to the wall. The poster was dotted with dark splotches, like grease spots, which mystified me until I realized the guards had been in the habit of masturbating directly *at* the picture. Prison guards, as species, feel anxious if they lack an object for their urges. And thank God they had one, for otherwise I wouldn't be sitting here today.

In one corner of the room, tied up in a silver garbage bag, was a red suitcase, its lock and zipper torn away, concave as an old man's chest. It held three folded pairs of underpants, a blue checked shirt wadded into a ball, and a thick, much-thumbed book with a spiral binding. A city map, divided into a grid: hundreds of squares, hundreds of pages. There was no cover, but I knew what it was. Only one city in the world was so large that the human eye needed an entire book to see it, and that was the city named not for one angel but for all of them.

Released, I wandered the streets of the capital city, eating food pressed into my hands by garbage pickers, until I found myself at a gas station on a road that led to the international highway. One truck led to another; a half-loaf of moldy bread led to three cigarettes, to a tourist's discarded disposable camera with three frames left, to a stale Snickers bar; and so I passed border upon border, fence upon fence, until I stumbled under the streetlights in the 1300 block of Sepulveda, between Las Palmas and La Cienega, just north of the Santa Monica Freeway. A countryman driving a cab from the airport picked me up and brought me to the dispatcher, and in a month I had the dispatcher's job.

The patron saint of my village must have approved of me belatedly, because there was no one else in the world who could give directions to any location in our colonial language and in three indigenous dialects. Rarely in life, and never in my own experience, were a person's abilities so exactly and appropriately necessary. This was the province of miracles, coherent governments, functional systems of higher education, none of which I ever believed existed.

Nonetheless, I stopped praying. I wanted nothing more than to be left alone.

In the daylight hours of my imprisonment, I had studied each square of the map like an eager seminarian with a page of scripture. Beginning in the top left corner, I worked my way through the grid: not imagining streets or buildings, intersections or coastline, so much as pure shapes—curves, bulges, drooping triangles, rigid rhomboids. At night I engraved each feature on the backs of my eyelids in gold, molten emerald, ocher, lapis lazuli. Each name a precious thing. *Norco. Culver City. Torrance. Fillmore. Thousand Oaks.* Here was a world that fitted together with unspeakable elegance. I loved the insouciant way Palos Verdes knuckled out into the Pacific; the elegant scimitar's curve of Interstate 5 down the coast to San Diego. I could shut my eyes and see the shape of the city dangling in perfect gravitational balance from a point near Altadena.

How can I describe my emotions when I reached this city of my imagination, like a gnat landed in the middle of an illuminated manuscript, or upside down on the ceiling of the Sistine Chapel? My sinuses ached; my head felt stuffed with sawdust. The sheer disorder, the rotting buildings, the dusty abandoned storefronts with brown paper peeling away, and the hot white glare that fell equally over everything, that hammered my eyeballs to a sheet of metal and left them broiling, flattened, in the sun! I could hardly walk without staggering. It wasn't a crisis of perspective: I could hold the whole in my mind as well as always. I had been betrayed by an image, that was all. In my innocence I still believed in meaning. I hadn't realized that if you love a book you should climb inside it and refuse to leave.

• • •

On my way to work one morning, I saw a neon sign that read *Body Art. Tattoos. Piercings. Modifications.* Two weeks later, after finishing a shift and polishing off two beers in the alleyway behind the office, I got off the bus early and made my way inside. There was a receptionist. I said to her, in our colonial language, I have an unusual request.

No, she said. They won't do that.

Go and ask them anyway.

They'll think you're crazy. They'll think *I'm* crazy.

But I insisted. I wouldn't go away.

And the man—who was covered in blue reptile scales from head to foot—came out and stared at me for a long time before saying anything.

Who told you to come here? Who said we would do that?

No one, I said. It was just an idea I had.

The woman they sent me to worked behind a curtain at the back of a hair salon in Hermosa Beach. She wore leather chaps over frosted blue jeans and had sandy blond hair that cascaded nearly to her waist. Renny, her name was. She squatted over the back of a chair as I explained what I wanted. I had written the sentences out on a piece of paper, using a dictionary. So, I said, when I had finished, is it possible?

Nearly anything's possible, she said. I'm not sure if it's *legal*. Have to check the state code on that one. You'll have to sign a waiver.

I had lost her by the third sentence. When can we start, I asked. Tomorrow? Monday?

I have to think about how to prepare.

If you need so much time maybe I should find someone else.

Look at me, she said. No, really. *Look* at me.

She stood up and put her hands or her hips. I saw, to begin with, that her waist was too small, a girl's waist. One of her hips jutted slightly to the side. Her breasts nearly disappeared beneath her wide, flat shoulders. There was a mole on the side of her chin, a very visible spot, and her teeth were tobacco-stained. Other than that she was unremarkable. A mixture of appealing and unappealing, like most of us. Not repulsive. But only a man of very particular tastes would be drawn to her.

Go on, she said, tell me a story about how the love of your life died and you can't bear to ever look at another woman. Even me. And I'm no prize.

No, I said. I'm not good at lying.

It was two weeks before she called me back; I assumed she'd forgotten. There was no law on the books, she said, one way or another. The waiver would have to cover it. She wouldn't tell her boss; I'd pay her in cash, of course, plus a finder's fee for the man in the scales. It's amazing what you can do to someone if they promise not to sue, she said. Makes you wonder what laws are for, frankly. I can't believe I'm doing this. But the procedure itself is easy. I looked it up on the Internet.

On the desk in front of me, in the car service office, I had arranged little piles of American coins, as well as one, five, ten, and twenty dollar bills. I was teaching myself to tell the difference by rubbing my thumb across them with my eyes closed. A pickpocket's trick. I hoped one day soon it would be useful.

Look, she said, first I want you to do something for me. Come out with me. I want to take you somewhere. It's nothing dangerous. Just come with me in my car tomorrow afternoon and I'll bring you back by nightfall.

All right, I said. What else could I do?

When she picked me up she tied a black bandanna around my eyes. I want this to be a surprise, she said. Her breath smelled of egg rolls and orange soda. Plus, she said, you should get used to the idea.

We drove west to the ocean, that much was obvious, with the sun full in our faces and the sea wind coming in through the open windows. Then there was a cloverleaf interchange, and I couldn't tell, for ten minutes or so, whether we were headed south or north. She had rolled up the windows and put on the air conditioning, and I couldn't locate the sun's heat. The bandanna was made of some kind of thick oily cloth, and she had tied it expertly. Of course, I was used to it.

We're on the Pacific Coast Highway, I said, bluffing, headed north. To our right is Pacific Palisades. In a minute we'll be at the Topanga Canyon intersection.

Good guess.

It's not a guess. We had turned east and were rising up into the hills. I could smell the desert; I licked my lips. I think I know what you're doing, I said. And it's not going to work.

Be patient, she said. Relax.

When the car finally stopped she untied the blindfold and I stumbled out into the light. There was a picnic table, it must have been some kind of rest area, a scenic view, though at first I was so dazzled I could see only long distances: the clay-colored haze over the city and the great indistinct stain of the ocean that seemed to come up to my knees.

Turn around, she said.

Someone had painted on her, I thought, when she spread her arms wide and I could see the rows of leaves that began on her wrists and marched straight across her shoulders and down around her breasts in spirals. No one could do that with a needle, I told myself, until I came up to her, got down on my knees, and touched the jacaranda tree that seemed to support her left breast. It was ink; it was in the skin. A skein of jasmine flowers floated across her stomach and descended between her legs where hair should have been.

Keep going, she said. Keep looking.

There was a tiny figure of a boy, sitting on her left kneecap, gazing up, and through some trick of perspective, an entire mountainside rose up along her thigh, a shaggy tropical forest that almost concealed a series of waterfalls and pools, little terraces spilling down to a lake, and the boy was, I saw now, perched on a rock on the edge of the lake, with a fishing rod across his lap.

My eyes were filming over; I wiped them with my sleeve. Why did I feel so certain that he was staring up at that marvelous landscape only out of obligation, when he would have preferred to look down at the tiny knot he was making in the fishing line, securing the second hook four inches above the first? My own childhood had been like that. I detested nature. As a child, I was sent to gather firewood every day before lunchtime; I walked on paths where the slightest shiver of wind caught the broad leaves of the trees and sent the morning's rainwater sluicing down the back of my shirt. If I passed a still pool, filled with orange salamanders and flickering tadpoles, I stomped in it. Even then I rejected this world! My imprisonment, my banishment, my exile, had nothing to do with it. My spirit had always been bruised.

I looked up at her, at the little bright orbs of her eyes, like ice-glazed fruit.

Don't feel bad, I said. I'm not afraid.

I don't understand why *you* have to suffer, she said. Her face, her very ordinary face, had the most extraordinary expression: a kind of gentle, impersonal bafflement. As if she were astonished that the world had produced me. I keep thinking, she said, *there must be something I can do.*

It's all I've ever wanted, I told her. Wouldn't you—I jutted my chin at her thigh—wouldn't you rather be *there*, too? In that world, the world you made?

I don't have a choice.

Then call me lucky, I said. Call me the lucky one.

• • •

After my shift, which lasts from seven in the evening till nine in the morning, I have one of the drivers drop me at the Las Palmas library, just a few blocks from my apartment. In the cool of the morning I sit on a bench in the park next to the library, kick off my sandals, and rest my feet in the grass. There is no greener feeling than one's feet in the grass in a desert climate. I have the long cane across my knees, which keeps anyone from speaking to me. No one speaks to the blind unless it's to say, *can I help you cross the street, sir? Or can I open that for you, sir?* My solitude is sealed tight as a coffin.

Around eleven a pickup truck pulls a metal trailer around the far side of the playground and I can smell, fifty feet away, immediately, the meat-filled pastries I first ate as a small boy on our trips to the market town. I have to count the minutes until I allow myself to stand and slowly amble in the direction of that smell, and the woman who stands there, with the trailer, after her husband has roared off to make other deliveries, addresses me in the dialect of the fishing villages of my own country, saying, You again, how was your night, did you lose anyone this time?

And I say, all our people are present and accounted for.

And how did we come to be here, in the first place? Well, at least I could find my way back. I feel sorry for you.

Don't worry about me, I say. I have no place to go back to.

What pleasure there is, sitting there in the shade, testing the hot pastry in its wax-paper envelope for the precise moment when it has cooled enough to eat, and then biting into it eagerly, the flaking skin yielding to the savory ground meat, the wave of heat from the chilies, the slightly sweet gravy, scented with oregano! I thought I would never regain the concentration I had as a child.

Renny, too, has developed a taste for these pastries; when she comes to visit me here she always takes home half a dozen for her freezer, and she insists they taste just as good as fresh, if you reheat them carefully in the oven, wrapped in foil. We're on the other side of town from her house, and it takes an hour fighting lunchtime traffic to get here. Don't bother, I tell her, but she wants to take me to her car, turn the air conditioning on full blast, and peek under my sunglasses, to see how the scars are healing.

It's fine, I tell her. I don't feel a thing.

Pity we have to keep this secret, she says. I mean, you should be a case study or some such. I was sure you'd be dead of an infection in six weeks.

Then why didn't you stop me?

Because you wanted it, she says. And this is America, where everybody gets what they want.

I remain just long enough to bask in the afterglow of the meal, and then bid her my goodbyes and walk back to the library entrance. I spend the afternoons inside, in a kind of alcove between the main reading room and the children's library. There are comfortable chairs, and pairs of headphones, and a stereo that plays a different selection of CDs every week. I put the headphones over my ears and quietly unplug them from the stereo. Sometimes I sleep. No one disturbs me. At four-thirty my special buzzing watch arouses me and I go home to make breakfast.

But who am I to be telling you such things, when you yourself have seen me there? You lingered behind the current magazines rack, pretending to read a copy of *Scientific American,* as if a blind man could see you staring at him while he was in any case asleep, his dry lips cracked, his chin tilted up at the ceiling. You stared at his dark hands with the reddish tinge and the little fringes of black hair on the fingers, a mellow color you might have compared to old bourbon or varnished walnut. You stared at the scabby white tips of his toes, visible peeking out of his sandals, and noticed that nearly all of his toenails seemed to be missing. There are so many stories to be told in this world, you thought, and so many stories lost, discarded, ignored. You who think the mountains in front of your face are real. How would you know that you are nothing more than a filament, a speck, a bit of frayed string, too small for me even to pick up, too small even to fit in the whorls of my fingertips, only here in this world, in this story, for a moment? How would you know that the warm wind at your back is my voice speaking, bearing you away?

THE HOUSE THAT DOESN'T GROW

from "The Winchester Series"

Alexandra Teague

T HE SPIRIT ROTS in the house that doesn't grow,
and so the builders build a hall of mirrors—dazzling as ice
    refracted back to snow—
then wall it in (reflections scare the ghosts)

and start a staircase in the dining room below
each step an inch toward heaven, nothing more...that infinite
    ascent, measured and slow...
The spirit rots in the house that doesn't grow,

and so the roofers roof the chimney hole,
then frame a ballroom with a stained-glass door (imported on a
    ship to riverboat)
then brick it in (bright light unnerves the ghosts)

and hang two windows etched with Shakespeare quotes:
These same thoughts people this little world.   *Wide unclasp*
    the table of their thoughts.
The spirit rots in the house that doesn't grow,

and so the workers work all night to close
the seventh cupola before the coming storm, their windchime
    hammers ringing in the cold,
then open it (the dark disturbs the ghosts)

then close it back, unnail the hallway cove;
then, for the flowers watered through the floor: a long zinc
    trough to catch the overflow.
The spirit rots in the house that doesn't grow
and grow (forever and everywhere, the ghosts)

POET-BASHING POLICE

Robert Hass

L IFE, I FOUND myself thinking as a line of Alameda County deputy sheriffs in Darth Vader riot gear formed a cordon in front of me on a recent night on the campus of the University of California, Berkeley, is full of strange contingencies. The deputy sheriffs, all white men, except for one young woman, perhaps Filipino, who was trying to look severe but looked terrified, had black truncheons in their gloved hands that reporters later called batons and that were known, in the movies of my childhood, as billy clubs.

The first contingency that came to mind was the quick spread of the Occupy movement. The idea of occupying public space was so appealing that people in almost every large city in the country had begun to stake them out, including students at Berkeley, who, on that November night, occupied the public space in front of Sproul Hall, a gray granite Beaux Arts edifice that houses the registrar's offices and, in the basement, the campus police department.

It is also the place where students almost 50 years ago touched off the Free Speech Movement, which transformed the life of American universities by guaranteeing students freedom of speech and self-governance. The steps are named for Mario Savio, the eloquent undergraduate student who was the symbolic face of the movement. There is even a Free Speech Movement Cafe on campus where some of Mr. Savio's words are prominently displayed: "There is a time... when the operation of the machine becomes so odious, makes you so sick at heart, that you can't take part. You can't even passively take part."

Earlier that day a colleague had written to say that the campus police had moved in to take down the Occupy tents and that students had been "beaten viciously." I didn't believe it. In broad daylight? And without provocation? So when we heard that the police had returned, my wife, Brenda Hillman, and I hurried to the campus. I wanted to see what was going to happen and how the police behaved, and how the students behaved. If there was trouble, we wanted to be there to do what we could to protect the students.

Once the cordon formed, the deputy sheriffs pointed their truncheons toward the crowd. It looked like the oldest of military maneuvers, a phalanx out of the Trojan War, but with billy clubs instead of spears. The students were wearing scarves for the first time that year, their cheeks rosy with the first bite of real cold after the long Californian Indian summer. The billy clubs were about the size of a boy's Little League baseball bat. My wife was speaking to the young deputies about the importance of nonviolence and explaining why they should be at home reading to their children, when one of the deputies reached out, shoved my wife in the chest and knocked her down.

Another of the contingencies that came to my mind was a moment 30 years ago when Ronald Reagan's administration made it a priority to see to it that people like themselves, the talented, hardworking people who ran the country, got to keep the money they earned. Roosevelt's New Deal had to be undealt once and for all. A few years earlier, California voters had passed an amendment freezing the property taxes that finance public education and installing a rule that required a two-thirds majority in both houses of the Legislature to raise tax revenues. My father-in-law said to me at the time, "It's going to take them 50 years to really see the damage they've done." But it took far fewer than 50 years.

My wife bounced nimbly to her feet. I tripped and almost fell over her trying to help her up, and at that moment the deputies in the cordon surged forward and, using their clubs as battering rams, began to hammer at the bodies of the line of students. It was stunning to see. They swung hard into their chests and bellies. Particularly shocking to me—it must be a generational reaction—was that they assaulted both the young men and the young women with the same indiscriminate force. If the students turned away, they pounded their ribs. If they turned further away to escape, they hit them on their spines.

None of the police officers invited us to disperse or gave any warning. We couldn't have dispersed if we'd wanted to because the crowd behind us was pushing forward to see what was going on. The descriptor for what I tried to do is "remonstrate." I screamed at the deputy who had knocked down my wife, "You just knocked down my wife, for Christ's sake!" A couple of students had pushed forward in the excitement and the deputies grabbed them, pulled them to the ground and cudgeled them, raising the clubs above their heads and swinging. The line surged. I got whacked hard in the ribs twice and once across the forearm. Some of the deputies used their truncheons as bars and seemed to be trying to use minimum force to get people to move. And then, suddenly, they stopped, on some signal, and reformed their line. Apparently a group of deputies had beaten their way to the Occupy tents and taken them down. They stood, again immobile, clubs held across their chests, eyes carefully meeting no one's eyes, faces impassive. I imagined that their adrenaline was surging as much as mine.

My ribs didn't hurt very badly until the next day and then it hurt to laugh, so I skipped the gym for a couple of mornings, and I was a little disappointed that the bruises weren't slightly more dramatic. It argued either for a kind of restraint or a kind of low cunning in the training of the police. They had hit me hard enough so that I was sore for days, but not hard enough to leave much of a mark. I wasn't so badly off. One of my colleagues, also a poet,

Geoffrey O'Brien, had a broken rib. Another colleague, Celeste Langan, a Wordsworth scholar, got dragged across the grass by her hair when she presented herself for arrest.

I won't recite the statistics, but the entire university system in California is under great stress and the State Legislature is paralyzed by a minority of legislators whose only idea is that they don't want to pay one more cent in taxes. Meanwhile, students at Berkeley are graduating with an average indebtedness of something like $16,000. It is no wonder that the real estate industry started inventing loans for people who couldn't pay them back.

"Whose university?" the students had chanted. Well, it is theirs, and it ought to be everyone else's in California. It also belongs to the future, and to the dead who paid taxes to build one of the greatest systems of public education in the world.

The next night the students put the tents back up. Students filled the plaza again with a festive atmosphere. And lots of signs. (The one from the English Department contingent read "Beat Poets, not beat poets.") A week later, at 3:30 a.m., the police officers returned in force, a hundred of them, and told the campers to leave or they would be arrested. All but two moved. The two who stayed were arrested, and the tents were removed. On Thursday afternoon when I returned toward sundown to the steps to see how the students had responded, the air was full of balloons, helium balloons to which tents had been attached, and attached to the tents was kite string. And they hovered over the plaza, large and awkward, almost lyrical, occupying the air.

STANZAS IN THE FORM OF A DOVE

Linda Norton

O N T H E W A Y to Yosemite, September 17, 2001, sheep the
color of filing cabinets, wrath on the radio,

religious war—save me, Robert Frost on tape, Groucho Marx,
"Your Show of Shows"—

Men and women in pick-up trucks honking at flags draped from
the overpass near Sacramento

one woman has flags painted on her cheeks—we're boxed in by
patriots and warriors—

Things open up at twilight

we pass rows and rows of trees

uprooted   on their sides   no leaves

an orchard napping

Donald Antrim in the *New Yorker:* "Is the United States now
part of the rest of the world?"

October: Yom Kippur in Oakland. A girl in a T-shirt that says,
"By Any Means Necessary" plays cello

at chapel. Bach, and then we take the children for a walk down
to the lake. We cast our bread upon the

waters. The pelicans glide in to eat our sins. This part of the park
smells like honey.

The morning the World Trade Center was attacked, parents and
children convened at chapel.

The smallest children, mine included, laughed and fooled around
in the pews. No one wanted them to

know what had happened. The eighth graders looked old that
morning.

Stanzas in the form of a dove—

BORGES, from *Invocation to Joyce*

I caught a whiff of Isabel last night, realized she needed a bath.
I was so tired, but I gave her a bath,

helped her with her pajamas, put her to bed. Just before she fell
asleep—I was asleep next to her, I

thought she was asleep—she said, "Mom?"

"Yes?"

"I have a question about being good or bad. I know you should
be good, but if you're not, what can

they do to you? I mean, my question is: Do I always have to be
good?"

Does she always have to be good? When I was a girl, I knew I
must always be good. Because I was bad.

The filth. Look what original sin has done for me.

So I say to her: "No. You don't always have to *be* good. You *are* good."

She breathes a sigh of relief. "Thank you!" Then falls right to sleep, smelling so sweet.

In the morning I drop her at school, then pass a sign at a gas station:

CLEAN PARTS ARE HAPPY PARTS

The smell of cold hair   cold car   home   I carry her up the stairs

The people downstairs are in love

I can hear them

I have a fever

I put my daughter to bed

breathe her in

and wonder

from *THESE DREAMS OF YOU*

Steve Erickson

B UT YEARS LATER, on a night in early November, when the wind comes in like a swarm, Alexander Nordhoc sits in the rocking chair—that he borrowed but never gave back—where his wife used to breast-feed their son.

It's eight o'clock where he is, in one of the canyons on the edge of Los Angeles. It's ten o'clock in Chicago, and thousands of people sweep across the TV screen and the same park where, forty years ago, police and protesters rioted at the scene of a great national political convention, and Nordhoc's country questioned all its possibilities.

Alexander's four-year-old daughter Sheba, adopted nineteen months before from an orphanage in Ethiopia, sits on his lap. Sheba is the color of the man on the television, in whose form the country now has imagined its most unfathomable possibility. Alexander, who goes by Zan, is the color of everyone else in the family, including his wife Viv and his son Parker, whose twelfth birthday happens to also be on this day.

With the announcement of the man's election, bedlam consumes the living room. "He won!" Parker explodes, leaping from the couch over a low white formica table that's in the shape of a cloud. "He won! he won! he won!" he keeps shouting, and Viv cheers too. "Zan," Parker stops, baffled by his father's stupefaction, "he won." He says, "Aren't you happy?"

On the television is the image of an anonymous young black woman who, in the grass of the park, has fallen to her knees and holds her face in her hands. Do I have the right, Zan wonders, as a middle-aged white man, to hold my face in my hands? and then thinks, No. And holds his face in his hands anyway, silently mortified that he might do something so trite as sob.

It's a country that does things in lurches. Born in radicalism, then reluctant for years, decades, the better part of centuries, to do anything crazy, until it does the craziest thing of all. But it's also a country—inherent in its genes—capable of imagining what cannot be imagined and then, once it's imagined, doing it.

Six years before, another president, a white privileged Texan, swaggered across the deck of an aircraft carrier in a pilot's jacket, a banner unfurled behind him proclaiming the end of a war that, in fact, was only beginning. It was an image that the country embraced almost as much as it believed it. Now, a black Hawaiian with a swahili name? It's science fiction, Zan thinks. Or at least the sort of history that puts novelists out of business.

At the radio station the next day, from where Zan broadcasts four times a week a three-hour music show, he announces following the first set, "The Sam Cooke record—the greatest ever made—was for what happened last night. Forty-five years after the song was recorded...but then all the song says is that a change *will* come, not how fast, right?" By the time the song was released as a B-side, the singer was murdered in an L.A. motel under tawdry circumstances. "But is it just me," Zan asks, "or when he goes from that bridge into the final verse, does he redeem not only anything he ever did—including whatever it was that got him shot—but everything I ever did too?"

• • •

The national anthem of dreams deferred, sung from the grave by a ghost who doesn't know he's dead. "Everything else," Zan goes on, "was for the kids. The hip-hop manifesto about brushing the dirt off your shoulder, that's for my twelve-year-old son who's gone gangsta lately, though at this point I'm sure he thinks the song is impossibly old-school, being as it's more than half an hour old. And the really old-school one about the lovers at the Berlin Wall— 'What's the Berlin Wall, Poppy?'—who get to be heroes just for one day? That's for my four-year-old Ethiopian daughter, who I guess can't get enough of British extraterrestrials in dresses."

Zan has no idea if anyone actually listens to him. The station has about a megawatt to its name. Viv catches the broadcasts on her car radio for the thirty seconds she's in range while driving the canyon boulevard; when she drops off Parker at school, the boy turns the radio down because the possibility some of his homies might hear it is too appalling. He furiously denies that it's his father's voice.

The four-year-old Ethiopian glam-rocker is the only one in the family not thrilled by the election result. Sheba has been the household's sole supporter of the opposing candidate, a man the age of grandfathers and the color of snow, neither of which the small girl has known.

Zan has three theories about Sheba's enthusiasm for this candidate. The first and most comfortable is that in fact he does remind her of Viv's father, who died two years before she was born and whom she sees in all the family photos. The second theory, more vexing if not too unsettling, is that she's just messing with everyone's heads.

The third and most troubling theory is that in her four-year-old soul she's already come to believe the color of snow is preferable to the color of…well, pick your racist poison—chocolate? coffee?

mud? With what brown does she associate? Since she came to live
with the Nordhocs, she's noted more than once that her skin is one
color and Zan's, Viv's and Parker's another. How come, the girl
asks resentfully, returning from preschool where there are no other
black children, you get to have light skin while mine is darker?

Dismayed, Zan isn't sure he's heard right. Was that really the way
she put it? "Yours is lighter," she points out again, pulling at his
arm and thrusting her thumb in her mouth.

"It is lighter," he says, "yours is darker and it's beautiful. Some
people have light skin and some have dark. Some have light hair
and some have dark."

"The man who sings the hero song has red hair."

"Yes."

"Mama has blue hair."

"There you go. Turquoise, actually."

"What's turquoise?"

"A kind of blue. Blue-green."

"Is it really blue or did she make it blue?"

"She made it blue."

"Why?"

"She likes it. It matches her eyes. Some people have light or
dark eyes. Some people are tall and some aren't."

Is this the way to answer the question? Is it better than "Because
you're black and we're white," if she doesn't yet have a concept of
black and white? Or is it an answer that only a naïve white person
can give?

On the other hand, Sheba was adopted in the first place out of
white naïveté, though less on the part of Viv who lived in Africa as
a girl. Viv's father was the city manager of Mogadishu—between
Ethiopia and the sea—a freelancer whose career back home in the

Midwest was subject to local elections, hired to bring running water and passable roads to a city half a world away. For Viv that was the year (her twelfth, which is to say when she was Parker's age) of other kids' parents abducted in the night never to be seen again, public hangings that were a social occasion, the ocean's edge lined with the innards of gutted camels that attracted sharks when the reefs were breached, and, on a beach against the Indian Sea under an African moon, movies broadcast against a slab of rock. When Viv saw the movie about the monolith surrounded by apes who hurl a bone into the sky that becomes a space station, it actually was on a monolith.

No white sentimentality invents, and no hard-nosed street wisdom disputes, the preternatural awareness of the four-year-old adopted child who shares with other abandoned children a perspective verging on the otherworldly. "Oh, yeah," says another father at Sheba's preschool when Zan identifies her as his, "the little girl who talks like she's twenty." The night that Zan takes Parker to the emergency room with a broken hand and loses his car keys, he's still railing at the experience an hour later behind the wheel when, from her infant's seat in back, Sheba advises, "Poppy, let it go," before plopping her thumb back in her mouth.

Sheba dazzles everyone she meets. Eyes big enough to center whole swirling solar systems, her charismatic entrance into every room brings it to a halt. Not unlike her new brother she's an irrepressible goofball, walking around with small stickers stuck to the end of her nose, spitting water across the dinner table in a stream like the stone water-breathing lion she saw in a fountain—a mimic who spins off her own original permutations. Lovingly seizing on a word like, say, buttocks, enthralled by both its emphatic sound and the unmistakable impact on those who hear it, soon she transforms everything into a variant. When her brother's feet stink, they're footocks.

Eventually the mimicry becomes not only more precocious but blacker, inevitable less because she herself is black than because her white brother—like all kids in the Twenty-First Century, or maybe all kids since the first white boy or girl heard Louis Armstrong blow his horn—is blacker: "Hey there, girlfriend," or "What up, sweet cheeks?" to people who probably shouldn't be greeted in that fashion. When she high-fives, she follows it with the sweep of her hand across her African head and declares, *"Smooooth."*

Those few whose reaction to her is openly malevolent are all the more conspicuous for it. In a western Michigan restaurant during summer vacation a woman shoots daggers at them, and it's all Viv can think about for days, rather than the hordes who welcome the girl. "You can't get too defensive about this stuff," Zan says, as the entire Nordhoc family tiptoes across minefields.

The sternest look Zan has gotten is on the afternoon he carried Sheba from the pediatrician's office and, having received her first round of immunization shots, she wailed in betrayal, "DOCTOR SHOCK ME, POPPY!" A black man at a bus stop on the corner closely monitored the father and daughter the entire walk to Zan's car, the two fixed in his gaze, and only as Zan struggled to strap the outraged girl into the backseat did the penny drop: *I'm a middle-aged white guy hustling a screaming little black girl out of a building.*

Sometimes the color confusion has its advantages. When Sheba slams into a grocery checkout line and the person in front whirls around furiously, Zan studies the architectural wonders of the supermarket ceiling as the aggrieved party searches in vain for a wayward black mother to chastise. Then there's the time on Melrose Avenue when a young black guy comes up to Zan and says, "Hey, man, just want you to know you have two beautiful kids," and though its obviously Sheba who's caught his eye, Zan is touched that he includes Parker in the compliment. Now the only way that Zan knows to conclude the conversation with Sheba about the difference between his skin and hers is to say some squishy white liberal thing like, "You're beautiful," silently adding to no one, You come up with something better. Sheba takes her thumb from her mouth, locks his eyes with hers, and draws a finger across her throat.

Of course when she first starts doing the finger-cross-the-throat thing, it's alarming. Now she does it all the time, little brown buccaneer, to convey irritation at whatever parental lapse has transpired.

Zan thought they were going to get a shy little Dickensian orphan girl. *Please, sir, may I have some more?* with empty porridge bowl lifted pitifully to a merciless world; and when Viv first met her at the Ethiopian orphanage, Sheba seemed exactly that. She barely spoke, only looked at Viv when she thought Viv wasn't looking. Viv would lie with Sheba until the child fell asleep, but when she rose from bed, the girl's hand shot out and clutched the mother's wrist in a death grip.

From California to Ethiopia, Viv brought to the girl pompoms and a toy giraffe and a photo of Zan and Viv in a bag with pictures of cherries on it. The girl cast all of it aside except for a picture of Parker that she kept day and night. She slept with it and woke to it. No one could take it from her.

So the first time that the shy little orphan girl emits more volume per capita than any single body Zan has heard, it's like a boombox in a confessional. Planting her small feet in the middle of the house, Sheba rears back and roars whims and needs, complaints and demands. She engages Zan, Viv and Parker in discourse about everything under the sun.

Early on, Zan assumes this is Sheba's bountiful curiosity, the expressions of a turbo-wonderment. She sweeps through the house picking up everything within reach and turning things on and off, pushing every button of every machine, appliance and device until all are rendered digitally senseless. This drives Zan to distraction, maybe because it feels a little too representative of the way everything else about their lives is falling apart. "Lighten up," Viv advises, until she finds her new digital camera has been similarly sabotaged, summing up perfectly the way her photography career has flatlined as well.

Soon Zan realizes that, for the four-year-old, the substance of communication is beside the point. "It's like she's afraid," Viv says, "that with the first break in a connection, everything and everyone around her will vanish." Sheba kneads her fingers into Viv's body like a kitten, expanding and contracting its claws. She presses herself into her mother as though to meld herself physically.

Before Sheba came home from Ethiopia, Zan and Viv worried that the shy little orphan girl would be traumatized by the family dog Piranha, a demented mix of jack terrier and chihuahua called a jackahuahua. Named as a puppy by Parker, Piranha so terrorizes the neighborhood—attacking other dogs, chasing neighbors' cars, holding UPS men hostage on their trucks—that an electric fence has been installed around the yard and the dog has been fitted with an electric collar, this in spite of Zan's doubts that Piranha can be restrained by any mere voltage once used to execute Soviet spies. "He's a sociopath," Zan scoffs to Viv, "an electric fence? That dog?" pointing at the animal. Piranha's head jerks up expectantly; he's practically vibrating. "Sniper fire wouldn't stop this dog."

"Aren't all animals sociopaths?" says Viv.

"Maybe I mean psychopath."

"Is there a difference?"

"I think one doesn't know the difference between right and wrong, and the other knows but doesn't care."

"Which is Piranha?"

"Which is Piranha? *His name is Piranha.* Oh, he knows."

"That doesn't make sense," Viv says. "Piranha fish know it's wrong to eat people?"

"He knows," Zan assures her, "and he doesn't care." When Viv left for Africa to go get Sheba, figuring out what to do about Piranha was one of Zan's tasks back home. The canyon's local dog expert, mistress of all breeds and their mutations, told him flatly, "You're going to have to get rid of that dog—he'll terrorize the poor child." From Ethiopia, Viv wrote in an email, *She's so sweet I'm afraid the dog will terrify her.*

Piranha never knew what hit him. Throttled by the small girl within half an hour of her arrival until his eyes bulged, the animal soon was darting shell-shocked from one hiding place of the house to the next. Only when he was hopping up and down the stairs like shrimp on a grill, as if trying to get out of his own fur, did Parker figure out that Sheba had pushed the button on the wall-unit that controlled piranha's electric collar. Originally set at four, the monitor now was at nine, the dog zapped silly from one end of the house to the other.

Soon Sheba and Piranha struck an accord. Now Sheba howls out on the deck and the dog howls with her, the two craning their necks and turning their mouths skyward.

Of course Sheba's name isn't really Sheba. "Should we really be calling her that?" says Viv.

"As in queen of," says Zan.

"Yes, I know who the Queen of Sheba was," says Viv, "that's not my point."

"I was only explaining it to Parker," says Zan, though at this moment Parker listens on his headphones to the small fluorescent-green music player barely bigger than a stick of gum that hangs around his neck.

Viv says, "But still." On the birth certificate that came with the adoption, Sheba's name is shown as Zema, which in Amharic means...well, Zan and Viv aren't precisely sure what it means. The closest variation means "melody" or "hymn," but from what Zan understands, Ethiopian names only derive meaning from adjoining names, like tarot cards derive meaning from the surrounding cards. Only by putting all of a person's names together do you complete the meaning.

Zan never has been to Ethiopia but somehow this thing with the names seems typical of everything he knows about it. Ethiopia has an extra month of the year and, as best Zan can understand, its own clock, falling half an hour between the time zones of the world.

It isn't so much that Ethiopia invented its own time zone but that its zone is the original time, the temporal referent against which all other zones have contrived themselves. Within weeks of coming to L.A., Sheba has mastered English but, after more than a year, notions of time remain elusive. She has no comprehension of time's terminology. "We'll go to the park tomorrow," Zan says.

"O.K.," says Sheba, and minutes later still waits. "Poppy, let's go!" she says.

"Where?"

"THE PARK!"

"Tomorrow."

"Yes," she nods, and a minute later, "Are we going? WHY AREN'T WE GOING!" Even as she grasps other subtleties, she continues to be confounded by distinctions among weeks, days, hours, minutes. She believes her birthday both precedes and follows whatever day she occupies—not wrong, of course, technically speaking—appropriate for a child of civilization's ground zero, the land where God placed Adam and Eve, the burial place of the oldest human fossil. "We are all Ethiopians," Viv likes to say.

To the family, Sheba's emotional need seems like a dark well that falls to time's center. It sets in motion dynamics compounded by Sheba's singular measure of things. "He's number one!" she protests, pointing at Parker, "I'm number three," and Zan can't be sure if this is errant math, Ethiopia's own system of measurement like its own calibration of time, or whatever manipulation knows to leave out two.

From the beginning Sheba has had an affinity for music. Because this is so much the stuff of racial cliché, Zan barely can tell people about the more earthbound aspects—the girl running for a piano like other kids to a scooter, warbling cheerfully in the yard of the orphanage back in Addis Ababa to the lightning in the sky—let alone that the girl's small body literally hums with song.

Within a week of Sheba's arrival, the family noticed it at the dinner table when everyone heard from her, barely audible, a distant music. "Sheba, we don't sing at the table," Viv gently tried to admonish her, until one day the mother is driving in Hollywood with Sheba in the backseat and picks up Zan's broadcast from the canyon that usually she can't get half a mile from the station. The girl transmits on Sheba frequency. Zan calls her Radio Ethiopia.

Up until around the time of Sheba's adoption, Zan taught popular culture and Twentieth Century literature at a local college. The popular-culture course began with the year 1954, because that was when a white nineteen-year-old truck driver wandered into a Memphis recording studio—only weeks after the Supreme Court ruled racial segregation unconstitutional—and instinctively, unconsciously miscegenated, in the language of the time, white and black music. Caught up in the sweep of a story, by the end of every semester the students invariably shed their old-school/new-school distinctions to afford Zan an ovation. It's the closest he's come to telling an epic; he doubts he's told a story better, certainly not any of his own.

The rest of the teachers in the department were childless and, as certainly was the case with Zan before he had children, there was little comprehension of the infinite variables that children bring, the way that children lay waste to rational odds, how one always has to err on the side of the long shot. Someone who doesn't have children may grasp the volume of time they take up but can't understand the way children won't be compartmentalized, the way children can't be consigned to their own rooms in the city of one's life. Children are the moat that surrounds the city, the canals that run throughout. They get everything wet.

from *BROTHER AND THE DANCER*

Keenan Norris

E RYCHA WAS SIX years old. Erycha was six years old and a girl. Erycha was six years old and a black girl. Erycha was a little six-year-old black girl. Erycha was a little six-year-old black girl living in a poor, cramped under-lit little apartment on the other side of town. Erycha was a little six-year-old black girl living in a poor, cramped under-lit little apartment on the other side of town with her unmarried and impoverished parents: her father, who drifted in and out of the apartment and in and out of her life; her mother, who enabled his transience and unreliability with her forgiveness and by paying the bills on time and on her own. Their daughter, being only six years old, took things as they came.

Erycha was a poor little six-year-old black girl living in a poor, cramped under-lit little apartment on the other side of town whose distracted mother would occasionally pay her surprising affection, would buy her a book about ballet or let go an hour in first-grade gossip, rubbing her feet. Erycha was a poor little six-year-old black girl living in a poor, cramped under-lit little apartment on the other side of town whose changeable father, though unreliable and often unemployed, never was away from home for more than a few hours at a time, never truly absent. Erycha was a poor little six-year-old black girl living in a poor, cramped under-lit little apartment on the other side of town who took advantage of her parents' distracted ways, escaping the cramped under-lit little apartment house by walking out the apartment, down the stairwell, across the walkway, and over the gates. Standing there, on the empty avenue, she could see where her Del Rosa Gardens apartment complex ended and the empty street stretched on indefinitely. Erycha was a poor little six-year-old black girl living in a poor, cramped under-lit little apartment on the other side of a beautiful new town called Highland. And she was learning.

"Fresh food," her mother would say. "*Or-ganic.* What's so hard to understand about that word?"

"Best I could do."

"O'viously. If you actually payin me attention an' still cain't buy *the expensive ones that say organic on the label.*"

"Those the only two options, either I'm stupid or not payin you mind, huh? I'm tryin to save you some money. That's the way I think, practical. I'm not no boojie gentleman like you want me to be, Evelyn. Jus a roughneck, I suppose."

"Really, now?"

"I'm jus sayin."

"I'm just askin, why not help me out, make some damn money so's we don't gotta go buyin this low-grade unhealthy shit?"

"I been explained this: Messicans take e'ry damn job where they ain't gotta show papers, which is e'rything but security, an' you know my paperwork won't stand up to that background check."

"Mexicans mess up *your* papers? Mexicans the reason you gotta mark 'yes' where they ask if you been to jail? I never had to trouble over that question, Mexicans or no Mexicans."

Erycha would hear her father's heavy steps nearing the apartment door, then the slow apprehensive opening of that door, and finally its close and lock. Then her mother's voice would again scorch the air with questions. It was always this way, a known protocol: even when he was working and there were no issues around government assistance or staying away when the welfare woman came, even when he was bringing checks home consistently, there'd still be a fight if he brought the wrong groceries, or did something else that could be judged unreliable. Erycha hated it but she was used to it, too, how her dad would come back home after however long away and walk slowly in, sit himself down with that pain in his slouch, and commence to look down darkness. And how her mom would come from her kitchen with suspicion in her voice.

"Takes you this long to get groceries?"

"Stepped out."

"Been steppin three hours now. Long time to shop. Short time to go to the casino with my paycheck money, though."

"Wadn't at the casino. I just don't like shoppin in the daytime is all. A man shouldn't go shoppin while it's light out, all them girls at the stores, makes him feel unemployed. But you wadn't even home three hours back so how you think you know how long I been gone?"

"Right, of course. I was at work. But Erycha said you left while it was still light out." She nodded at the child.

"Babygirl." Her father shook his head. "Dime-dropper."

"Don't bother her. She playin."

"Solidarity, babygirl. We locked down together."

"You think you're funny."

"I'm truthful."

"Truthfully broke."

"Warden."

"*Con-vict.*"

Erycha remembered her father actually had been a convict at least one time in his life so she knew the joke was a joke with cutting power. The way his story went, he hadn't infringed on the law in a felonious manner, he'd just lost control a little bit and ended up with his car in somebody's else's front lawn, a small Cupid statue severed at the loins. Early '80s East Oakland was apparently so insane and calamitous with drugs and gunfire that drunk joyriding and minor vandalism wasn't worth much police attention, let alone jail time. But when he was unable to pay his fine he ended up in the county pen. As this was not the first time that they had looked up and found him in County, his loved ones used up all his phone time counseling him about how he needed to find a higher purpose in life. Religion. Or something like that.

He said that this time he spent his first free Sunday at Allen Temple Baptist Church trying to find that higher purpose. But instead he found the mechanics of praise and worship more boring than the Good Book itself. All the gospel music in the world couldn't hold a candle to a good Ant Banks record burning up a club past midnight, the most animated preacher's sermon had nothing on the three in the a.m. testament of a girl moaning something that sounded like his name. The only worthwhile thing about church, he decided, was that there were so many fine young ladies there. Of course he knew these were morning, not night women, but he found them irresistible nonetheless. So he spent each Sunday morning getting dressed as sharp as possible and showed up on the church steps just as the worshippers were filing out. He would pad at his face with his fingertips, whistle loud like the spirit was just too down deep inside him, and would generally pretend that he too had come from the House of God weary with worshipping. Then, he said, he would go about meeting the righteous sisters with the blessed backsides. Maybe at eighteen, and impressionable, Erycha's mother had been too naïve to realize that he had worn more orange jumpsuits than church clothes. But seven years had smartened her.

"*Con-vict*...You know what, Morris? I love you. I love you, I love Erycha, 'n that right there's my problem. That's my one sole problem in this whole world. If I could just escape that, go off, do my own thing, be my own person, not have to worry bout, bout, all this. Just escape."

"That food's still fresh, warden."

"I, I know, I know it is."

Erycha knew this dance, knew its rhythms. She'd studied its intricacies of condemnation, forgiveness, and eventual seduction, and she knew its every last step. So even though she'd yet to learn the difference between a relevé and a Chevrolet, she could already sense the music and move out of her parents' way, out the door, down the stairwell, across the walk. Up over the apartment gate, past the corner boys who posted like sentinels or statues along Del Rosa Avenue, across that street and into the scrub forest that lay in the narrow little gully there. Maybe after years of education and refinement, professors and critics would praise her for the naturalness of this art. But she was only six years old and for now the world was blind to her talents. Her parents had closed a door between them and her. The statues and sentinels remained blind, too. Only the small scrub forest hidden from the street seemed to know that she even existed, but it welcomed her as its child. Maybe because the forest was as unseen as she was, it became her private comfort, a shaded grove for imaginative play where the figures indifferent and dangerous that composed her usual life became dream-things. Where rude corner boys became goblins and her parents the comic jesters of the court, and she, of course, the queen.

Who knows. But Erycha conducted this shadow symphony from one thicket of scrub to the next. Piles of vegetation that to outside eyes would look like dead heaps turned into something more once she knelt down and gazed into their intricate work of dry brown branches and leaves. Then she saw the unique tangles and secrets in each. The most secret of all was the thicket where she found the white pagoda and its bullfrog: here, shadowed by a mound of abandoned construction work, gravel heaps, broken boards and such, she had chanced upon the pagoda. Gazing at it, looking it over absorbed her completely. Now she didn't even need to use her imagination. The pagoda was about a foot high. Its white paint had begun to chip away in flecks, exposing the grayed wood from which it had been sculpted. She had seen pagodas before, in pictures in books, and always admired their spiraling design, the dragon twisted around the twisting tree, and the open house completing it. The only difference was that this one was painted white instead of black, and a bullfrog lived within its open house. Sometimes it would shade itself inside during the days and she would see it then. Other times she would have to stay awake till long after her parents and everyone else in Del Rosa Gardens, even the corner boys, had gone to bed, and then she would listen as its weird croak filled the silence. The sound mushroomed out and out, a gentle explosion. She imagined the way its head and gills had to fill up with air to make that sound. In the days when she found it stooping in the open house she would run her fingers carefully across its notched, dry skin, trying to learn its secrets.

The bullfrog never liked her touching him, though, and he'd bluster if she kept at it too long; then his body would expand, his eyes would get big and bright like she imagined them in the dark. But the croak never came except at night and from far away.

One night, he didn't come home for a long, long time.

Her mother cooked dinner. They ate and waited. They took showers. Talked to Miss Simms on the telephone. Knelt and prayed for his eternal soul and ephemeral body, for their own souls and bodies, and waited for him.

About the time Erycha was used to hearing the bullfrog croak, instead she heard a different sound waking her from what had only been a light sleep. It was her mother. "Uphold momma in somethin, OK, sweetie?" the sweetness-tinged voice asked from across the couch. "OK, Erycha?"

Her mother was a thin woman yet her face was girlish with baby-fat and tenderness sometimes. But looking at her across the space of couch where they'd fallen asleep, it was like God had painted her in blacks and blues: her looks had hardened and chilled with the night.

Erycha wasn't sure what it meant to uphold a person in something and she didn't want to ask. It was best not to ask adults, just do as they said. She didn't even ask what needed upholding. She followed her mother into the bedroom—the apartment's only true bedroom, her own being an improvisation consisting of a makeshift curtain, some bedsheets, two pillows, and an inflatable mattress—and let her eyes do the asking.

In the dark room she could make out a pile of her father's things. They sat out like so much unbagged trash. Socks and shoes, two pairs of jeans, several pair of slacks, shirts and vests and thin coats; hats, a beret, a fluffy white Kangol, an open jar of Sulfur 8, a necklace and silver-colored promise ring. His car and girl magazines, his few, damaged albums. His manly supplies: cases of beer, a bottle of cologne. And maybe even his smell, she imagined.

His things lay heaped. It was strange that a man as big and impressive-looking as her daddy could get reduced so fast, to so little.

"Let's gather this mess." Her mother nodded at her. "As much things as he's put me through."

Erycha took a load of his things in her arms. She tucked the awkward objects in the crook of her arm like a great big football and tottered out to the center room.

She heard her mother's voice behind her, over her shoulder. Keep it movin, girl. Keep movin. She noticed that the front door was open. The winter wind escaped inside, its quick jets stinging her skin. Her nostrils filled with the smell of freshly frozen air. She shuffled across the apartment and out onto the porch, where she waited for her mother again. She saw the boxes rowed one after the next leading down the steps and the miscellany of objects contained in them: now she caught on and understood what would come next. She didn't want to put him out, not like this. She just stayed there, staring at each different-marked box.

"As much things as he's put me through. Since the beginning, I had his back, Lord knows why. Cut my roots for this nigga. Didn't judge him. Didn't play him short. Not once. Not even when I's eighteen an' stupid an' I's cuttin from my roots, leavin home for a nigga in prison." Her mother stopped and glanced fast at Erycha, like she was trying to judge something about her girl. Erycha was so confused now, she was half-ready for the world to end. She didn't know why her mother was looking at her like this, or why she was putting her man out, or why winter was the beautiful season where she lived. Everything from plain little words to the turning earth was a mystery.

They started down the stairs, packing first the Salvation Army box, then the Goodwill box, then another Salvation Army box. They had scavenged so many clothes and things from Goodwill and the Salvation Army that now they had plenty of moving boxes, enough boxes to travel across the country and back.

As she went back up the stairs, Erycha heard a faint rustling just above her head, like the flutter of birds. But it was nighttime and no birds were out, only the moon and the stars. The sky and the street below and everything seemed wrapped in the same silence and emptiness, and she remembered again that she should have heard the bullfrog by now. She wondered when he would come back.

Re-entering the apartment, she asked "Why idn't he back yet?"

Her mother bobbed her braided head as she bent down to gather up the last of his things. "It's what he gets for leavin the civilized labor force"; which didn't answer the question.

"But why cain't he come back?" Erycha wanted to know.

"Ask him."

How could she ask him if he wasn't home? How could she ever ask him if he never came home? Erycha wanted to know. But she could tell by her mother's hardening face that she probably shouldn't ask. It was such a tired, frustrated face. Erycha watched the face and the woman with it struggle out through the open door and down the stair-steps one careful one at a time and decided against any and all questions. She figured her father couldn't stay away forever. He'd get hungry or cold eventually, just like the bullfrog would eventually return to the pagoda: as many times as he had left, he had come back home. She looked up into her mother's eyes as she returned through the open door and closed it behind her, pushing back the frozen night.

By the time he returned, the bullfrog was croaking again. Erycha was listening for the occasional croaks and she almost didn't hear her father's small, resigned knock-knock noise on the apartment door. Then she heard it only faintly. But as she listened closer, she heard her mother rolling over in bed. How she made that old contraption creak and wail in ways that no inflatable air mattress ever could. She listened to her father's retreating steps down the staircase and on to the cement walkway where in the silence he fumbled clumsily through the cardboard boxes. But she didn't hear him leave. She didn't hear his brogans go down that walkway any farther. The sound of his shoes told her where he stood and where he walked, and for now they made no sound and no stand at all, as if he had simply stopped.

She heard the bullfrog croaking.

She reached her head over the bedsheets and looked around. It was safe to come back into the world, she decided. When she pulled out of the sheets, the mixture of silence and sound felt strange in her ears: it was easing her through sleep and calling her out into the world all at once.

Excitement thrilled through her as she slipped out of the bedroom that was not a bedroom and past her mother's closed door, out the apartment and down to where her father lay sleeping in amongst his scattered life. This was another new dance she'd made for herself, except now she had a partner to hold her in his arms.

Then, dawn. The boxes were looking down at them from the staircase when they came awake in each other's arms. She noticed that some had been turned on their sides, their contents spilled along the steps. But despite all that, her father started in thanking God and Stevie Wonder and Raphael Saadiq: he made it seem like a miracle that he got to wake up with his stuff all put out of doors just as long as no one had robbed or cut him and his daughter up. "Thank you," he mumbled. "Thank you. For not lettin these niggas do nothin. For not lettin none of these heartless-ass people take us out. Thank you."

Erycha had never been afraid of her neighbors or her neighborhood day or night. It was her neighborhood, her home, after all. So it surprised her to see her big strong dad getting all thankful for divine protection when all that had happened was that they went to sleep and woke up. What was there to be frightened of? She wondered. Scanning their quiet, familiar surroundings she didn't see anything new or exciting or scary. "Why you scared?" she asked, looking into his dancing eyes. "What's wrong?"

He shook his head real slow. "Because." She waited for more, but he didn't elaborate.

Because. It was the kind of answer Erycha heard all the time in her classes and on the playground. It didn't seem appropriate for any adult to be saying it and plain wrong for a dad-adult. Her teachers told her not to begin sentences with that word, and he told her to listen to her teachers, so why didn't he have to, too?

"Because what?" she challenged him.

He looked at her with surprise and hurt. "Babygirl," he said, his lips parting in the silence, his boyishly handsome face dropping as if suddenly loaded over with responsibility, "Babygirl."

She stared back at him in frustration.

"Don' turn into one a them type women. Please. For my sanity sake."

It was only morning, but she already noticed his mood darkening over like a lowering sky: she could see the future as he saw it, not one but two women berating him. Telling him when to come and when to be gone, when to speak and when to elaborate even though he felt like he had already said enough. She was coming into intuition like into a bad cloud: her dad would never really leave. She realized that. He was too scared of something out there in the world to leave, and he was not enough of whatever it was her mother wanted him to be to make peace at home. He would always be somewhere between staying and going. Her poor daddy. He was about to go back up those stair-steps, pick up the boxes, and return to whatever waited for him inside.

She felt him stir and then stand up, raising her off the ground with him. He held her there for a second, like a jewel, his and not his.

"OK, Erycha, I'ma drop you. We bout to go back up the stairs, K? Ladies first."

"K." She nodded. She seemed to have all the answers and he all the questions. "OK."

She squirmed in his grasp, a signal to let her go. But he didn't, not right away. She had the sense that he didn't want his hands empty. She squirmed some more, but he kept her tucked in his arms. After her, there would only be boxes for him to hold and at that point he might as well be empty-handed. She wondered if her mother was waiting on them right now and listened for her call. She thought of the pagoda and the bullfrog, wondered if he was still in his little chamber, waiting for her too. It was nice to think that people and things thought of her and waited for and wanted her. Many years later, after she had become a college student and left her mother's home for the last time, Erycha would buy a baby iguana that ate the rose petals from off the walls of her apartment building. The iguana would eventually grow to six feet in length counting its tail, and every day when she woke and left her room the iguana would see her and whack the thin wall with its thunderous tail, making the apartment shudder just a little. It was, she figured, its unique way of saying good morning and breaking the loneliness that was her life, just as the bullfrog of her girlhood had kept her company at night with its own reptilian kindness.

TRANSCEND

Cheryl Strayed

DEAR SUGAR,
I'm torn. I feel like I have to decide between the two things I love the most. My wife and I have an eighteen-month-old daughter. Our marriage has been rocky for years. My wife is a heroin addict who relapsed (post-baby), after seven years of recovery. She had been breastfeeding and snorting opioids until the night I caught her.

I come from three generations of addiction from both my parents. I got sober myself when I was a teen and turned my life around while living at a boys' home, which I consider partially my home. I now work as a drug counselor at this very place. I have become a walking example for the Los Angeles street kids I work with, who are much like me. This work is my calling. It has even inspired me to write my novel, which has become the most stolen book at the boys' home where I work.

Here is where the tear in my soul begins. My wife is from a small city in the South. I met her there. My mother died when I was living there. My wife was there for me. That city healed me. Recently my wife got an opportunity for a job that's based in that city. All of my wife's family and support are there. She just had her second interview and is probably going to be offered this great job.

I'm confused about what to do. Things are progressing for me professionally. I'm halfway through my master's degree in social work and momentum is building in my life. Right before my wife got this job opportunity, she had confessed to being on methadone (prescribed by her doctor) for the last three months to wean her off her heavy addiction. She chose not to tell me even though I have been supportive and had been asking for connection since her relapse. It might not make sense, but I felt more betrayed by this than I do by her relapse. I just want her to have a connection with me.

If she gets the job, I don't know if I can make the commitment to go with her because of my lack of trust in her and the positive direction of my life here in Los Angeles. I want my wife to be happy and near her family (I don't have family to offer her as support), but I cannot even bear the thought of being away from my daughter. I don't want to be like my father.

I'm torn and distraught. Should I be with my daughter and my wife or continue the path of my calling with the boys' home among the LA street kids I love?

Please help me think this through, Sugar.

Signed,

Torn and Distraught

Dear Torn and Distraught,

I teach memoir writing occasionally. I always ask my students to answer two questions about the work they and their peers have written: *What happened in this story?* and *What is this story about?* It's a useful way to see what's there. A lot of times, it isn't much. Or rather, it's a bunch of what happened that ends up being about nothing at all. You get no points for the living, I tell my students. It isn't enough to have had an interesting or hilarious or tragic life. Art isn't anecdote. It's the consciousness we bring to bear on our lives. For what happened in the story to transcend the limits of the personal, it must be driven by the engine of what the story means.

This is also true in life. Or at least it's true when one wishes to live an ever-evolving life, such as you and I do, sweet pea. What this requires of us is that we don't get tangled up in the living, even when we in fact feel woefully tangled up. It demands that we focus not only on what's happening in our stories, but also what our stories are about.

There's a sentence in your letter that matters more than all the other sentences: *I don't want to be like my father.* It's strange that it matters since I don't know precisely what you mean by it—nowhere in your letter do you tell me what your father is like. And yet, of course I understand. *I don't want to be like my father* is a story I know. It's code for a father who failed. It's what your story is about.

If you do not want to be like your father, do not be like him. There is your meaning, dear man. There is your purpose on this earth. Your daughter is the most important person in your life and you are one of the two most important people in hers. That's more than a fact. It's a truth. And like all truths, it has its own integrity. It's shiningly clear and resolute. If you are to succeed in fulfilling your meaning, everything that happens in your life must flow from this truth.

So let's talk about everything that's happening.

Your first obligation as a parent is to protect your child. Allowing your daughter to move across the country without you when you know that her mother is a drug addict who is struggling mightily with her recovery is a bad idea no matter how many grandmothers and uncles and cousins live across town. Until your wife is clean and strong in her recovery, she should not be the primary caregiver of your child. I don't question the profound love your wife no doubt has for your daughter. But I know addicts and you know addicts and we both know that no matter how wonderful and loving your wife may be, when she's in her addiction, she's not in her right mind. For that, your daughter will suffer and has suffered. It is your duty to shield her from this to the greatest extent possible.

The struggle your wife is engaged in right now is essential and monumental. Everything is at stake for her. Her ability to get and stay clean is directly connected to her ability to mother your child and remain your partner. Her addiction can't be cured by a job or a new town, though those things may ultimately play a role in her recovery. It can only be cured by her desire to stay clean and explore the underlying issues that compelled her to become an addict.

I strongly encourage the two of you to step back from the frazzled excitement of a possible job opportunity in a far-off and beloved town and focus instead on the monster that's hunkered down in your living room. What support and resources does your wife need? What role can and will you play in her recovery? Is your marriage salvageable? If it is, how will you as a couple reestablish trust and connection? In what city would you like to build your life together and what does that decision mean for each of you, professionally and personally? If your marriage isn't salvageable, how might you lovingly proceed in the direction of divorce? How will you negotiate custody of your daughter?

Those are the questions you need to be asking right now. Not whether your wife and daughter should move across the country without you in the midst of this already tumultuous time. There are other jobs for your wife. There are other jobs for you (much as you love yours, there are boys all over the country who would benefit from your leadership and wisdom). There are other times one or both of you may decide to move back to her hometown or stay in LA.

Choosing not to ask these questions right now doesn't mean that you won't ask them later. It's only putting a pause button on what's happening in your story so you can figure out what it means instead. It's opting to transcend—*to rise above or go beyond the limits of*—rather than living inside the same old tale.

I know you know what it means to transcend. You did it in your own life when you made a whole man out of the fractured boy you once were. But the thing about rising is we have to continue upward: the thing about going beyond is we have to keep going. You have only begun to understand what it means to not be like your lather. Keep understanding. Do not fail yourself on this front. No matter what happens when it comes to your marriage or your work life or your geographical location, there is no being torn when it comes to your daughter unless you choose to rip the fabric yourself. She wins every time.

Yours,

Sugar

from *BLUE NIGHTS*

Joan Didion

O N T H E D AY her adoption became legal, a hot September afternoon in 1966, we took her from the courthouse in downtown Los Angeles to lunch at The Bistro in Beverly Hills. At the
courthouse she had been the only baby up for adoption; the other
prospective adoptees that day were all adults, petitioning to adopt
one another for one or another tax advantage. At The Bistro, too,
more predictably, she was the only baby. *Qué hermosa*, the waiters
crooned. *Qué chula*. They gave us the corner banquette usually
saved for Sidney Korshak, a gesture the import of which would be
clear only to someone who had lived in that particular community
at that particular time. "Let's just say a nod from Korshak, and
the Teamsters change management," the producer Robert Evans
would later write by way of explaining who Sidney Korshak was.
"A nod from Korshak, and Vegas shuts down. A nod from Korshak,
and the Dodgers suddenly can play night baseball." The waiters
placed her carrier on the table between us. She was wearing a blue-
and-white dotted organdy dress. She was not quite seven months
old. As far as I was concerned this lunch at Sidney Korshak's banquette at The Bistro was the happy ending to the choice narrative.
We had chosen, the beautiful baby girl had accepted our choice, no
natural parent had stood up at the courthouse and exercised his or
her absolute legal right under the California law covering private
adoptions to simply say no, she's mine, I want her back.

The issue, as I preferred to see it, was now closed.

The fear was now gone.

She was ours.

What I would not realize for another few years was that I had never been the only person in the house to feel the fear.

What if you hadn't answered the phone when Dr. Watson called, she would suddenly say. *What if you hadn't been home, what if you couldn't meet him at the hospital, what if there'd been an accident on the freeway, what would happen to me then?*

Since I had no adequate answer to these questions, I refused to consider them.

She considered them.

She lived with them.

And then she didn't.

"You have your wonderful memories," people said later, as if memories were solace. Memories are not. Memories are by definition of times past, things gone. Memories are the Westlake uniforms in the closet, the faded and cracked photographs, the invitations to the weddings of the people who are no longer married, the mass cards from the funerals of the people whose faces you no longer remember. Memories are what you no longer want to remember.

[...]

Some of us feel this overpowering need for a child and some of us don't. It had come over me quite suddenly, in my mid-twenties, when I was working for *Vogue*, a tidal surge. Once this surge hit I saw babies wherever I went. I followed their carriages on the street. I cut their pictures from magazines and tacked them on the wall next to my bed. I put myself to sleep by imagining them: imagining holding them, imagining the down on their heads, imagining the soft spots at their temples, imagining the way their eyes dilated when you looked at them.

Until then pregnancy had been only a fear, an accident to be avoided at any cost.

Until then I had felt nothing but relief at the moment each month when I started to bleed. If that moment was delayed by even a day I would leave my office at *Vogue* and, looking for instant reassurance that I was not pregnant, go see my doctor, a Columbia Presbyterian internist who had come to be known, because his mother-in-law had been editor in chief of *Vogue* and his office was always open to fretful staff members, as "the *Vogue* doctor." I recall sitting in his examining room on East Sixty-seventh Street one morning waiting for the results of the most recent rabbit test I had implored him to do. He came into the room whistling, and began misting the plants on the window sill.

The test, I prompted.

He continued misting the plants.

I needed to know the results, I said, because I was leaving to spend Christmas in California. I had the ticket in my bag. I opened the bag. I showed him.

"You might not need a ticket to California," he said. "You might need a ticket to Havana."

I correctly understood this to be intended as reassuring, his baroque way of saying that I might need an abortion and that he could help me get one, yet my immediate response was to vehemently reject the proposed solution: it was delusional, it was out of the question, it was beyond discussion.

I couldn't possibly go to Havana.

There was a revolution in Havana.

In fact there was: it was December 1958, Fidel Castro would enter Havana within days.

I mentioned this.

"There's always a revolution in Havana," the *Vogue* doctor said.

A day later I started to bleed, and cried all night.

I thought I was regretting having missed this interesting moment in Havana but it turned out the surge had hit and what I was regretting was not having the baby, the still unmet baby, the baby I would eventually bring home from St. John's Hospital in Santa Monica. *What if you hadn't been home, what if you couldn't meet Dr. Watson at the hospital, what if there'd been an accident on the freeway, what would happen to me then.* Not long ago, when I read the fragment of the novel written just to show us, the scrap in which the protagonist thinks she might be pregnant and elects to address the situation by consulting her pediatrician, I remembered that morning on East Sixty-seventh Street. *Now, they didn't even care any more.*

[...]

There are certain moments in those first years with her that I remember very clearly.

These very clear moments stand out, recur, speak directly to me, on some levels flood me with pleasure and on others still break my heart.

I remember very clearly for example that her earliest transactions involved what she called "sundries." She invested this word, which she used as a synonym for "possessions" but seemed to derive from the "sundries shops" in the many hotels to which she had already been taken, with considerable importance, dizzying alternations of infancy and sophistication. One day after she had asked me for a Magic Marker I found her marking off an empty box into "drawers," or areas meant for specific of these "sundries." The "drawers" she designated were these: "Cash," "Passport," "My IRA," "Jewelry," and, finally—I find myself hardly able to tell you this—"Little Toys."

Again, the careful printing.

The printing alone I cannot forget.

The printing alone breaks my heart.

Another moment, not, on examination, dissimilar: I remember very clearly the Christmas night at her grandmother's house in West Hartford when John and I came in from a movie to find her huddled alone on the stairs to the second floor. The Christmas lights were off, her grandmother was asleep, everyone in the house was asleep, and she was patiently waiting for us to come home and address what she called "the new problem." We asked what the new problem was. "I just noticed I have cancer," she said, and pulled back her hair to show us what she had construed to be a growth on her scalp. In fact it was chicken pox, obviously contracted before she left nursery school in Malibu and just now surfacing, but had it been cancer, she had prepared her mind to be ready for cancer.

A question occurs to me:

Did she emphasize "new" when she mentioned "the new problem"?

Was she suggesting that there were also "old" problems, undetailed, problems with which she was for the moment opting not to burden us?

A third example: I remember very clearly the doll's house she constructed on the bookshelves of her bedroom at the beach. She had worked on it for several days, after studying a similar improvisation in an old copy of *House & Garden* ("Muffet Hemingway's doll's house" was how she identified the prototype, taking her cue from the *House & Garden* headline), but this was its first unveiling. Here was the living room, she explained, and here was the dining room, and here was the kitchen, and here was the bedroom.

I asked about an undecorated and apparently unallocated shelf.

That, she said, would be the projection room.

The projection room.

I tried to assimilate this.

Some people we knew in Los Angeles did in fact live in houses with projection rooms but to the best of my knowledge she had never seen one. These people who lived in houses with projection rooms belonged to our "working" life. She, I had imagined, belonged to our "private" life. Our "private" life, I had also imagined, was separate, sweet, inviolate.

I set this distinction to one side and asked how she planned to furnish the projection room.

There would need to be a table for the telephone to the projectionist, she said, then stopped to consider the empty shelf.

"And whatever I'll need for Dolby Sound," she added then.

As I describe these very clear memories I am struck by what they have in common: each involves her trying to handle adult life, trying to be a convincing grownup person at an age when she was still entitled to be a small child. She could talk about "My IRA" and she could talk about "Dolby Sound" and she could talk about "just noticing" she had cancer, she could call Camarillo to find out what she needed to do if she was going crazy and she could call Twentieth Century–Fox to find out what she needed to do to be a star, but she was not actually prepared to act on whatever answers she got. "Little Toys" could still assume equal importance. She could still consult her pediatrician.

Was this confusion about where she stood in the chronological scheme of things our doing?

Did we demand that she be an adult?

Did we ask her to assume responsibility before she had any way of doing so?

Did our expectations prevent her from responding as a child?

I recall taking her, when she was four or five, up the coast to Oxnard to see *Nicholas and Alexandra*. On the drive home from Oxnard she referred to the czar and czarina as "Nicky and Sunny," and said, when asked how she had liked the picture, "I think it's going to be a big hit."

In other words, despite having just been told what had seemed to me as I watched it a truly harrowing story, a story that placed both parents and children in unthinkable peril—a peril to children more unthinkable still because its very source lay in the bad luck of having been born to these particular parents—she had resorted without hesitation to the local default response, which was an instant assessment of audience potential. Similarly, a few years later, taken to Oxnard to see *Jaws,* she had watched in horror, then, while I was still unloading the car in Malibu, skipped down to the beach and dove into the surf. About certain threats I considered real she remained in fact fearless. When she was eight or nine and enrolled in Junior Lifeguard, a program run by the Los Angeles County lifeguards that entailed being repeatedly taken out beyond the Zuma Beach breakers on a lifeguard boat and swimming back in, John and I arrived to pick her up and found the beach empty. Finally we saw her, alone, huddled in a towel behind a dune. The lifeguards, it seemed, were insisting, "for absolutely no reason," on taking everyone home. I said there must be a reason. "Only the sharks," she said. I looked at her. She was clearly disappointed, even a little disgusted, impatient with the turn the morning had taken. She shrugged. "They were just blues," she said then.

IMPERFECT EULOGY
FOR ELMER MORRISSEY

Shanthi Sekaran

April 14, 2012. On the 100th anniversary of the Titanic's collision with an iceberg, the eight crew members of the Low Speed Chase set off on a day-long yacht race. When the 38-foot boat took a turn near the southern edge of the Farallon Islands, erratic and powerful waves threw the crew from their vessel, into the ocean beyond the San Francisco Bay. Three sailors made it onto the island, where the small yacht crashed, and were rescued. One was found dead in the water. Four are still missing.

I'VE BEEN WAKING up in the earliest hours of the morning, before sunrise. From my window I can see the distant bay and the bridges that cut across it. It's almost too dark to see the ocean, but I know it's out there. And I know that somewhere in it is Elmer Morrissey.

I ask myself if the sea is less beautiful for having taken away my friend. I wonder if I have the energy to be angry at the Pacific Ocean. I try to think of what Elmer might say. I decide that Elmer would see the ocean for what it is: a roiling stage of life and death, a setting, not a being. I decide that Elmer would forgive.

I was a little bit in love with him, in the way you can be with someone you're not romantically attracted to. Is that just love? It feels more like something in between love and in-love. I might have told Elmer this when he was alive. I might have said, "I'm a little bit in love with you, Elmer, in a platonic way that straddles the boundaries of love and in-love." A simple "I love you" would also have sufficed. But how often do we really say this to our friends? I never throw out a casual "Love you!" at the end of a phone call. I might have said it to Elmer, though, and meant it fully. But I never did, because I'm too damn awkward with that sort of thing, and so I'm left saying it to my computer in a silent and rambling essay.

We found out on Sunday morning, the day after the accident, that Elmer was missing. Our two friends stepped through our gate and stood on our porch, red-eyed and shaking, to tell us the news. At that point, the search was still on. We measured the day in phone calls and Chronicle updates. We tried to act normal for our son. That evening, we stood on our balcony to watch the sun dim and the sky blush. "Stay with me," my husband said. The search would continue until sunset. He would keep an eye on the horizon until the light was gone. Elmer was alone out there.

A vapor trail shot up beyond the Golden Gate. It rose vertically, burning orange and aiming for the sky. "It's a flare," we said. "Maybe he's sent up a flare." We waited for a phone call. We waited for the news. We stood on the balcony and watched it, our son playing quietly indoors. Nothing happened. What we saw was no more than a fiery finger of cloud, pointing heavenward. We stayed out on the balcony until the evening grew cold and vanished into night.

Part of me, the over-thinking part, thinks that this essay may be self-indulgent, that by focusing on my own experience, I exclude the grief of others. I call this an imperfect eulogy because most eulogies are written to capture a general sense of loss, to bid to the departed an elegant and public goodbye. This is not that. This is my personal and flawed goodbye.

Each of Elmer's friends misses him in his or her own way. We aim our anger, our confusion, our disbelief in unique directions. When Elmer was alive, the group of us ate together, drank together, worked together, ran together, climbed together; but when Elmer left, we each took on a solitary cocoon of struggle. That's why we gather for things like memorials and barbecues. Events organized around the death of a friend have an angle of the absurd to them, but they serve a purpose. Not only do they make it more likely that we manage to eat, but they give us a way to pile our sadnesses together. We gather because we understand each other's long silences, because no one minds when we trail off mid-sentence, or talk endlessly about football because it's the only thing that will prevent us from thinking about what we're really thinking.

There's also the matter of Elmer's physical absence. Nobody's found him. He's missing, and somebody—the newspapers, the rescue crews, the rest of us—have presumed his fate. There's a minuscule possibility that he's still alive. Until we know for sure—if we ever know for sure—I've considered a few alternate endings. Option A: Elmer has found a hidden cave populated by feral spear-wielding cave children. He is their leader. Option B: Elmer has discovered a sparsely populated island, and founded a city-state of the New-New World. He is learning to cultivate a delicious and highly nutritious fungus. Option C: Elmer was rescued by a Soviet submarine. He's told its inhabitants about the fall of communism, and they are not happy. To transition them to a new capitalist reality, he's teaching them to make and play ukuleles. Option D: Elmer is the crown-prince of an underwater kingdom. He has forged an active sex life with a mer-woman in a cockle-shell brassiere, with whom he "feels a connection." Option E: Elmer comes walking in. He's alive. He wants to know why everyone looks so glum. We feel foolish. How fantastic it would be to feel like a fool.

Eventually, the concept that Elmer really is gone will settle into my head and stay there. Over the past few days, the idea that he's died has come and gone and come back again. The immediacy of it can recede for hours, and then, as I'm rummaging for my keys or putting a head of lettuce back in the fridge, it hits me. I brace myself for months of this, for the realization to come at me in sudden, unstoppable waves. I also dread the day when the reality will start to feel comfortable, when the thought of Elmer's death will not yank my heart into my throat. Before that day comes, I'll make a mental record of the things I must never forget about him. And because I don't trust my mental records, I will write these things down.*

Since I found out that Elmer was missing, my days have slowed down considerably. Unable to work, unable to think of much else but him, I've started to notice things I haven't before. I notice people's ages. I divide people I see on the street into those who've lived longer than Elmer, and those who are still catching up. In the garden, I notice a worm with a tapered head. In the kitchen, the cap on a bottle of canola oil pops right off, all by itself, and plinks onto the stovetop. In bed, my cat chews on the knuckles of my left hand— first the pinky finger, then the ring finger. He gnaws gently, like he's trying to communicate rather than attack.

I look up a picture of the southernmost Farallon Island, the one that holds the remains of the boat that Elmer and his seven crew-mates sailed. I notice that it looks like an upside-down left

---

*13 things not to forget about Elmer Morrissey: 1. The gap in his front teeth. 2. The way he pushed the sleeves of his tracksuit jacket all the way up to his elbows, so that the fabric belled out over his forearms. 3. His fear of touching his eyes. 4. How his height never failed to surprise me. 5. The fact that he owned a Groupon for trapeze lessons. 6. The night he drank four bottles of ginger beer, and couldn't stop smiling. 7. The fact that he read my novel—on his cell phone. 8. The honest, woodsy timbre of his voice. 9. How he thought his name sounded feminine. 10. How he trained himself for a month to confront a boy at school who'd continually bullied him for crying, and then beat the shit out of him. 11. How his singing voice was so much gentler than his speaking voice. 12. How he wouldn't have minded me saying that. 13. The time I smashed my finger in my car door outside of Chester's, just as he arrived. He hopped off his bike, examined the bloody, pulsating wound, and told Spencer I'd need a butterfly bandage. I dunked my finger in a cup of ice water, and the water turned immediately red, and kept getting redder, until it looked exactly like a vodka cranberry.

hand. And I wonder if Elmer was speaking to me through my cat, telling me where to find him. I wonder if Elmer rests at the northeast corner of the southernmost island, between the pinky and ring fingers of rugged brown rock. But then I remember that Elmer was terribly allergic to cats, and I question whether he'd really choose Toady as his medium. I don't think it's odd that I'm searching for signals and significance wherever I can find them, to explain a reality that doesn't make sense.

As the days pass and my sorrow becomes less urgent, I find myself trying to recapture the moment when I found out about the accident, from two friends who stood at my door. I try to feel again the transitional seconds when Elmer went from being unquestionably alive to incomprehensibly lost. This was when I felt most acutely connected to him. Now, just a week later, my memory of Elmer begins to let go, surrenders to the tides, grows smaller and quieter.

As I write this, I look up at my mug of tea. I notice, for the first time, the way the steam curls up and into the room, tending left at first, and then right, pulling itself into mushroom-shapes and jellyfish. On a normal day, a happy day, I would have swigged my tea and seen nothing but the screen before me. I would have missed watching the way steam dances. Elmer talked a lot about living in the present. The idea connected with his meditation practice, but also with his own life story. He was adopted as an infant, and growing up with this knowledge, he learned that interrogating the past can be a cruel and fruitless game, that the only way to live is to live forward.

The final time I saw him, for lunch at the Epicurious Garden, he said this: "The only thing to do is live for the moment, and make the best of it you can." The logic of this comes back to me now, and hauls into its orbit the gut-walloping truth of Elmer's death. I think he would like it best if I focused on life post-Elmer, on the things and people who remain. He'd prefer me to push on through the heavy sands of sadness, until pushing on becomes less of a struggle, until the day when the thought of him brings more joy than grief.

Still, when I see an email titled "In Memory of Elmer Morrissey" the words sound ludicrous. They are of another dimension, a farcical dark fantasy. But is it possible that Elmer himself has accepted his reality? What happened the other day at his memorial barbecue, when the dense evening cloud cover gave way to rays of sudden sunshine, and a spray of rain-pellets fell down upon us? This could have been Elmer's doing. It could have been Elmer telling us that he's made it to a good place, after all. It could have just been the weather. We take from the moment what we need, and we push on.

Elmer, I love you. Goodbye.

Post-publication addendum: Elmer Morrissey's body was recovered several weeks after the crash of the Low Speed Chase. He now lies in rest near his family home in Glounthaune, County Cook, Ireland.

SERVING OYSTERS TO M.F.K. FISHER

Rachelle Cruz

*"All the Filipino servants, pretty little men-dolls
as mercurial as monkeys, and as lewd."*

— M.F.K FISHER, AMERICAN FOOD WRITER,
1924, "THE FIRST OYSTER"

WE SLIDE PAST the wooden crates stained with salt,
crowding the service entrance.

We pry open the question of lids: slippers of oysters waiting
for a tongue to kiss.

We freeze our hands scrubbing their algaed coats, pristine
from the thickness of our bristles.

We mimic the Pacific's sharp bite and overtake, salt shaking
free from our hands.

We shuck and snap with our pointed knives, unlock, twist the
collection of God's gnarled doors.

We cut the muscle under the shell, inhale the liquor we can't
drink.

We serve gloved young women waltzing, oyster in one hand,
the other on wide shoulders.

We remember our first oysters grown on the ghosts of coconuts,
slithered in by submerged ropes.

We remember the quickburn of rum to chase these heartbeats of
ocean, brining our bodies, cruel.

from *TACO USA*

Gustavo Arellano

S UCH A SIMPLE, brilliant meal: a tortilla wrapped around a stuffing. No utensils needed. The taco. That's it. Oh, modifications are possible: fold the tortilla in half and deep-fry it to create a taco dorado, what Americans know as the hard-shelled taco. Roll it like an enchilada, deep-fry it, and you have taquitos (also called flautas). Eat them at breakfast? Breakfast tacos. Fine for lunch and dinner. As a snack. As a full meal. Serve them with one or two tortillas. From a truck, from a grill, from fine china. Sprinkle some salsa, maybe some cilantro and onions. Grasp and grub. That's it.

Tacos have existed since there was a tortilla, even if they didn't exist by that name (the earliest mention of "taco" as a food dates only to the late nineteenth century; previously the word stood for everything from a pool cue to a hammer to getting drunk.) They now cover the United States the way chili and tamales once did— the world, really. They're huge in Sweden, popular in Japan, big in Peoria, where El Mexicano offers them to city residents with chorizo that shines the shade of orange you want transmission fluid to reflect.

What's so remarkable about the foodstuff's odyssey, however, is its delayed start in this country. Unlike the enchiladas, frijoles, tamales, and beef stews that dominated the travelogues of American visitors to Mexico and the American Southwest, tacos didn't merit a mention in American literature until a Los Angeles socialite traveling in Mexico City came across them, describing the dish as a "fried turnover, filled with chopped, highly seasoned meats." Tacos originally migrated to California and Texas in the 1920s, and only made it into scattered Mexican cookbooks written by Americans in about the 1930s. They didn't become easily available nationwide until Taco Bell and its numerous imitators rushed to colonize the United States during the 1960s, selling tacos that the average Mexican derided as inauthentic but the average American gobbled with gusto.

Such a delay is almost counterintuitive. The taco is now the quintessential Mexican meal in the United States, so wedded to Americans' perception of the cuisine that even Irish pubs will sell corned beef tacos during Cinco de Mayo served by lasses wearing T-shirts boasting "Irish I Were Mexican." But the ballad of tacos in the United States and their subsequent globalization is also the story of modern-day Mexican immigration to this country—and the eternal fascination Americans had with the treats of their southern neighbor.

The American taco can boast of two birthplaces: Los Angeles and San Bernardino, California. But its baptismal font is the pan angrily bubbling with oil at Cielito Lindo, a tiny stand in downtown Los Angeles named after a classic *ranchera* song meaning "Beautiful Little Heaven." From here come taquitos filled with shredded beef, grabbed fresh from that roiling pan, then anointed in a creamy salsa, more pureed avocado than chile. The cooks hand them to waiting customers in a container better suited for a hot dog, two for three dollars. These taquitos last a minute: people grab them with one hand and chomp, shattering their purchase into shiny shards with the faintest of bites; the shredded, fatty beef hangs off the end of the last bite like tendrils.

Cielito Lindo is the first business people see when entering the northern section of Olvera Street, a stretch of Los Angeles that has evolved along with the city's sense of itself. When the business district first opened in 1931, Los Angeles was simultaneously looking forward and backward. The city was booming, exponentially increasing its population nearly every decade as industries sprang up and boosters lured the nation with images of orange groves and movie stars, sun and sand. The Olympics were just a year away, and the eyes of the developed world prepared to focus on the City of Angels—a dramatic coming of age for a city that just fifty years earlier was still predominantly a Mexican-dominated cow town.

With progress came nostalgia, and the lords of L.A. pined for what the progressive historian Carey McWilliams dubbed California's "fantasy heritage," the idea that the Spaniards and Mexicans who had once ruled the state, before the Mexican-American War, truly lived the good life, and that modernity was laying ruin to paradise. One of those women, a northern California transplant named Christine Sterling, became enraged when she discovered city planners wanted to raze the old adobes and buildings around the Plaza de Los Angeles, the acknowledged birthplace of the city. The socialite gained citywide notoriety by placing a sign in front of the Avila adobe, the oldest in the city, that read in part, "Los Angeles will be forever marked a transient, Orphan city if she allows her roots to rot in a soil of impoverished neglect."

Sterling solicited the help of Harry Chandler, owner and publisher of the *Los Angeles Times,* the mighty daily whose incessant drumbeat for the region influenced the city it covered in a way few newspapers have before or since. Chandler's use of his paper to promote projects around the city—many in which his family and friends had a financial interest—had already turned Los Angeles into one of America's rising cities, and he used the pages of the *Times* to push forth the idea of El Paseo de Los Angeles, a reimagined Olvera Street for approved vendors to sell *mexicanidad* via artisan crafts and food for curious Americans. But to do that, Sterling,

Chandler, and other boosters had to try to kill once and for all the Mexican food scene that had dominated the area since the 1880s with tamale wagons.

Given Los Angeles's spread-out geography even in those embryonic days, wandering tamale men didn't take hold in L.A. as they did in the rest of the United States; a cart or a wagon was necessary, not only to travel from home to downtown but also the better to procure a spot on the bustling streets. The origins of the city's tamale sellers are murky, although newspaper accounts place them as far back as the 1870s, and by 1880, a *Los Angeles Herald* article commented, "The experience of our Eastern visitors will be incomplete unless they sample" a Los Angeles street tamale.

As dusk fell, a cavalry of two-by-four pushcarts and eight-foot-long wagons with walls that opened up to reveal cooks inside wheeled their way toward the Plaza and its vicinity, setting up shop until last call and beyond. On the menu was everything from popcorn to pigs' feet, oyster cocktails to sandwiches, but the majority of them carried tamales prepared elsewhere and kept warm in steam buckets.

By 1901, more than a hundred tamale wagons roamed Los Angeles, each paying a dollar a month for a city business license. "Strangers coming to Los Angeles," reported the *Times* in 1901, "remark at the presence of so many outdoor restaurants, and marvel at the system which permits men…to set up places of business in the public streets…and competing with businessmen who pay high rents for rooms in which to serve the public with food."

Not everyone appreciated the food scene, however. As early as 1892, officials tried to ban them outright; in 1897, the City Council proposed to not allow tamale wagons to open until nine at night, at the behest of restaurant owners who didn't like the crowds the tamaleros attracted. Four years later, Police Chief Charles Elton recommended tamale wagons close at one in the morning because they offered "a refuge for drunks who seek the streets when the saloons are closed for the night." And in 1910, a hundred downtown businessmen signed a letter asking the council to prohibit tamale wagons because they didn't reflect well on the district.

The constant attempts at legislating the tamale wagons out of existence didn't succeed initially, however, because they were just too popular. And the tamaleros—knowing what they meant to their fans—pushed back against even the smallest slight against them. In 1903, when the council tried to outlaw them altogether, tamale wagons formed a mutual-aid society and presented the council a petition with the signatures of more than five hundred customers that read in part, "We claim that the lunch wagons are catering to an appreciative public and to deprive the people of these convenient eating places would prove a great loss to the many local merchants who sell the wagon proprietors various supplies."

The time of the tamale wagons was waning, though. "They belong not to the new order of things," the *Times* editorialized in 1924. "They were born of the pueblo—they perish in the metropolis." By then the wagons sold more than mere tamales—the biblical wave of migrants from Central Mexico due to the Mexican Revolution and other problems over the previous twenty years had introduced other Mexican delicacies to the city largely unfamiliar to the region: *birria* (goat stew), menudo (soup made from cow tripe), and different preparations of pork, chicken, and beef, best eaten snuggled in a tortilla: the taco.

That experience with mobile food had long-lasting repercussions for the region. The idea of a movable feast prefigured the drive-throughs that dominated the 1950s. And though Olvera Street developed and pushed out unsanctioned street vending from the area to make way for sit-down eateries such as La Golondrina Cafe, where Chandler and the city's power structure finally found a place to eat Mexican food in a refined atmosphere to their liking, it was simple meals such as tacos that resonated with the public. When Chandler enlisted a Latino writer to pen a piece extolling the authenticity of Olvera Street, even the shill had to plug the tacos.

"I see Mexico in every 'botellon' and 'serape' on the Paseo," the author wrote, "I taste it in the 'tacos,'" which he went on to describe as a "tortilla, folded over meat and vegetables and roasted a little."

Their portability and easy preparation made tacos favorites of workers, who took them everywhere, from the factories to the fields. Tacos made their way onto the menus of the Mexican restaurants in town to become a hit for the working classes and blue bloods alike. Entrepreneurial immigrants as well as Americans saw opportunity in tacos. One of those was Aurora Guerrero, who left her village in Zacatecas during the 1920s to look for her husband, who had earlier settled in Los Angeles. She found poverty instead, and survived by cleaning houses and working the fields until finding an opportunity on Olvera Street selling taquitos from a stall out of a restaurant before renting a spot. Guerrero had to ask for Sterling's blessings to start a business; the matron of Olvera Street agreed with the condition that they sell "something different." And thus arose Cielito Lindo's taquitos.

Guerrero turned them into a living; a daughter, Ana Natalia, branched out with her mother's approval and opened a chain of Anitas restaurants across Los Angeles, taking with her the family's taquitos recipes and opening Las Anitas on Olvera Street, not far from Cielito Lindo. Competitors copied those taquitos, along with Mexican restaurants across the region, and the modern-day taco took its infant step toward supremacy.

The efforts of Chandler and Sterling worked; Olvera Street became a sensation. But it came at a cost. Sterling forced all the vendors to dress in "native" costume and affect the pomposity of Spanish dons and señoritas; those who refused faced eviction. Los Angeles's authentic Mexican street food scene had been replaced by Mexicans who played the role assigned to them by white patrons, who looked on in approval while chowing down tacos.

BOYLE HEIGHTS

Jen Bergmark

FOR CLASSICAL GUITAR, I need strong fingernails on my right hand. Washing dishes, all this water, it's ruining me. I use gloves, but after awhile I take them off, because it's hard to pick up stemware wearing rubber paws. And my hands get hot. Sometimes I want to scratch my nose.

I scrape a half eaten crab cake into the garbage pail. I peel a spent teabag from a cup. Waiters rush in and out with blasts of air conditioning from the dining room. Before work I spent a half hour shaping my fingernails with an industrial diamond file. Now my thumbnail has chipped. I found the broken piece embedded in a Brillo pad and I have it in my pocket. It's a clean break; maybe I can reattach it with Crazy Glue. The door swings open and the owner enters the kitchen, standing with her hands on her hips like the queen of something.

My diamond in the rough, she says, patting me on the back. She moved here a year ago from Armenia—took over this place before the stamp on her passport was dry. She likes that I can play Bach. She thinks twenty-one is not too old to get my GED. She's rooting for me.

Has Arthur played guitar for you yet? the owner asks Jolene, the cute new waitress. Jolene—a stack of folded napkins in her arms—stops and frowns, a little confused. I introduced myself as Arturo. The owner Americanizes everything, even with her fancy accent. She's got this we-speak-English-only-in-my-kitchen thing. She says she wants us all on the same page.

He plays classical guitar, the owner says.

My dad was a guitarist. He played every concert hall in Los Angeles. My mom took me to his performances when I was a kid. I wore a clip-on tie. My dad's dress pants had creases ironed so sharp I could see them from our row. Someday I'll be onstage with him, I used to think, father and son.

I lift the machine's hood and roll out a tray of water glasses.

I'm not very good, I say.

He is *very* good, the owner tells Jolene. He'll play for us later, won't you, Arthur? She sweeps her arm to take in the kitchen.

Sure, I say. But I'm not that good.

I bet you're good, Jolene says, looking me right in the eyes. I'm embarrassed. Jolene. It's like she surfed in on a golden surfboard. The guys in the kitchen fall all over themselves every time she picks up a tray.

Before this, I worked in the file room of a law firm downtown five minutes from home. I could take the bus. One day as I sat there collating, my heart revved like I was running a race. At first I just sat there, feeling the sudden reverberations in my nervous system, and then I was floored by a fear so amazing that I could think only to run. I stood but my legs folded. I couldn't breathe, couldn't stop shaking. I lay on the carpet in a fetal ball. It felt like I was dying. Somehow I managed to drag myself out of there, almost losing consciousness during the elevator ride to the lobby. There was an endless wait at a bus shelter. An actress on a billboard leered at me. The sun bleached the sky. Finally the bus arrived and I sat in the last seat, forehead pressed against the window to stop the shaking. I didn't go back.

A few weeks ago it happened in a movie. One minute I was sitting quietly in the dark and the next I thought my ribcage would blast open. I ran out the back of the theater—the door locked behind me—and I vomited on the sidewalk.

When the last customers leave, the owner sets a chair in the corner facing the dining room. Everyone on staff gets a beer and they all sit around like an audience.

Attention, the owner says, clapping her hands with a big clank of bracelets. Tonight, she says, we bring you Arthur. She's like an emcee. A swoop of sleeve in my direction. There's a round of applause. Jolene whistles.

I play a Sor study—*Estudio En Mi Menor.* My ragged thumbnail rasps the E string. I'm not sure I'll be able to fix it. Glue. An acrylic nail. Some players cut out a sliver of ping pong ball. Nobody seems to notice, but I cringe. After awhile though, the guitar takes hold and I stop hearing the brittle sound. I sink to the place I go when I'm playing, like going underwater, that kind of peacefulness and isolation. I'm alone, weightless; the guitar hums through me. Minutes go by and I'm not sure if I've taken a breath. Then the piece is over, and I resurface—first a relief to inhale, then disappointment. My head is full of distracting sounds. I'm back in the world again.

They applaud. The waiters cheer, *You.*

Our dishwasher the genius, the owner says, raising her glass. Everyone claps again.

It's really nice, all this, but it also makes me feel a little sick.

When you listen to guitar, really listen, you hear more than the notes. You hear the space where a note hangs until it fades to a small, intense emptiness before the next note. The little space fits inside you. There's a reason for everything. If you are really listening, you forget about your bank account or your health. Forget about anger and fear and sorrow. You're solely a container for music and silence.

It takes dedication. My dad had plenty of dedication for playing and nothing left over. He moved out when I was thirteen, forgetting one guitar. It's the one I play, the most expensive according to my mom, made by a luthier to my dad's specifications. She thinks he overlooked it because he played it so rarely. In his hurry, his guilt, he forgot to look in the back of the bedroom closet where it was stored for protection. I probably shouldn't drag it around with me, expensive as it is. I should be more careful about humidity and temperature. I like to have it with me, though. I like to think he left it on purpose as a gift for me. But who knows why people do things.

On my way home from the restaurant it happens again. It's never happened while I'm driving. I'm about to clear the off-ramp when my heart starts pounding. My field of vision narrows to a pinprick. I swerve off the road onto an embankment. The jolt of the tire hitting the curb sends me out of my seat and my head bumps the ceiling.

Some instinctual self-protection kicks in: I switch gears from drive to park. I crouch in the well under the steering wheel, shaking like I've been tossed naked into snow. I try to focus, think ordinary thoughts, like: *it smells like feet down here.* But my brain ticks off a grim slide show—an earthquake fissure yawning open, mountain lions descending from the hills. A list of ways to die. I know I'm not dying. I'm safe inside this car. I'm blocks from my house. There are poppies growing here on this embankment, pushing their orange petals up through the garbage and car exhaust. There's nothing to be afraid of. But a refrain keeps repeating. A small voice whispering, *this moment's your last.*

It takes me an hour to get off the car floor. When I get home, my mom's still awake, in the living room watching TV. She likes real-life crime shows, where episodes follow the wife and husband from their wedding day until the wife's body turns up in a ravine.

There's pizza in the fridge, my mom says without looking away from her show. The pepperonis are curled up and the cheese is dry. My mom used to cook dinner in the old days. She made pastries from scratch. I'm not hungry anyway. I can't stop shaking though the house is warm. I look for a blanket in the hall closet, pushing aside photo albums and clothes. I find a carton of adult diapers with several diapers missing.

Each morning my mom sits at the kitchen table with a plastic hand mirror, putting on mascara, rubbing powder on her cheeks. She thinks the light's better than the bathroom. I wonder what she's trying to see. No matter how long she sleeps she looks tired. When she smiles there's a tinge of gray at her gum line. She's going to lose teeth. She's forty-seven.

I go to the living room with the blanket around my shoulders.

Do you know a doctor? I ask.

Mijo, what is it? she says. She straightens up and reaches for the remote.

My parents were married before they moved to the U.S., when my mom was just a teenager. She was happy. She had parties in our backyard for neighbors. She covered the picnic table with a linen tablecloth she'd embroidered herself. After my father left, she stopped inviting neighbors over. We didn't have money, she said. I dropped out of school during senior year to work. My mom got a job in a stationery store stockroom. Women from the store called the house to invite us for dinner. We never went. At night, when she thought I was asleep, I listened to her crying in her bedroom. She was sad all the time, and there was nothing I could do.

As I get undressed for bed, I put the scrap of paper with the doctor's phone number on the dresser. I didn't tell my mom what's wrong with me. I take the torn piece of fingernail out of my pocket. I get my gear from the top drawer—tweezers, glue, emery board.

With the tweezers I grasp the broken bit of nail and fit the sliver in place against my thumb. My hands won't keep still. The sliver looks like a pale, sad crescent moon. The glue would probably only hold it for a week. Fuck it. I toss the piece in the trash and file my nail down.

Have you heard of panic disorder? the clinic doctor asks. He pats the pockets of his white coat, looking for a pen. I sit on the examining table, shirtless so he can prod me.

I think I need an x-ray, I say.

The examining room walls are the same beige as the linoleum floor. The doctor writes something on a pad.

It's neurophysiological, he says. Fight or flight response. It's not uncommon.

I think it's my heart, I say. I press my hand against my rib cage.

I can give you an x-ray, the doctor says, but this is nothing to be ashamed of. You say chest pain, right? Heart palpitations? Nausea? Chills? Dizziness? Fear that you're dying?

Without waiting for an answer, he tears the prescription sheet from the pad. Okay, he says. This medicine is addictive so take it only when you need it. I see folks doped into zombies. Any big changes in your life? You get married, have a kid, anybody die?

No, I say. No changes.

The doctor scratches his face. Okay, he says. Here you go. He hands me the prescription. You should find a psychiatrist.

Is it temporary? I say.

Ideally, says the doctor. But some suffer their whole lives.

The pharmacy cashier gives me a waiver that says the pharmacist explained the proper dosage. The pharmacist is in the corner scraping capsules into a tray. It's a formality, the cashier says, pushing a pen across the counter.

I'm late for work. I blame traffic. No one will question that. It's Friday and we're busy. Producers, directors, lawyers. All celebrating the successful end of another workweek. Our customers name-drop freeways. There's a pile up on the San Diego, a Sigalert on the Ventura. They complain about congestion on the Santa Monica.

The kitchen smells like garlic. Entrees sizzle in pans. The owner's in the dining room making sure everyone is happy. I tie my apron, slide a rack of dishes in the machine and pull the hood down. Jolene comes in for a break. She's got a soda and a dinner roll stashed on a metal storage shelf.

Hey, sweetie, she says.

Her face. Her ass. Jesus Christ. Makes me want to open doors for her, hold an umbrella over her head, carry her around so her perfect feet never touch ground. The chef watches as I sneak looks at Jolene sipping from a straw. She heads out to the dining room. I scrub a scorched pan.

Champagne tastes, the chef says.

So what, I say.

She won't go for you, says the chef. Where does she live? West-wood?

She's in school, I say. Yeah.

And you?

I'm in Boyle Heights, I say. I keep scrubbing the pan.

Tell you where she'll live after school, he says. Brentwood.

I look at him.

Dream on, *Boyle Heights,* he says, and gives me a big smile.

Fuck off, I say under my breath.

Oye, the chef says. *No quiero bronca contigo.*

English, I say. Same page. Remember the rule.

By night's end everyone's calling me Boyle Heights, including the prep chef, who usually barely utters a word.

I can name-drop freeways. The massive East L.A. Interchange is in Boyle Heights. The Golden State, the Hollywood, the Pomona, the

San Bernardino, the Santa Ana and the Santa Monica freeways all meet in my hometown. Used to mean Boyle Heights was a place people wanted to go.

Back home after my shift, there's a package of Oreos waiting on the counter. A blue TV glow seeps under my mom's bedroom door. I pour a glass of milk and take the cookies and pharmacy bag to my room. Even though my heart feels pretty normal, I wash a pill down with milk and wait. A car driving by throws a flash of headlights across the wall. I don't feel any better. I don't feel different. I just get tired and fall asleep. I dream that my hands are sweating inside dish gloves, and when I pull the gloves off to get some relief, my skin peels off too, flopping wetly into the restaurant sink basin. The bones of my knuckles are slimy white knobs. Blood drips slowly into the sink, and then it comes faster, like a faucet. The water turns red.

I'm careful, during my next shift, to keep on the gloves.

Hey, cuteness, Jolene says, passing my station with an appetizer order.

Hey, baby, she says later, sitting on a barstool counting her tip money while I sweep.

I'll take you for a beer, I say.

I think I've surprised her. She stops counting with a little half smile. Okay, she says.

I take her to a beach bar with sawdust on the floor, a pool table and a popcorn machine in the corner. I buy a couple of Rolling Rocks and fill a basket with popcorn. Jolene racks the balls and chalks her cue stick. When she leans over the felt to shoot, her shirt rises up to reveal a little edge of lace panty. Everyone in the place is watching her and they can all see that she's with me.

After last call I drive her to her car, parked in the alley behind the restaurant. Haze has rolled in off the ocean. The power lines hiss. I turn on the wipers to swipe condensation from the windshield.

You ever go over there, walk around? Jolene asks. She points.

Where? I say.

The canals. Over there.

There are canals over there? I say. I lean toward the windshield. In the alley there's nothing to see but the dumpster.

That's why it's called Venice, she says. I thought you grew up here.

I did.

I'll show you sometime, she says. We sit, facing the dumpster. I can feel my heart rattling a little in my chest.

Thanks for the beer, Jolene says. She starts digging in her purse for her keys, taking her time, and then she gives me a look. In two seconds I've switched from my seat to hers, and her seatback's reclined, and my tongue is in her mouth. I reach under her shirt and slide my hand across her stomach. She wiggles her hips under me. She's gives a sexy little chuckle every time I kiss her neck.

Later, driving home, I smell her perfume on my skin, and underneath that the steam of the dishwasher.

My next shift, the owner flutters around the kitchen as the night gears up, tasting specials, making sure the busboys have their shirts tucked in. I'm getting through the first round of dishes. I slide a rack into the wash tank. I pull the hood down and lean against the rumbling machine. Jolene rushes in, catching my eye and smiling as she grabs an order. The owner wants me to play later. I hold up my thumb. It won't sound good, I say, until I grow this nail in.

You'll use a guitar pick, she says.

It doesn't work that way, I tell her.

She wants me to apply to music school. She says I'll get a scholarship. I need that GED first, but she tends to jump ahead. The other night she dragged me into the dining room to meet someone from the board of the L.A. Phil. He was a decent guy. He shook my damp hand. The owner said he needed to hear me play. She was so amped up. The guy sat there smiling. Neither of us had the heart to tell her there are no guitars in an orchestra.

I will find you a guitar pick, the owner says.

She folds her arms and watches her kitchen. Her jewelry rattles even when she's not moving. The chef sends one of the busboys into the walk-in to grab something and the busboy calls back to him in Spanish. The owner whirls toward the door of the walk-in. Maybe she worries about what we might say about her. Maybe she's investing in me because she's afraid her new country will reject her. Who knows why people do things.

I take a batch of clean glasses to the bar. A guy approaches, wearing a UCLA sweatshirt, khakis, styling crap in his hair so he looks like he just rolled out of bed. He sees that I see him but he clears his throat in a way meant to get my attention.

Jolene here? he asks.

I think to myself, *She's busy and not interested.* I jerk my head toward the kitchen and just then Jolene comes through the swinging doors. The guy perks up. Jolene looks from me to the guy and grins, cool as can be. She hoists her loaded tray above her shoulder. She motions for the guy to meet her outside. He leaves and a moment later Jolene follows, the empty tray tucked under her arm. I put the wine glasses away slowly, so I can wait for her. When she comes back she looks flushed. I corner her before she can get to the kitchen.

Your table in back wants their check, I say. Who was that guy?

Study partner, she says, without a blink. She presses past me into the kitchen. So that's how it's going to be.

The rest of the night she pretends to be too busy to talk to me. During clean-up, as I'm bringing garbage out to the dumpster, I see her heading down the alley to her car.

Hey, I say.

When she turns there's a flash of annoyance on her face that she quickly hides with a big smile. Arthur, she says.

You never gave me your number, I say. I'd like your number. So we can talk sometime.

She does a coy tilt of her head. I don't give it out, she says.

Bullshit, I say. And her smile disappears.

Arthur, she says. I like you.

But, I say. Finish your thought, Jolene.

I feel almost sorry for her as she stands there, looking helpless, a little trapped, her balled-up apron in one hand, her car keys in the other.

Clean-up runs late. It's after midnight when I drive home but the freeway is crowded; people are always heading somewhere. Downtown looms: the financial district, the garment district, Little Tokyo, Skid Row. Then Mariachi Plaza and my neighborhood. I had no idea there were canals in Venice. I know what's on the postcards: the Hollywood sign, Grauman's Chinese Theater, the Library Tower lit up purple and gold for the Lakers. There's an old pop song playing on the radio. *Desire, despair, desire,* the singer sings. I want something different. I want to want more.

After his Boyle Heights joke, the chef told me I had real talent.

That guitar, you should do something with that, he said.

I should, I said. All roads lead to Boyle Heights.

He looked at me like he'd forgotten about the joke.

Or they lead out, he said.

So maybe I don't really want things to be different. Maybe I want to be okay with what I've got so I don't have to carry a pocket full of blue pills.

At home I throw my work clothes into the hamper and go to the kitchen for a glass of milk. I'm standing barefoot at the sink in my boxer shorts when my mom comes up behind me and puts an icy hand on my shoulder. I almost hit the ceiling.

Are you sick, *mi corazoncito?* she says. I turn to face her. She grips the back of a chair, as though bracing herself to hear I have cancer. Her nightgown is buttoned to her neck.

No Ma, I say. I just wanted a checkup.

You don't eat enough. Look how skinny, she says.

Ma, I'm fine.

Her face tells me she's not buying it. I gulp down the milk.

What about you? I say, thinking of the diapers in the closet. You okay?

Don't worry about me, she says, taking the glass from me and reaching for a dish sponge. I'm your mama, she says. I'm on this earth to worry about you.

The following weekend, the night winds down and I'm going through the motions, not thinking anything in particular, when I drop a dinner plate. It bounces off the slip-proof rubber mat and smashes on the tile.

Jolene passes with a tray. A second later she's back with the broom and dust pan. *Thanks for nothing,* I think as I sweep up the broken porcelain. I'm turning to dump it into the garbage bin when there's an explosion inside me, like my heart's a grenade and someone pulled the pin. I freeze. Every inhale is a ragged gasp. A little voice says, *not here.* I manage to empty the dust pan before it falls from my hand and clatters to the floor. I look up at the bank of fluorescent bulbs, where the light wavers queasily, and I crumple to the ground by the sink.

Arthur? Jolene says.

The floor is wet and cold. I try to breathe as slowly as I can. My hands throb in the dish gloves.

Arthur, Jolene says again, louder this time. Are you okay?

I need the pills in my jacket, I say. I see Jolene's sneakers scamper away to the storage closet and then back and then my jacket lands on my feet.

What's going on? the chef calls from across the kitchen.

I think we need help, Jolene says.

I pull the gloves off, wrestle my prescription out of my jacket pocket and struggle with the child-proof cap. *Don't die,* I tell myself while I tug at it. With a scrap of clarity I think: *someone could break a fingernail on this.* Then the pharmacy bottle springs open and pills scatter everywhere.

Shit, Jolene says. She drops to her knees to pick them up. They're down in the holes of the perforated floor mat and melting on the wet tile. I salvage one and choke it down.

What the hell? the chef says. He heads around the prep table. What are you doing on the floor? he says.

Arthur's hurt, Jolene says.

Arturo, the chef corrects her. Like suddenly he's had it with being on the same page.

I feel like I'm outside myself, hovering near the greasy ceiling. I can see Jolene crouching beside me and the chef looming over us with a spatula in his fist.

Get me out of here, I whisper. Then I'm in my body again.

Are you bleeding? the chef says, but Jolene's tugging my arm and we're stumbling down the back hallway. The metal door flies open and we burst outside. The air is cool, which calms me a little. There's a full moon. The alley looks phosphorescent. I sit in the passenger seat of Jolene's car with my feet against the dashboard, my apron bunched around my waist, my head between my knees. Jolene stands beside the open car door.

I was hoping this wouldn't happen at work, I say.

It seems to be over, though there's a murmur in my veins. I'm nauseous but the medicine is slowing my pulse. My heartbeat is like a tire hitting a pothole, over and over. There's a breeze. It smells like the ocean and the garbage in the dumpster.

You okay? Jolene says. She's either concerned about me or she wants to go.

These should help, I say. I hold up the pharmacy bottle with a few wet tablets gunked together at the bottom. The rest are disintegrating on the kitchen floor. My voice sounds slow. Maybe I took two pills instead of one.

Is it nerves or something? she asks.

You could call it that, I say. I close my eyes and then open them again when the restaurant's back door opens. The owner rushes out, looking for us.

Did you cut yourself? she yells. Everyone thinks I chopped my arm off, even though there isn't a drop of evidence. When a waiter sliced his hand on a broken glass, there was a bloody trail from the bar to the bathroom.

Arthur was trembling, and then he sort of fainted, Jolene says.

The owner pokes her head into Jolene's car and looks at me. She puts her hand to my forehead. No fever, she says. It could be hypoglycemia.

She sends Jolene to the kitchen for orange juice. I don't like orange juice, but I'm worn out enough to accept it, as well as the owner's offer of a ride. Jolene makes herself scarce after delivering the juice carton and a glass to the owner, muttering something about needing to tip the busboys. So there's my answer. She wants to go. *Yeah,* I feel like telling her. *So do I.*

The owner drives a boat of a Cadillac with a pine air freshener swinging from the rear view. We hurtle east on the Santa Monica freeway and I doze against the headrest. The owner hums to herself and at one point reaches over and pats my knee. Eventually she pulls alongside the curb on my block and stops the car. My mom's house is one in a row of square stucco houses with dry patches of lawn. The windows are dark.

Drink lots of orange juice and play your guitar, the owner says. Get a good night's sleep.

I will, I say. Thanks. The owner pops the trunk so I can get my guitar case.

I walk behind the house instead of going in the front. I feel hazy and tired but I want to practice a little. The old picnic table is back here, the wood faded and split. I should sand and re-stain it. I should plant grass, or flowers. The yard is just packed down dirt with tufts of weeds. The fence is clogged with ivy. We never come out here anymore.

I try the Torroba piece I've been working on. My bad thumbnail buzzes the strings and sounds thick. It will take weeks to get that bright, clean sound again. I'm going to have to go back to that doctor to get more pills. To convince him that I didn't take them all, that I didn't sell them to my friends. Then my nail will break again. It will go on and on like that.

I grab the guitar by its neck, swing it behind me, and slam it down against the table. There's a bang and a crunching sound, and then it's quiet. What have I done? I turn the guitar over. There's a hole punched in its rosewood side. I feel like I might start crying. I put the guitar back in its case and sit with my hand on the black hard-shell. *I'm sorry,* I think. *I'm sorry, guitar.* My heart is pounding hard, but at least it's beating fast for a reason.

There's a helicopter nearby. I hear its low, mechanized hum. Tomorrow I will take the bus to pick up my car. The next day I'll put my battered guitar in the back seat and I'll leave here. Later, maybe, I'll come back.

IN THE LONG RUN: HOW THE BATTLE OF THE SEXES CHANGED PORTOLA JUNIOR HIGH SCHOOL

Kevin Hearle

T HE BATTLE OF the sexes came to Portola Junior High School in Orange, California, one day in the spring of 1973. When the bell rang for nutrition break in the middle of that morning, the entire student body poured out of the classrooms and marched across the basketball courts and football fields to the track on the far side of campus.

"What's going on?" I asked.

"They're going to race," someone told me.

"Who's going to race?" I asked.

Paul Hargrove, a sprinter and the ninth-grade varsity quarterback, and Dave Galloway, a sprinter and the eighth-grade starting tailback, were going to race a mile against a girl.

I knew about long runs. To my classmates, I was the egghead who wanted to be an athlete. Captain of the history team and backup center on both the varsity football and basketball teams, I was six feet tall and broad-shouldered—but terribly near-sighted. In many ways, I was still the kid the school psychologist had described five years before as "the most uncoordinated child I have ever tested."

But spring was track season, and I was the second-best long-distance runner in the school. Unfortunately for me, long-distance running wasn't a popular sport in Orange or in the U.S. In 1970, the New York Marathon had a budget of $1,000, and only 55 competitors crossed the finish line. In the spring of 1973, even as I was winning races and opposing coaches were working out strategies to box me up in dual meets, I knew that the third-best hurdler and the fifth-best sprinter at Portola Junior High School would get far more respect for their athletic accomplishments from our fellow students than I did.

My problem wasn't only that long-distance running was weird and unpopular. What probably most hurt my case for being considered a real athlete was that the best long-distance runner in the school was a girl. That her nickname was "Little Mary," and that the moniker was appropriate, didn't make things any easier. Mary was short even for a fourteen-year-old, and she was so leanly muscled as to seem scrawny to junior high students whose idea of a real athlete was a quarterback or halfback.

In the early 1970s, today's explosion of opportunity for female athletes wasn't visible on the horizon. Some girls played sports, but everyone knew that girls weren't athletes. Girls were cheerleaders. After any football pass that came up short, or any baseball throw that bounced before reaching its target, at least one opposing player or fan was all but guaranteed to say, "You throw like a girl."

Both sports and American society were changing, though. In 1972, Frank Shorter, an American, won the gold medal in the marathon at the Munich Olympics. That same year, the Boston Marathon—the oldest race of its kind in the United States—permitted women to compete for the first time. Until then, race officials had always denied applications from women on the grounds that no woman would be capable of running that far. Internationally, the prejudice against women lasted even longer. As late as 1980, the longest running event for women in the Moscow Olympics was 1,500 meters—the so-called "metric mile."

Not only women's liberation but also the backlash to it hit the world of sports hard in 1973. Bobby Riggs—a 55-year-old former

Wimbledon and U.S. Open champion and world number-one—began to mouth off in the press about the ridiculousness of the very idea of equality between the sexes. Women's tennis was a joke, according to Riggs, and he'd recently challenged the great women's champion Margaret Court to a match. Although he'd been coached for many of his teenage years by one of the top women tennis players in Los Angeles, Riggs played the old man-versus-woman angle for all the publicity it was worth. Later that spring—playing a game of tactical lobs and spin shots—Riggs would beat Court.

That morning at the track, though, I was still trying to figure out what this race between two boy athletes and Mary was all about. I spied Mr. Burnett, the head boys' P.E. coach, a bit ahead of me and to my left. I cut over and picked up my pace. "Why are they the ones who're going to race her?" I asked.

"Because they're the ones who challenged her," he said, and then he shook his head.

I think Coach Burnett and Miss Hawkins (the girls' P.E. coach, whom Mr. Burnett later blamed for setting up the race) might have been the only ones that morning who didn't expect the guys to win. Well, them and Mary.

That is: my classmate Mary Decker.

Actually, I had a sense that Mary was going to win, too. My junior high classmate was already competing against—and beating— adult women in international track meets. But when I discovered that the two guys were running a relay, their consecutive half-miles to her mile, I had my doubts.

The race started, and Hargrove, the ninth-grade quarterback, took off at a dead sprint. He was pulling away, and the crowd was enjoying itself as it cheered him on. His speed didn't last long, though, and after maybe half a lap Little Mary began gaining ground. The cheers turned to shouts of, "Come on, Paul. You can do it!" Then the exhortations turned to groans as Mary Decker passed Hargrove without a glance. When Hargrove finished his half-mile, Mary Decker's lead was larger than Hargrove's had been at the peak of his sprint.

The exhortations picked back up a bit when Hargrove passed the baton to Dave Galloway, the eighth-grade tailback. Galloway took off quickly, but—having seen what had happened to his predecessor—he paced himself somewhat. He gained a fair amount of ground on Decker in his first hundred yards. But, with every hundred yards he ran after that, the distance he was gaining diminished until, on her fourth and final lap, Little Mary Decker began to expand her lead.

Most of the girls were cheering for her now. Aside from a few muttered curses, most of the guys in the crowd had fallen silent. As Mary crossed the finish line to mostly muffled applause, the second sprinter—glorious representative that he was of male athletic dominance—wasn't even on the final straightaway. Most of the crowd was already heading back to the blacktop to buy a snack or get ready for their next class by the time Galloway finished the boys' relay.

The next week, across town at the final dual track meet of the season at Cerro Villa Junior High School, near the end of the three-quarter-mile race, I heard something I'd never heard before. My teammates were cheering for me. And this time it wasn't just the coach and my buddy Vince Deveney, the sarcastic shot putter, urging me on. To my amazement, as I began my kick past the last of the Cerro Villa runners just after the start of the final straightaway, it kept getting louder. The whole team was shouting.

"Come on, Hearle!"

"Go! Go! Go!"

My supporters were the same guys who six months before had tossed me out of the back of the gym without my clothes on (in full view of one whole row of classrooms), locked the door behind me, and stolen my favorite shirt out of my football locker.

I sprinted to the finish line for a victory, and, for the first time all season, my schoolmates came up en masse, clapping me on the back in congratulations. "That was great! I thought he had you beat until the last hundred, but you showed him. Way to go. Really, way to go."

I was flabbergasted. It hadn't occurred to me that Mary Decker's trouncing of the two sprinters would change how anyone thought about me. I'd never run with her or against her. We'd never had a class together, and I don't think we ever had occasion even to speak to each other. But Mary Decker had shown not only that girls could be athletes but also that long-distance runners were tougher than sprinters, and in the process she had changed the way our corner of the world saw me.

Mary Decker Slaney went on to far greater victories. A year after her race against the boy sprinters of Portola Junior High, she set her first three world records. Eventually, she would set thirty-six U.S. records, seventeen world records, and—in the same meet in 1983—win World Championships at both 1,500 meters and 3,000 meters. She is the only athlete ever to have held the American record in every competitive distance between 800 meters and 10,000 meters.

Thanks to Mary Decker, I finally learned what it felt like to have a crowd cheering me on. I never won another race. The next school year, at my new high school in Irvine, I blew out my knee early in cross-country season, came down with mononucleosis and encephalitis during track season, and decided perhaps the world didn't need me to be a great athlete. But that fall, when Billie Jean King crushed Bobby Riggs on national TV in the Astrodome, I was rooting for her all the way.

from **ELSEWHERE, CALIFORNIA**

Dana Johnson

I LOVED BASEBALL WHEN I was a child. And I do now. But more than the statistics of baseball, the endless facts, I loved the ceremony of baseball. I loved Vin Scully's reassuring voice on the radio—calm, matter-of-fact, full of possibility or resigned deference: *And the 3/2 pitch? Foul ball.* No matter what was going on, I had a place to be in baseball. Then and now, always, Vin Scully. I loved Dodger Stadium because you never met a stranger. The people in our section, wherever we sat, we were happy together when the Dodgers were winning and in steadfast denial when they were losing, but it was always okay because there would always be another game, another year. And anything was possible in baseball. In baseball, everybody was the same because we all bled Dodger blue. Who was this person giving me a high five? There was no way to tell, except we were all on the same team.

Keith, the older he got, decided that baseball was not the sport for him. Too slow. Too white. "Ain't nothing happening," he'd say, whenever I forced him to watch or listen. He was turning toward the money and flash of the Lakers. So glamorous, glittery, and Hollywood. The only Laker I ever liked was Kurt Rambis, which Keith said figured. But sometimes, still, my father would take Keith to games too, since Keith had no father and no other man to do such things with, no other man to show him how to be. My father tried.

The sun has gotten too hot, and Hank Williams has stopped singing, and so I get out of the pool for a hat and to change my music. My favorite hat to wear is a tattered Dodgers cap. Massimo hates the hat, mainly because it's tattered and because whenever I wear it, I look like a man. My face, free of dangly earrings and makeup, looks like it couldn't possibly belong to a woman, couldn't possibly be the face of the woman that Massimo is fucking. I have heavy eyebrows and a strong chin. And my lips can belong to any gender until they are covered in color. The enormous breasts of my body don't match what I am told is the masculinity of my face. A delicate and fine-featured masculinity, but still. Once, driving in the car with Massimo, I got pulled over when I ran a red light. The cop looked me squarely in the face and called me sir. Massimo looked at the officer and then at me with wide eyes, as if horrified to suddenly find himself with a black man. "Avie," Massimo says now whenever we're out and about and I'm wearing my Dodger blue. "Lipstick at least. I don't want people to think I'm a fagoni."

In the entrance of our hallway, hanging against an otherwise stark white wall, is a portrait of me and Keith. Whenever Massimo stayed the night and was made miserable by the sparseness of my apartment, the thing that made him the most miserable was this portrait. In the portrait, Keith and I are naked from the shoulders up, and we are kissing in what I have always thought to be an innocent way, both of our lips puckered and stuck way out so that our lips are barely touching. We are both wearing Dodger caps, which Keith would no doubt protest. I am looking at Keith and Keith looks out of the corner of his eye with a hint of fear, as though someone or something is about to be upon us. In my apartment, the portrait was positioned so that as I lay in bed, alone or with someone, Keith was watching. I liked that about the painting, but I was also most proud of the colors I managed to get right. I am darker than Keith with yellow undertones and a hint of gold. Keith is light skinned, with a pinkish cinnamon undertone I always used to call red. Keith was not a "black guy," painted in nondescript brown or literal black, as I had seen time and time again. He was cinnamon and saffron and I was burgundy. The Dodger caps were, of course, the true blue.

"It's creepy," Massimo said one night as we lay in bed in my apartment. He had finally eased up on his relentless charm and allowed me to see him irritated.

"Why?" I looked at the portrait and smiled. "Don't you like it?"

Massimo rubbed his belly, pulled on the coarse black hair. Then he stroked himself absently while he looked at the portrait. He was almost hard again. "I don't like looking at you kissing some guy. Some black guy," he said.

"Aww." I propped myself up on my elbows and winked at him. "Jealous. It's not some black guy," I said. "It's my cousin."

"Oh," Massimo said. "Okay. That's normal."

Now the portrait hangs in the hallway because Massimo refused to hang it in our bedroom. He finally consented to the entrance hallway after I yelled and yelled that I was bringing nothing to his house that I owned except my clothes, a few books, and my paintings, and couldn't he see that I had to try to make this place something of my own or else I would disappear?

When I pass the portrait on the way to the stereo, I lift the bottom left corner to straighten it out, and as I walk away, Keith's fearful eye follows me down the hall.

School is out in a week and we are all going to Tennessee later this summer to see our people, but for now Aunt Janice said to Mama can you and Darnelle take Keith for the rest of the summer because I am about through with him. She say Keiths daddy came around to see him, aint seen him for five years before this, and Keith is just acting a fool for no reason. Say his daddy took him out to eat and bought him some clothes but then he was gone again. Keith done stole a bike, money from Aunt Janice, and run the streets when he should be at home. His mama is through with him. She tired, she say. That boy aint but eleven. She tell Mama she work two jobs and between making pancakes at the International House of Pancakes and working at her factory, she cant keep up with him running wild. Im tired, she keep saying to Mama. Im just so damn tired.

He a smart boy and he think he slick, Aunt Janice say. Maybe Darnelle can snatch a knot in his ass, make him act like he got some sense, Aunt Janice say. She say, He running around with that white boy John getting into shit, but he aint like John with a lawyer for a daddy.

But I know that sometimes Daddy gone too but he always come back and Keith act like he dont care about anybody making him do anything. Only once did Daddy tell Keith to watch himself, and that he wasnt going to tell him again, that he didnt talk back to Daddy. Not ever. But still, Daddy has taken us to three Dodger games, the zoo, and Huntington Beach. Owen came too, except for the zoo because he said he was too old for all that. And the Dodgers. He say hes too old for them too. Plus hes got all his new friends from high school who think hes cool because hes tall and acts like he the king of everything.

Today Keith and Brenna and me cant find stuff to do. Schools been out for a week but we feel like its boring already. We walk up and down the streets of the neighborhood playing my K-tel Disco Dazzler eight-track. Its hot and the sun is so bright and none of us have sunglasses on. We just squint and hold our hands over our eyes all day. We all like that song Float On. Float float on. Float float float on. We pick the parts of all the guys who sing in the song. Everybody wants to be Larry because his voice sound the best and he gets to say the best lines. We all sing, Cancer and my name is Larry, and I like a woman that loves everything and everybody.

We already been down to the school on the swings but it got too hot, and anyway, Brenna say, What a bunch of dumbasses we are. Back at school. Keith laugh at everything Brenna say and he tries to get her to laugh at everything he say. I can tell he likes her even though she tells him stuff like, Shut the fuck up man. Or Fuck off, dude. Youre a fuckin liar. Brenna dont ever think about what she saying. But at my house she do. She dont say stuff like that around my house because Mama heard her once when we was in my room playing music. She open my bedroom door and she ask Brenna, What did you say? Mama looked at me like I said it. Mama say again, What did you say? Nothing, Brenna say after a minute and look down at the floor. We dont speak like that here, Mama say. But I wanted to say that she do, Daddy do, and Owen do. Just not me. Im the only one who would get into trouble. Thats why I like Brenna too. She gets to do and say whatever she wants. Just not at Mamas house.

We decide to go back home and be bored at my house because its too hot to keep walking around. I can see Joan watering her lawn. Her lawn is the kind of grass thats hard and tough feeling under your feet. Hey Joan, I call out, and wave real big. She wave back big, like me. When we get to her, she smiling. You kids look hot, she say. Brenna and Keith just look at her, but I say, Yes, yes, Joan. We are hot.

Brenna and Keith look at me funny.

Would you and your friends like to swim? Joan stick her thumb in the water hose to make it spread over more grass and some of the water get on us. It feel real good, even though I usually hate water.

Yeah, Keith say. I want to get in the water.

Me too, Brenna say. She pull all her red hair to the back and then hold it up, away from her neck.

This my cousin, Keith, I say, but I forgot a word. So I say it again. This is my cousin Keith and this is Brenna. I talk slow and concentrate on every word I say. Joan still smiling at us. Nice to meet you both, she say. You kids come over whenever you like. Now, even.

Thank you very much, Joan, I say.

Brenna tell us that she gone be back in five minutes. She got to go home and get her swimsuit. When we get to my house to put swimming clothes on, Keith say, Yes, yes, Joan, we are hot, and he make a face at me. You sound stupid, Keith say. All retarded.

I tell him, Thats how you speak right.

Lovely is a word she use. I never known or seen anyone who say lovely in real life. But lovely is the right word to describe Joans house. It smell new. The dark green carpet smell new. The furniture is nice colors like light brown and pink. It smell sweet like flowers every time I been over. It never smell like my house, like grease and collard greens and ham hocks and cigarette smoke. And I like her backyard. It got a picnic table and a garden with roses. Our yard got roses but they all tangled up and got a bunch of weeds and bugs in them. Because nobody has the time to pay attention to the outside of the house. Caint nobody see it nohow, Mama say. But I wish they were like Joans roses that are perfect like fake ones.

Joan left us in the yard by ourselves to make us a bite, she say. So we float in the water and just play around in the pool. She dont have the big kind, the real kind you see on TV. She got the kind thats on top of the ground and all of us can touch the bottom and still not get our heads wet. Im glad because I dont really like being in the water that much and I dont want to get my hair wet. Mama pressed it two days ago and if I get it wet its going to get hard and nappy and be hard to comb and Mama wont do nothing to it until the weekend.

Brenna wearing a bikini. I never seen her almost naked before. I seen the freckles on her arms and face and on her legs, too, but all together with just a bikini on all them freckles look strange like Brenna got polka dots all over. Im not sure what Im thinking about them polka dots. I dont think they look bad. But they dont look good, neither.

After a while, Keith say, Lets play something, yall. Lets close our eyes to find each other in the pool. If you touch somebody, see if you can guess who it is without opening your eyes.

I look at Brenna to see what she says. I dont want to be in the water with my eyes closed and feel like Im drowning. I say, I dont want to play that. Keith say, What about Brenna though. She want to play maybe.

I dont even care, Brenna say. She lean back and float across to the other end of the pool. Her hair float out around her like orange ribbons, and I wish I could do that, just lay my head back and float and not worry about my hair turning hard and nappy.

Awright, then, Keith say. Everybody close your eyes.

After he say that I watch Brenna close her eyes. But me and Keith, we dont close our eyes. He moving over to where Brenna is floating and he move quiet and slow with his hands like claws and high in the air like he playing boogie man. When he get to Brenna, he stand over her and wait, and then he put his hands under the water like he helping her to float. Brenna smile and open one eye. They cant see that Joan is standing behind them looking through her sliding door. I wave at Joan and smile but she dont smile back. Thats when Keith put both hands on Brennas titties. Boo, he say. Youre a dumbass, Brenna say, but she laughing. Thats when Joan open the door. She look at Keith for a long time. Kids, she say, and her voice sound different than usual. Like she worried. Come out of the pool, kids. Have some lunch, she say. Ill bring it out to you.

When she bring out the lunch, we dont know what all it is. I know a tuna sandwich and the little bowls of tomato soup, but she also got three little plates with something on them that look like little hard green plants. She give all of us one with our sandwich and soup and put a bowl of yellow cream or something in the middle of the table. We just stare at everything and look at each other.

I know, Joan says. All kids hate vegetables. But I thought you might like to try. These are going to go bad if I dont get rid of them. Eat, kids, Joan say, and sit with us at the little picnic table and drink her coffee.

Im thinking and thinking. How you eat this?

I aint eating that green thing, Keith say.

Joan put her coffee down on the table. Thats an artichoke. Youve not had an artichoke?

Keith shake his head and make a face like something stink. Joan say, Avery?

No, Joan, I say quiet. I have not had an artichoke.

Joans face get red. She looks at Brenna. Well, she say, I know Brenna has. She can tell you. Its good, isnt it?

Brenna make the same face Keith make. No way, she say. We have normal food at my house. Good food, she say. Out of a can. Like Spaghetti Os.

But I pick up my artichoke because Joan look like she feel bad. I bite into it. Avery! Joan shout, and I drop it back on the plate. Spit the rest out.

Kids, Joan say and she frown, but she laughs too. For heavens sake. You pull out a leaf and then you dip it in this butter. Here. Look. She pull one off, dip it in the sauce, and eat a little bit off the bottom. She dont eat the rest of the green part. Mama and Daddy yell at me if I dont eat all the food on my plate like that. Try it, Avery, Joan say. I do what she tell me and its not nasty but it dont taste like food. It taste like you have to eat a hundred artichokes to be full and it still only taste like the sauce anyway. Like butter. I'm not going to ever eat another artichoke if I can help it. I decide I do not like them. I say, Its really good Joan. I like it. Thank you very much.

Keith and Brenna laugh and then Joan face turn pink. She laughing too. Honest to goodness, she say. Eat your soup and salad then. You dont have to eat this if youd rather not. Youre right, arent you? Of course you wouldnt like this. Then she snatch up the artichokes and walk into the house.

You a lie, Keith say. You know it takes like dookie. I like it very much, he say, trying to sound like me. Yeah, Brenna say. Kiss her big ass, why dont you. And I dont know why they getting mad at me. I didnt do nothing. They the ones being rude to Joan. Shut up you guys, I tell them.

Avery eat anything anyway, Keith say. Porky Pig.

Brenna laugh at Keith again. He been trying all day and now he made her laugh twice. I sit and stare at my sandwich. They make me feel bad about eating it. I put it down. Brenna eat her sandwich with a big smile on her face and Keith eat his sandwich, just staring at her like he want to eat her up. Im the only one not eating and I get so mad. Both of you assholes can eat shit and die, I say. Nappy-headed nigger. Polka-dotted honkey.

Avery! Joan say. Shes standing at her door again and the way she look at me make me feel like I want to die. She look at me like Im ugly. She say, You talk like that? Brenna and Keith put their faces down in their soup. Joan look at all of us like she dont like anything she see. I think you kids better leave, she say after awhile.

I tell Joan Im sorry and she say its okay but I can tell that its not really okay. We all walk through her house and Im looking at all her matching furniture and all I can think about is please Joan dont tell Mama and Daddy because they will be so mad. Mama will beat me for sure and Daddy will look at me for a long time like he figuring out a punishment but then he wont punish me because he never does. He will just probably say, Avery. You know. You know better than that. We taught you better. But when he say the we, it don't sound like he just talking about him and Mama. It sound like theres a whole bunch a people somewhere that I have never even met and they watching me. They disappointed in me because they all taught me better than what Im doing.

• • •

Owen hates school but he likes West Covina all right. He always say that he glad he only had to do one more year of high school when we moved because he wants to go out and make some dollars. School cant do nothing for him, he say. Daddy aint happy that Owen aint going to college. *Isnt* going to college. Daddy say he and Mama work like dogs cause thats the choice they had. Work like a dog and lie down and die. Daddy say Owen and me got more choices than being dogs and dying, but Owen head hard, Daddy say.

But Daddy let Owen have a graduation party at the house, make Owen pay for it with his own money he saved from his job at the market down by the high school. Im glad about the party because I get to spend the night at Brennas house so I can be out of the way. Mama have rules about me going over there, though. Dont go over there being loud and tearing up anything, Mama says. Eat what they put on your plate but dont be eatin up all they food. Clean up after yourself and do everything that Brennas mama tell you to do. She and Daddys main rules for Owen is they dont want people tearing up they house but even Owen isnt that crazy that hes going to let somebody do that. Even if he eighteen and taller than Daddy, he would get whupped for sure. There are going to be people from L.A. that we have not seen in so long. Owens old friends from L.A. High coming too.

But Id rather be at Brennas, just down the street from my house. We got the same house, too, shaped like a barn, but it doesnt feel anything like my house. Brennas mama and daddy look young, not like my mama and daddy. Brennas mama look like a sister, same size and everything. Same freckles. She always got a cigarette in her mouth and she let Brenna light them for her sometimes. She says, Do me a solid, kiddo, and hand Brenna a cigarette, that Brenna light up on the stove or with matches. Then she take a puff and pass it to her mama. She dont even care.

Now she got a cigarette hanging in her mouth while she open a can of beans. She let Brenna and me make hamburger patties that Brennas daddys cooking outside.

Like this Ma? Brenna hold up one.

Too small, kid, Colleen say. She hate being called Mrs Kiersted. I called her that when I first got here. She say, I dont care what else you call me, kid, but Mrs Kiersted sound like a fucking old lady, dont you think? I said, Yes maam, and she looked over at Brenna and told her, Maam. Manners, kid. Those are manners. And she bumped me on the hips with her butt and smiled at me.

I hold my hamburger up. What about this one? Perfect, Colleen say. Beautiful Ave.

When we done we sit in the backyard and watch Brennas daddy grill our hamburgers. He plays the radio loud and sings to it. He looks like a high school guy to me, like Brennas brother Tate. His hair is blonde and long down his back. He looks like a surfer. He always wear a baseball cap. Angels. Wear his pants low like they falling off. I stare and stare at him because he kind of look like a rock star to me. Like Robert Plant who is a stone fox. He dont ever see me staring because he hardly pays attention to us when were around. He hardly ever home because he drive a truck all the time. He open up another beer, turn over our hamburgers, and sing about how your cheating heart is going to tell on you. He point to them with his big fork. You girls ready to eat? Got you some killer burgers over here. Tell your mom, he say to Brenna. Its ready. And then he wink at me, and it make me feel like he and me got a secret.

Sometimes the way Mama and Daddy talk about white people make me think all white people be practically the same, but here its not like at Joans house where she set the table and put everything out nice. At Joans house she take things out of the boxes and plastic they come in and then she put it on another plate so it look good on the table. Here its more like my house. Brenna and me get our paper plates and then just get us some beans out the pot. We get everything ourselves and go to Brennas room.

In Brennas room, we can do whatever we want. It looks like Brenna spill trash all over the place. Shoes on the floor. Bowls with dried up Cheerios on her desk. Clothes on the floor and not hanging in the closet. Papers and books inside the closet, on the floor in the closet, and not on her desk. I think its a good thing that my mama is not Brennas mama. Brenna can have John Travolta and Lorenzo Lamas posters everywhere. Daddy wont let me put up nothing, wont let me put up anything, because he says it mess up the walls, but what if I could stare at Lorenzo Lamas all day? How sweet man. But the last time I had tried, Daddy made me take Lorenzo down. Daddy passed my door, saw Leif Garrett and Lorenzo and Shaun Cassidy. Avery, he say, Who in the hell are all these white boys? Get that shit down off those walls right now, Daddy say. So I did.

Brenna turns on her radio and Disco Inferno is on. This song sucks, she says. But I like it. I like to dance to it in my room like Im on Soul Train. Ugh, Brenna say. She say, Rock and roll is here to stay, throw that disco shit away. She turn the station. You light up my life, Debbie Boone sing. Brenna can sing the whole song in pig latin but now she says, This song makes me want to barf. She needs a stiffy for reals. When Queen comes on, Brenna is happy. We are the champions, my friend! she scream and hug me so tight she make me drop my hamburger on the carpet. I pick it up and its got stuff on it now, look like lint. Look what you did, Brenna. She say, God made dirt and dirt dont hurt. Kiss it up to God, she say, hold her burger up after she kiss it. I cant eat mine, though. I just cant and I can hear Mama. You did what? Ate a hamburger off the *floor?* Now you know you know better.

We should be at your house, she say. Tates there. We could be spying on some babes right now.

Like who?

Brenna shrug and put her burger down and leave it lying there. She never finishes her food. I want it, but I dont want to ask for it. I dont know, she says. Maybe theres a guy who looks like Leif Garrett.

Owen never ever went to school with anybody who looked like Leif Garrett, but I dont tell Brenna that.

We stay up late because nobody tells us we have to go to bed. Nobody tells us anything. We hear Tate talking, so we come out and pretend to get some soda.

How was it, Colleen say. She on the couch in the living room, watching TV and drinking a beer. Youre home early, kid, she say.

Tate take the beer from Colleen and drink some. Some asshole called the cops, he say. Brenna and me look at each other and Colleen frown. Why? What happened? Tate rub his eyes. Theyre red because hes a stoner. Thats what Brenna say. Tate take off his Vans and pull his T-shirt over his head. I try not to look at his back, but it looks soft and I wish I could touch him. Dont even ask me, he tells Colleen. I dont know why. They said we were too loud but we werent. It was kind of lame, he said. Owen kept telling people not to mess stuff up and not party too hard. And there were a lot of brothers there, too. Like a lot of black dudes. Colleen look at me and say Tate! Goddamn it. Watch it. Sorry, Tate say to me, and go to his room. He didn't mean anything by that Avery, she say. That kids got a big mouth. But Im not even sure what he said that was bad. If there were a lot of black people there, then thats the truth, isnt it?

When Im home the next day I ask Owen what happened, and he say that the cops say that his party was disturbing the peace. Yeah, Owen say. He was taking down trash to the curb. Member that, Aye, he say laughing. Too many niggas always disturb the peace. But I dont know why hes laughing. Thats not funny to me.

• • •

Mama and Daddy have a party too. Well, not a real party. Just people that used to live in our building in L.A. Four people. Mr Channey and his wife Bonnie, her brother named Dash and their daughter Cassandra. But its not the same like when we lived on 80th Street and we used to just walk into each others apartments like normal. Like first, they walk into the house all quiet and keep saying, Dang Darnelle! Dang Vicky! This nice! Miss Bonnie look down at the floor when she first come in the house. This floor wet? It look like its wet. We supposed to be walking on this floor like this?

Mama say, Bonnie, girl, now you know this floor aint wet. Its just shiny. Got two coats of that Mop n Glo on it.

Sheeiit, Mr Channey say when he standing in the kitchen. He go to the sliding glass door and look out at the yard. This real nice.

We gone get some more furniture in here when we can, Daddy say.

Cassandra stand by her mama like she shy of me. Hey, I say. Hey Cassandra.

Hi, she say, but thats all she say.

Come on, I say. Come to my room and look at my magazines.

Go head on, her mama say. Stop hanging all on me. Miss Bonnie push her away and run her hands over her bun like she checking if a hair out of place. She still pretty. Light brown hair like Cassandras. I see how her fingernails match her lipstick. Bright red like orange. So Cassandra come to my room. We sit on the floor and I show her Robbie Benson and Leif Garrett pictures, but she dont like them. She say, They ugly. I say, What else you want to do then? Nothing, she say. She get off the floor and then sit on my bed. She sit perfect and straighten out her yellow dress.

Lets go outside and run around then, I say. Come on. Lets go. I grab her hand. We can run around in my yard. Its big.

I cant, Cassandra say. She smooth her hair just like her mama. I cant get dirty.

Why is she being so boring? I dont know what else to do so I just tell her, Im going back out to the kitchen.

But everybodys outside sitting on the patio, they not in the house anymore. I get a chair and pull it over to Cassandras mama. Come on over here, Miss Cassandra, Mama say. Sit next to me. And Cassandra does. She sit and kick her legs back and forth, and I stare at the shiny dress shoes she wearing. Cute, Mama says. Aint you looking cute? She looks alright to me. Not all that cute.

The grown folks are drinking and Mr Channey and Dash keep getting louder and louder. Dash got on a lot a jewelry. Lots of chains and a shiny red dress shirt. Its not orange red, though. Its red, red. He keep cussing real loud and Daddy say, Dash we got to keep it down out here, they real particular bout noise around here.

Oh, alright. Thats why you got Aretha playing so low we caint even hear her. Man, Dash say real loud. Fuck these white folks, and Mama look at Daddy and Mr Channey look at Miss Bonnie, like you better tell him something. Plus, Aretha is not playing low if you ask me. She loud. She sound mad. Some people want! she holler. But they dont want to give!

Dash, she say. Come on now. You done had enough I think.

And Ima have some more! he say. Why yall leave the bottle inside? He gets up and almost fall. He walk to the sliding glass door but when he get to it he dont stop. He walk right into it. Goddamn! he say. I thought this shit was open. Thought I was just gone walk through it. He rub his forehead and then Daddy standing right next to him. I didnt even see Daddy get up, but he there.

You all right man? Daddy put his face close to Dash face. Look like you already getting a knot above your eye.

What you a doctor now nigga? You gone diagnose some shit?

All right, now. All right, Mr Channey say. He get up too.

Yall leave me alone. Im cool, Dash say. Ima get me another drink, though. I know that much. He pull on the door but its locked.

Let me show you, Daddy say. You got to switch this latch thing right here.

I know, man. I know, Dash say. You think I dont know how to open a door negro? But he try it and it dont work for him. He keep trying but that door stay closed.

Here, Daddy say. He flip the lock real quick and slide the door open. Dash walk in but Mr Channey right behind him telling him he aint getting no more to drink and right after that, everybody else get up and they leaving.

Im glad, though. Dash scary. He make too much noise. And Cassandra is boring anyhow.

Mama says, Well. Dash crazy but I wish they could have stayed longer than what they did.

Maybe Jonathan and Bonnie could have stayed, Daddy say. He pour himself some more J&B. He take a sip. But, uh uh. Daddy shake his head. Dash need to stay his ass on 80th Street.

DAIRE NUA: THE NEW OAK GROVE

Elizabeth C. Creely

THERE IS A kind of acquired memory that gets formed from family artifacts—objects acquired accidentally or gained by inheritance—and from the small stories they contain. Things like a picture of a woman with a ridiculous hat. A gold ring that could never fit on any present-day finger, with an inscription attesting to eternal love. A rusty horse bridle with a large silver "C" engraved on it that hung in my grandfather's garage for years. (It now hangs on a wall in my apartment.) Most family artifacts come with a story, or with the hint of a story: I've always looked at the bridle and wondered what the name of the horse was that it was used to control.

These stories can feel like memory, embodied, experienced. They can feel like something you lived. False memory may shape you, just as surely as the geography of the place you live in shapes you.

But only if there is a story. What if there isn't one?

Stories can be hard to come by if one country was left for another because of disaster: war, for example, or in the case of my family, famine. If no one had stories of "home" to tell, or brought anything with them—and who had that luxury, amidst the stress and panic of something not quite deportation, but, well, very like deportation? If the people who left Ireland lived through a fear so intense that the conscious mind was ordered to face forward, it's likely that their living story was set aside and left behind, as something wholly unsuitable for the future. Why bring disaster with you?

In that sad and common case, the descendants of the emigrant will usually follow the example set for them: to never look back and never make any inquiry of what life was like, back then in those catastrophic and eventful times. They gathered their families together and ran.

This is the unspoken rule of the immigrant: don't look back while walking in uncertain terrain. And, while moving forward, don't engage in unreality. The immigrant Civil War soldier in the nineteenth-century song may wish he were in "dear old Dublin." But he knows that Dublin could not provide for him, could not accommodate his existence. He had to leave. What he remembers and longs for is not real.

I know much more about the Creelys than anyone else in my family, although I don't know much. I have casually researched the family name in Ireland (more than the actual family), using the usual lunch-hour search on Ancestry.com, an astonishingly easy and pleasingly quick method. Cobbled together from the research a cousin undertook twenty years ago, these researches have resulted in an incomplete profile of a family set in motion from Armagh to San Francisco by the combined forces of colonialism, disaster, and personal ambition.

But that's it: just big picture, impersonal stuff. Statistics, instead of story. No documentation. No letters, no photos. Just impenetrable silence, so typical of refugees. My great-great-great-grandfather, Patrick Creely, arrived in San Francisco in 1851, near the height of famine-induced immigration in America. To be something other than a man in flight would make him a statistical anomaly. If he had been that rare Irish Catholic who came to America in the mid-eighteenth century, untroubled and confident, I don't believe he would have kept his mouth shut so tightly.

Patrick did not talk. He passed on his silence intact and it became the inheritance. I imagine when he lived, one would have needed a crowbar to pry open his mouth...and even then, what might have emerged would have been a shadow, a void in which the enlightening words swirled around like dry leaves.

The Creelys became "real," traceable through a paper trail of wills, death notices, directory advertisements, in California starting in 1875. Their residences and businesses—a blacksmith shop on Folsom Street, a house on Shotwell—are listed in San Francisco city directories. There is a picture of Edward Creely's veterinary hospital in San Francisco at Golden Gate and Polk streets, intact just two months after the 1906 earthquake. There are pictures of family members confidently riding horses, at ease in a landscape that did not threaten them with scarcity. All real.

We choose from these stories carefully. Some have been edited out of the family telling as too indicative of family failings: alcohol abuse, cars crashing into gas stations, the horse in Healdsburg, California, that broke my grandfather's hip, laming him for life. His brother James slapped its flank and startled it.

(Was the horse wearing the elaborate silver bridle? Is that why my grandfather saved it?)

My own memories were acquired under the influence of California: its coastal hills, fragile riparian environments, tidal zones, the foundation of granite that shifts and moves and is visible as the magnificent Sierra batholith. The Creelys have variously abused and admired, bought cheaply and sold dear, the land of California. Early on, we associated in halls and in churches, but at some point we left these institutions behind and ventured outside into "nature": the backyard, the large field across the street, the nearby Santa Ana Mountains. We met there. Habit, rather than memory, was the medium through which old ideas, old words, and old images flowed, the mute conveyer of custom. We lived at ease and in relative confidence—free, we believed, from famine and the indifference of a colonial government, free from the predations of nature.

I grew up walking in the great green but, even then, rapidly vanishing wild areas of Newport Beach, and Costa Mesa, both smallish towns in Southern California at the time. My dad, Christopher

Creely, loved trees, rocks, and anything that was made by the combined forces of chlorophyll, geologic time, and weather. He walked his children everywhere, and while it was ostensibly for our health, I think his love of walking was also an atavistic urge descending on him, asking him to conduct a survey of the land he lived in.

Consider what is real, Christopher, something urged him. Look at the earth. Look at the sky. These things are real and constant. They don't change. Stay with the project: keep making discoveries about this place called California. Learn it by heart. (Did his great-great-grandfather Patrick Creely look at the coastal hills, and compare them with the drumlins of northeastern Ireland? When he looked at the San Francisco Bay, or the wetlands of the California Delta, what did he see? What did he compare these vast bodies of water to? How long did he rely on comparison in order to understand where he was?)

Christopher Creely and his five children walked on terrain that was under constant threat from real estate developers, who were displacing California's native flora and fauna—the gnatcatcher, mountain lion, condor, and other species too numerous to list—and replacing them with houses that sprang up on the freshly graded hills. The water that was requisitioned from California's rivers brought artificially bright lawns and non-native species to Southern California, with ecologically disastrous results—castor bean, pampas grass, ice plant, and hundreds more invasive species gone wild.

The first landscape I remember my dad taking me to, when I was four and he was about forty-two, was Upper Newport Bay or the "Back Bay," so called because of its location due east of the Newport Beach coastline. It's a tidal estuary, odiferous and a bit slovenly, full of rich black mudflats. It smelled hellish. Like many estuarine environments in Southern California, it was situated near an expensive housing development, built to take full advantage of the ocean view to the west, all the while polluting the watery mud at its feet with gray water runoff. Nitrogenous pollution from the nearby Irvine Ranch covered the waters of the estuary with a mat of bright green algae.

There were fish that swam in the estuary, mythological creatures who couldn't be seen, but whose presence I felt as a swarming energy. If I got too close to the mudflats and the water, my dad would grab me back, guarding me from the things in the murky bay: small sharks and stingrays. The place was uncanny and impossibly green. It surged with the full force of life. It was not benevolent and not malicious, but was solely concerned with its perpetuation: endangered and dangerous in equal measure.

(Years later, I would dream of stepping carefully across stepping-stones that paved a wide waterway filled with murky water: it was oil slicked and iridescent. The shapes of unfamiliar fish swam below its surface. *Come away, O human child, To the water,* the wild shapes called to me. In my dream, I ran from them.)

In the estuary I sensed, rather than saw, the churning intertidal system pursuing its own ends; in with the new and out with the old. The bay shivered and swayed in response to the pull of the ocean. I was a mote in its wild eye.

Once the grasping mud stole my shoe, my precious shoe. In spite of my best efforts, I stepped carelessly, and was suddenly treading slime, terrifyingly liquid, with nothing solid underfoot. I fell and continued to fall. Dad stepped over to me and with a great yank got me to my feet and onto dry ground. His foot accidentally stepped on my hand, which was buried in the muck. I watched the mud collect around my shoe, holding it for a moment as if it were inspecting a curious artifact. Clear water bubbled up around the shoe, which was framed in black. Then it sank slowly and disappeared.

I began to cry. I told dad that I understood that he had stepped on my hand as punishment for losing my shoe (I knew that shoes cost money). He had green eyes that intensified when the sun hit them or when he was moved by emotion. At that moment, they glowed at me like twin suns. "I would never step on your hand!" he said. "Jesus, what gave you that idea?" He picked me up and carried me away.

Later—clean, but still agonized over the theft of my shoe—I felt anger. Something had been taken from me, easily; candy from a baby. The Back Bay was capricious and unaccountable.

"Where is my shoe?" I asked dad that night at dinner.

"Gone," he said. "The bog got it."

"What's a bog?" I asked.

"It's a place like the Back Bay," he answered.

There were no bogs in Southern California. It would have been more accurate for him to simply call it the "Back Bay." Or he might have taken a pedagogical approach by introducing me to the term "coastal estuary." But, characteristically, he chose the imagination of romanticism over the precision of technical terms.

Sometimes, even a single word can open a window on the submerged past. While I was sniffing the air and picking up shells, my father's inherited mind and vision was engaged in a survey of the estuary, taking an unconscious inventory—mud, water, the stench of decay, the silent vigor of birds as they fed, the treacherous ground underfoot that had tried to snatch his child away—and matching the seen and unseen with something he'd heard about, but had never seen. He used the word "bog" ritualistically, knowing, at a level below conscious recall, that—but for great-great-grandfather's emigration—he would have yanked me out of the Irish mud in Armagh, where sphagnum bogs do, in fact, exist. In a place where there were no bogs, the word made one and forged reciprocity between the immigrant and the assimilated.

"Quagmire, swampland, morass: the slime kingdoms"—the words of Seamus Heaney, in a poem titled "Kinship," describe a layered landscape sunk under the acidic waters of a bog. The bog preserved artifacts from ancient Ireland: a skeleton of a huge elk and the remnants of fir tees, submerged thousands of years ago when Ireland's climax forests held great tracts of deciduous and coniferous trees that grew and grew and grew.

Our estuary was a time capsule, too, and it held ages in its grasp. The bog had got my shoe and would preserve it. The canvass would rot, but the rubber sole might not. Someone, thousands of years in the future, might lift the shoe from the depths of the slime and note its size and question my fate. Did the child survive?

Another landscape with my dad, almost forty years later. After he died of a heart attack (congestive heart failure is a direct genetic inheritance for all Creely men), I decided to scatter his ashes. I was living in San Francisco's Mission District—a stone's throw from my great-great-grandfather's house.

In the credulous culture of the New Age, as I've experienced it in Northern California, Irish and Celtic histories tend to get confused with each other, which has created some enduring myths about the Irish and what they worshipped and how. This cultural mash-up has always annoyed me—do people really believe the Irish consulted a tree zodiac?—but the eclecticism of the New Age ritual community can be hard to resist: I was persuaded, in spite of my preference for historical specificity, to lay down my defenses and find an oak grove in which to scatter my father's ashes. My dad, a bookseller by trade and temperament, was a quiet man who liked to escape the urgency of the twentieth century by reading widely, including (and especially) early Irish and Continental Celtic history and myth. Commemorating him both as an Irish American and latter-day Celt made sense.

My best friend Elyse thought she might know a place; she had spent her childhood exploring the Oakland Hills. We entered a trailhead one June afternoon with the late afternoon sun setting behind our backs. After twenty minutes of walking in Tilden Park, she directed my attention to the faint outline of a deer track, which ran up the side of a hill. We followed it into a small grove. A granite boulder sat in the dead center of a clearing. Over the boulder leaned an old Coast Live Oak. A group of graceful Bay Laurel trees lined the rear of the clearing. I inexpertly recited the chant of Aimhirghin, the oldest known Irish poem, for my father, a man who loved the great green world, and who was now in it and of it, peacefully.

For thousands of years, the stretch of coastal woodland in which I stood reciting Aimhirgin's words of perpetual becoming had been thick with native trees like Valley Oak, Redwood, and Bay Laurels. Under the pressure of urban development and natural disasters like the 1906 earthquake and fire, coastal woodlands were felled and used to build and rebuild San Francisco and other cities. A fatuous bar in San Francisco called the Redwood Room is an arboreal time capsule: the walls are paneled with old growth Redwood. California's trees tend to be entombed in buildings instead of bogs.

What remains of California's climax forests is a landscape punctuated by solitary trees. The iconic California oak tree—the city symbol of Oakland and subject of so many artistic renderings of the Golden State—sitting alone on top of a hill is a mark of tragedy. There should be many oaks instead of the lonely survivors so lovely, so desolate in their majestic singularity.

Singularity may yet be the fate of the California oak. In 1995, scientists at the University of Santa Cruz observed that large numbers of California oak trees were dying, quite suddenly. Closer investigation revealed the agent to be an unknown type of *Phytophthora*. Finding out that a *Phytophthora* pathogen was running amuck in California's coastal ecosystem didn't, as far as I know, cause a ripple of unease to spread throughout the Irish-American community of Northern California. But it frightened me. When I read the word

Phytophthora in the paper, I shuddered, having made an inherited gesture of comparison.

I knew what the implications of an active *Phytophthora* blight were. I had taken classes in Irish history. I recalled my teacher, the late Daniel Cassidy, using clinically accurate terms in the classroom when speaking of the blight that ruined the potato crop. *"Phytophthora infestans,"* he would intone in his New York honk, "was the name of the fungus, which only destroyed potatoes. The famine was man-made." The wild microbial world in which the Creelys—in our latter-day incarnation as Californians—had spent heedless hours walking and hiking in, had in the past been turned against us. *Phytophthora*'s fungal power was unstoppable, unappeasable: it played by its own rules. *Phytophthora* could exert its power to radically reshape cultures, communities, history itself. It had done so before, to my family and to millions of others.

I scoured the local papers for any news of the oak tree blight. I felt no surprise, only resignation (and real fear) when I read that scientists at Berkeley thought that the oak killer might actually be *Phytophthora infestans,* the ancient nemesis of the Irish. Was the killer mold that had destroyed the potato crops now bent on destroying California's oak trees? Was it stalking my family, taunting us with its invincibility? The oak tree has been a keystone species in every landscape my family has ever inhabited. The first occurrence of the patronymic "Creely" is found in County Derry, *Chontae Doire,* which is named after the great oak groves of Ireland. It all fit together.

It is now known that the oak killer is a cousin to the potato killer, a newer strain called *Phytophthora ramorum.* It is on the loose in California's coastal woodlands because of the preference of the commercial plant industry for nonnative species. It is rapidly killing the California oak. As of this writing, there is no known cure and no solution.

In the late eighteenth century, an anonymous Gaelic poet looked at the denuded woodlands near Slieve na mBan, in Tipperary, and asked, plaintively, *Now what will we do for timber / with the last of the woods laid low?*

The oak tree that bends over the granite rock in the center of my dad's grove is still there. But for how long?

The interconnected nature of the forest is a tool, expertly wielded by the pathogen, which depends on the trees' proximity to one another. A raindrop crashing down on the leaf of a laurel tree will run down the trunk and into the soil. The pathogen swims in the tiny waterways of the sodden soil, making its way to a nearby oak. A cankerous spot appears on the trunk and the tree weeps precious sap. The oak tree dies within one to two months. No respite, no bargaining: just quiet death by water mold: sudden, silent and remorseless. And then a great transformation will change California. Instead of an oak tree bending over a stony boulder, there will be some poor substitute and only incoherent recollections of what used to grow there.

If the oak trees die, will anyone know why? Or will we instead put that story down and consign the trees we knew and loved to the inflexible and terrible category of the past?

In the future, when I tell stories of the California that I lived in, and that I sometimes call, privately and inaccurately, Daire Nua, the New Oak Grove, will anyone think to ask me this question: Why didn't the trees survive?

LOSING DON PÍO'S PLACE

Michael Jaime-Becerra

THE ONE-TIME HOME of Pío de Jesus Pico IV, last governor of California during Mexican rule, is wedged between the 605 Freeway and train tracks, and crisscrossed overhead by jets closing in on Long Beach and Los Angeles International airports. Since 1927, it's been the site of Pío Pico State Historic Park. It had been one of 70 parks scheduled to close on July 1 because of cuts in state funding, but a major donation by the city of Whittier, along with the support of private donations, raised $40,000 to keep it open until the end of the year. It will take another $40,000 to keep it open until July 2013.

I've been by the park hundreds of times. Several years ago, I had the windows on my Honda tinted at the shop across the street (I felt mildly vindicated to see that the shop now displays an "Under New Management" sign—but that's another story). In high school we'd pass by the park's ivy-covered walls on our way to a liquor store that sold beer without asking our age. I knew some of Pío Pico's history, probably thanks to Huell Howser, patron saint of the modest California landmark, but the walls of the park had always presented themselves with the uninteresting and infrastructural familiarity of power lines, and I always drove past.

I visited on a recent Sunday and first discovered that the ivy isn't ivy at all. The park walls are topped with grapevines, and they give the place an air of serenity befitting a monastery or the sort of prison where crooked stockbrokers get sent. Even with the nonstop commotion of car traffic from Whittier Boulevard to the north and the freeway's faint din, I had the sense of being shut away from the larger world.

The park's north end is enclosed by a stand of tall, broad-leafed oak trees. I took a seat at one of the picnic tables to regard El Ranchito, the vaguely Western, single-story structure that Don Pío called home. It's made of adobe bricks and is coated in cracking white plaster. Surrounding it is a five-acre expanse of lawn and gardens dotted with young orange trees. There are more grapevines being cultivated on the west end of the property. It was easy to envision families from all over the San Gabriel Valley enjoying a weekend afternoon here, as El Ranchito is a picturesque sight. But when I started toward the house, the oranges revealed themselves to be undernourished, and I noticed that a third of the trees were dead, their branches withered to tinder. The grass underfoot was green, but it crunched as I walked.

The exhibits inside El Ranchito pieced together a trite, disappointing impression of life in Don Pío's time: bedside ephemera, shards of an old bowl, a sturdy plow once used to plant corn. There was an instructional diagram on adobe and small wooden blocks meant to be a hands-on demonstration of how El Ranchito was built. In the parlor, I passed a piano to enter another room with a dinner scene. One door opened to a screening room with crooked rows of folding chairs and a wall-sized screen displaying menu options from an unmanned video station. A messy stack of instructional DVDs lay atop it. A remote control had also been left out, but there weren't any instructions on how to use it.

Don Pío was a complicated figure, a proud Mexican whose walking stick bore the Spanish king's seal, a Californio whose indigenous and African and Italian bloodlines formed a complex family tree. Even after the Mexican-American War, he remained one of the richest men in California. Known for his grandiose hospitality, he built the most lavish hotel in Los Angeles. Eventually, though, he lost hundreds of thousands of acres of land by signing a contract that he was unable to read. In the end, irreversibly leveraged by a lifetime of extravagance and a weakness for gambling, Don Pío was evicted from El Ranchito at the age of 91 with whatever could be piled onto a horse-drawn buggy.

There was one smaller display attempting to present several facets of Don Pío's life. Composed of multi-sided panels, it seemed to be the most honest object in El Ranchito. The leftmost panel disdained him for seeming like a mule, while the rightmost one suggested that he should be a role model of perseverance and bravery. But the wheel to reveal the other panels was broken. And because the displays and literature in El Ranchito aren't forthcoming or direct about the details of Don Pío's life and the prickly implications behind them, I exited feeling insulted. I left feeling lied to.

The most peaceful place in the park is at the rear, near the train tracks, where a shaded picnic table overlooks a glen. Sitting there, it was easy to imagine Don Pío entertaining early Angeleno society in the Victorian-era clothing he favored. While the city of Whittier and the park's supporters have rallied to save Pío Pico State Park, it would be a shame to let the rest of the orange trees die this coming December, to let the grapevines dry out and wither. But in six months I will still be part of a society that routinely votes down initiatives that would keep parks like this open without the need for last-minute heroics, a society that instead encourages me to rent rims for my car and to try the new Taco Bell taco because the shell is made of Doritos. I will still be part of a society that doesn't read the fine print and instead prefers to think that the multitude of vacant storefronts and foreclosures around us is someone else's fault.

Don Pío's story ended tragically because of deep, human flaws: Indulgence. Pride. Greed. (And that's before we get to his desire to control the region's water rights.) But we don't really like that sort of story when it hits so close to home. Perhaps that's why people drive by Pío Pico's park without stopping in to visit—and why I was there alone on a sunny Sunday afternoon.

PALM SPRINGS

Mark Cox

IMPLODING CASKET OF leisure and skin cancer,
Bobsled of vanity, autopsy table
Of the dead marriage and midlife crisis—
Could the sun-gods tracked by shadow and angle
Across temple courtyards,

Could they have imagined the tanning bed,
Or how, here, in the endless operatic
Hospice piano lounge of our world,
We worship selves we want, but cannot be—
Intravenous drips of bile and self-pity—

Until the transplant ice chest opens
And the bartender scoops out the viscera,
Offering it once more, in the name of love,
To the body. Can someone explain to me why,
Once we have lain down in our self-made beds,

We choose to get up?
Why, having been divorced and jettisoned,
We insist on being useful again—
Each flagellant helping his neighbor,
Bringing, as it were, his expertise to bear—

Until each visitor is escorted, sedated,
From the asylum ward, committed again
To line dances and speed dating?
Fountains of perpetual joy and anguish,
We are but skin poured forth,

Caressed, and poured again.
The magician, whose wife has sawed
All he owned in half;
The physician whose husband has his ear
To the heart of the babysitter;

The field commander calling in the coordinates
Of his own suburban home;
The hanged suicide denied the kiss
Of his bludgeoned wife;
The voyeur cabbie, nibbling lettuce in his shell,

For whom dawn is a Dollar Store place setting
Minus a beloved to breakfast with.
Though, there are (or were), for all
The spa's pleasures: crystal healing, mud masks,
The vaguely urinous hot mineral springs,

And, of course, the tanning bed:
That flaming stretcher
On which we are borne narrowly along
Each wanton trench
To glory.

A GOOD DEUCE

Jodi Angel

I WAS ON MY second bag of Doritos and my lips were stained emergency orange when my best friend, Phillip, said he knew a bar in Hallelujah Junction that didn't card, and maybe we should go there. We had been sitting in my living room for eighteen or nineteen hours watching Robert Redford movies, where Redford had gone from square-jawed, muscled, and rugged to looking like a blanched piece of beef jerky, and we had watched it go from dark to light to dark again through the break in the curtains. The coroner had wheeled my mother out all those hours ago and my grandma Hannah had stalked down the sidewalk with her fists closed and locked at her side, insisting that a dead body had every right to stay in the house for as long as the family wanted it there. My mother was no longer my mother; she had become Anna Schroeder, the deceased, and my grandma Hannah had been on the phone trying to track my father down. The best we had was a number for the pay phone at the Deville Motel, and only one of two things happened when you dialed that number—either it rang and rang into lonely nothing or someone answered and asked if this was Joey and hung up when the answer was no. My grandma called the number twenty-two times, and the only thing that changed was the quality of the light, and my mother went out, and Phillip came in, and my sister, Christy, packed her things so she could go, and I did not.

I understood why my grandma didn't want to take me. There had been that time when I was eleven and smart-mouthed and full of angry talk and I had made her cry. I still thought of that sometimes, what it looked like to see her in her bedroom, staring out her window in the half darkness, and how I walked up beside her and said her name and then realized that she was crying. I can still smell the room she was standing in, talcum powder, stale lace, but I try very hard to forget what I said, though it hangs in my mind like the dust caught in the weak shafts of sun. It did something to my heart to see her like that, something that I can't explain, and it did something to hers, too, I guess, because after that she never looked at me directly with both of her eyes. And now Christy was handed a suitcase and I was handed a brochure for the army recruiter office in the strip mall by Kmart and told I could take my mother's car over as long as I gave it back when my bus left. Christy was thirteen, and I was seventeen, and what she had was no choice, and what few choices I had were being made for me.

"It doesn't smell," Phillip said. He was standing in front of my mother's room, both of his arms braced in the doorway so that he could lean his body in without moving his feet. From over his shoulder I could see the bed against the wall, and the flowered mattress stripped and the blankets on the floor. The bed stood empty and accusatory, waiting to be made.

It was Christy who'd found her, and I wished it was me—not because I wanted to spare Christy the sight of what she had seen, but because for the rest of Christy's life she could fuck up or give up or not show up, and nobody would hold it against her because *Jesus Christ, you know her mother died, and she was the one who found the body.* Christy had a free ticket to minimum. I came in when Christy called for me, but when your mother dies, there is no prize for coming in second. No one was ever going to keep some slack in my rope. The one who comes in second is the one who is supposed to spend the rest of his life cleaning up the mess.

"I keep feeling like I'm waiting for something and it isn't coming," Phillip said.

"I wanna go out," I said. My fingers were stained yellow, like weak nicotine or old iodine, and I thought about all the ways that iodine could cover and stain—clothes and fingertips, forearms that had gone through bedroom windows, scraped knuckles from walls. My grandma Hannah kept a jug of it under her bathroom sink, called it something in German that I could not understand.

Outside, a dog started howling, and I listened to its voice rise and fall, over and over again, and then I remembered that Oscar had been chained to the back fence since the paramedics came, and he had cried like that at the sound of the sirens, even though they were all for show and not for need, because my mother's lips were blue and there hadn't been breath between them for a while. I went out back and saw that his water bowl was tipped and his chain was wrapped around the post, and when he saw me he started straining at the clasp and coughing out barks because his throat had gone hoarse from the spilled bowl or the tight chain or a combination of both.

My mom's car was cold inside and smelled like tired cigarettes. Phillip wanted to drive, and I didn't care enough to fight about it, so we put Oscar in the backseat and I leaned against the headrest and closed my eyes. It was the first time I had done that in more than half a day and I realized my pupils felt grit-rubbed and sore. Phillip cranked the engine over a few times, pumped the gas pedal, and the car started and he gunned it a few times so that I could smell smoke from the tailpipe coming through my window. There were lights on in houses and my watch said six and there was a second when I couldn't decide if it was A.M. or P.M., and I thought maybe I could just make myself faint if I thought hard enough about it. It was a tempting thought, but Phillip couldn't handle surprises well, and I knew that if I fainted and let the whole damn mess go, when I woke up I would still be in my mom's car, breathing in the smoke stain that she had exhaled, and we would still be in front of the house, and it would still be this day, and nothing about anything would be changed.

"Let's roll," Phillip said, and he dropped the stick on the tree to drive, and when we pulled away from the curb, the wheels caught the wet leaves in the gutter and we spun in place for a minute, the back end trying to fishtail, and then the tires gripped the street and we put the neighborhood behind us, and in twenty minutes we put the town behind us, and if Phillip kept the car pointed east, we could put the state behind us, too, but east kept bending north, and then we finally turned west and the thought of escaping faded from a spark to an ash.

There had been rain, and the road was hard obsidian that threw back the reflection of taillights every time Phillip came up on a car. Hallelujah Junction was ninety minutes out of town and nothing but a general store full of hunting and fishing supplies and a roadside bar and a place for people to stop on their way to Bear Lake for ice or more beer.

Oscar ate dog chow from his bowl on the floorboards in back, and every now and then the radio picked up intermittent stations that came in when we broke through the pine trees for a minute or two, then turned to static over a voice as the signals blurred. The tape deck was broken, just like the heater and the window crank in back and the speedometer, but Phillip was able to wedge a Van Halen tape in place with a crumpled Viceroy pack, and we listened to side one over and over again as the road hairpinned and climbed until the asphalt thinned out and there was a gap in the trees and the sudden neon promise of cold beer. Phillip did not talk to me and I was grateful for that.

We got out of the car and stretched and kicked at the gravel for a minute. Neither of us wanted to be the first one through the door, and even though Phillip had been positive that we could drink here without a hassle, I could tell that he wasn't so sure now, and maybe he wished he hadn't opened his mouth back at the house and we were still watching movies in the dark and debating over a pizza, because when push meets shove, it's a lot of responsibility to have an idea.

"Let's give it a try," I said. The air was crisp and it snapped at my clothes in long sighs. I was showered and clean and new, and I had the bottle in the front pocket of my jeans, an amber cylinder with a name on it that was not my mother's shoved deep in the cotton that my shirt hem covered, half full of blue ovals the innocent size of Tic Tacs. When me and Christy had rolled my mom over, not for the first time, she still had the bottle in her hand, and I had to pry it loose because I didn't want her to be seen like that. People are quick to judge because sometimes it is easier to not understand.

We walked across the short parking lot and up to the building, and there was the steady increase in volume of steel guitar and snare drum, and when we pushed the door open there was a moment of huddle and wait that we had to fight before we stepped in far enough to let the door close behind us, and both of us stood there, blinking into the darkness, as if we had come in late to a movie and we were standing in the back, waiting until our eyes adjusted before one of us finally took the lead and made the brave walk in the dark to find a seat. The place was small and full, maybe fifteen people along the bar to the left and knots of men around the pool table at the back of the room. There was a handful of tables against the wall opposite the bar, and the center of the floor was clear and big enough to dance on if maybe the night was right.

I was immediately disappointed.

I had wanted the stuff of movies and TV, the mountain bar, the big men with shaggy beards and leather vests and a band playing loose and loud and a barefoot lead singer and a sea of hats bobbing in time to the kick. I wanted a fight in progress, breaking glass, splintered pool cues, and a lot of ducking of punches.

But there was no band, and the men at the bar were old and thick and slow, and what few women I saw didn't look as if they were in much need of having their honor defended. Phillip seemed as disappointed as I was, but he got over it faster and went up to a break in the barstools and leaned in far enough to get the bartender's attention. Phillip was six months older, four inches taller, and thirty pounds heavier, with shoulders broad from the football he thought he might someday play. I watched his mouth move without hearing the sound, and the bartender adjusted his greasy baseball hat, and Phillip pulled money from his pocket, and two bottles of Budweiser were uncapped and set down in front of him, and that was that. No emergency, no joke, no *get the fuck out of here*, no bouncer gripping our collars and tossing us to the gravel outside. Phillip brought me a bottle, and I swallowed as much as my mouth could hold, and it was over. I had my first drink in a bar.

We found a table in the corner near the jukebox and we both slid in, and I sat back in my chair and surveyed the room.

"I didn't know what beer to get," Phillip said. "I thought I was going to blow it. The guy said, what can I get you, and my mind went blank and I panicked for a second. Then it just came to me. Budweiser. Thank God for all of the fucking commercials."

Phillip raised his bottle in the gesture of a toast, and for a second I was afraid he was going to do it, drink to my mother or say her name or apologize and tell me how sorry he was about what had happened, and I braced myself, already uncomfortable and hating him a little bit for doing it now, like this and here, but instead he just held the bottle up by the neck, squinted at the label, and set it back down again. I drank as fast as I could, and hoped that the sooner the bottle was out of my hand, the less chance there would be for Phillip to make that toast and ruin everything. If he said one thing, even put her name in his mouth, I was afraid that I would drop my face to the table and press it to the sticky residue of the last beer that had been spilled and I would not be able to sit up again. It wasn't exactly because I was sad, but maybe just because I had a feeling that even with my mother dead, there would not be a noticeable difference between the then and the now.

"You mind if we sit with you guys?"

I looked up and there were two women standing next to our table, both of them with beers in each hand, and then Phillip nodded and raised his eyebrows in a silent expression of *why the hell not,* and they slid in next to us, one beside Phillip and the other beside me, and they each put a bottle in front of them and slid the second bottles toward us, and it took me a minute to realize that they had bought us beers. When they were settled in and drinking, they both leaned toward us and asked our names, so we went around the table—Veronica, Phillip, me, and Candy.

Candy leaned closer toward me, and I met her halfway. She asked me what I did for a living and I said that I worked construction, and she thought that was pretty great. I had never worked construction, but I had always been fascinated with the guys who did, with their ragged T-shirts and tank tops and tattoos and dark tans from working in the sun, muscular and dirty and smoking and blasting hard music over the sound of their hammers. Maybe I would work construction if I could.

Candy told me that she waited tables in Battle Creek, but she wanted to move to Humboldt and go to school, but she was getting older and there never seemed to be the chance to go. Veronica was her best friend, and they worked together, and Veronica had a two-year-old daughter whose name I did not catch. After a while, Candy got up and put some money in the jukebox, and after she sat back down the music changed to the Eagles and Candy clapped her hands. "I really love this song," she said. I could picture the album cover in my mind, one from the milk crate by the old stereo in the living room, eagles' wings spread over a desert at sunrise or sunset, blue sky over pink, and not a lick of a hint to give away whether or not the day was looking to start or finish. I had stared at that album cover half of my life, looking for a sign.

Candy and Veronica liked to drink and they weren't tight with their money, and the drinking led to talking and the conversation was as easily got as the bottles lining up in front of us. Candy had an open face and a wide smile, and when she laughed she had a tendency to bring one hand up and cover the top of her lip and look away.

The beer eventually got the best of me and when I got up to find the bathroom, Phillip slid past Veronica and followed me down the narrow hall until the smell of bleach and piss and mildew directed us to the right door and I pushed inside and was amazed at just how steady I could be on my feet.

"This is the best time," Phillip said. He looked at his reflection in the mirror and let the water run in the sink so that he could wet his fingertips and smooth down the front of his hair. We had been friends for five years, and he knew more things than I wanted him to sometimes; he had been around when there had been a steady ride from bad to worse, and sometimes I resented him for that, for the easy way that he could slide in and out of my house and my life and stay only long enough to stand as witness to some kind of shit coming down and maybe eat some of the food out of the cupboards, or an order of takeout, and then he would walk back home to his leather-furniture two-parent slice of existence, and I was the one who had to stay behind and live what he only had to look at.

"I'm a little wasted," he said. Someone had written *asshole* on the wall with one *s*. Part of me wanted to find a pen somewhere and correct it. "What do you think of the girls?" Phillip said.

I turned the water on in the sink and washed my hands. I looked at myself in the mirror and saw the dark circles under my eyes, and my skin had a shine that I had never seen before. "They're nice," I said.

"You like that Candy?"

I shrugged.

"You don't want to trade, do you?"

The water got hot, fast, and I let it run so that it blasted the porcelain and the steam rose toward the mirror. "What do you mean?"

"You know, when we get back to the table, I can swap sides with you if you want. Sit next to Candy. You can take Veronica." Phillip pumped some soap into his cupped hand and lathered up. The soap was a weak green color that looked toxic. "I mean, I'd rather keep Veronica, if it's cool with you, but I figure, hey, your mom just died…" He paused for a second. "I mean, you should at least get first choice, you know?" He let the hot water hit his hands and jerked them back so hard that his fingers hit the edge of the sink. "That's fucking burning."

I thought about Christy calling for me, yesterday? The day before? Time had turned soft, and minutes and hours felt stretched and pulled. I was no longer sure if it was Thursday or Sunday or if it had been just five minutes ago that Christy had called to me, *Roy, come here,* and there had been no sense of emergency or fear, just a voice even as blacktop, *come here,* and we had done what we had done so many times before out of habit, the rolling and the looking at what we would find, only this time it was different, more than different, less than different. Maybe this was what indifferent really meant. And then we had been running hot water, so much so that the steam banked against the wall, taking turns running water and soaking towels and cleaning up. There just seemed like so much to clean.

Phillip pulled a couple of stiff paper towels out of the dispenser and rubbed his hands dry. "I mean, they're about equal. Veronica's got the bad skin and mustache, but Candy's a good deuce, so I think it all balances out." He wadded up the paper towels, threw them toward the trash can, and missed. He did not pick them up and try again. "You don't mind a fat girl, do you?"

The room was hot and small and there was still steam in the air, and in my mind I could see Candy laughing with one dimpled hand hovering over her top lip.

"She's nice," I said.

"Yeah, she's great. She's funny, et cetera. It's like that fat girl joke—Hey, why is fucking a fat girl like riding a moped? Because they're fun to ride, but you don't want your friends to see you on one." Phillip laughed and slapped me on the shoulder. I stumbled forward. "But you know I don't care."

Phillip looked in the mirror and smoothed his hair again. "I would settle for a blow job from Veronica. I wouldn't say no to that," he said.

I didn't say anything. I noticed that the floor was cement and there was a drain in the center and everything had a gentle slope toward it.

Phillip scooped some water into his mouth, rinsed, and spit it back into the sink. He squinted one eye closed and picked at a dry whitehead high on his cheek. "If it's all right with you, I want to keep Veronica. I mean, no offense, but I can close my eyes and she'll feel just fine. Fat girls don't work that way."

When we got back to the table, there were more beers and the jukebox was stuck on the Eagles album, and judging by the stack of quarters on the table in front of Candy, it would be for a while. The crowd in the bar had thinned and emptied, but when I looked at my watch it was blank-faced in the dim light.

"Hey, you know what? Roy's grandparents were Nazis." Phillip leaned back and took a drink from his beer and put an arm around Veronica. "I'm not even kidding. Tell them. Tell them about that time you found the swastika armbands and all that shit in your grandpa's closet."

It was something I thought I had seen once, and maybe I had or I hadn't, I wasn't sure, and when I tried to remember what I had seen in that closet, and I put myself back in that room, all I could smell was talcum powder and see my grandma standing at the window, stiff and straight, staring out at nothing in the weak light, her back to me, the tears streaming because I had said it, I had said names, called her things, told her how my mother would disappear every time she got off the phone with her, my grand-mother with her thick accent and twisted language, harsh, guttural, clipped through the phone, and for seventeen years I never once remembered my mother asking me how I felt—not once—*how do you feel?* Because feelings, she said, were lies. The only truth was in what you could see.

"Were they really Nazis?" Candy asked. "That's crazy." Her blue eyes were wide and filled her face.

"Did they kill people?" Veronica asked.

"Kill people!" Phillip yelled. His voice put the music to shame. "Probably. Of course. Hey, tell them about that time you had to help your grandma kill all those kittens."

"Oh my God," Candy said. She was staring at me with her mouth open. I could see the way that her lipstick was cracked around the corners of her lips.

"His grandma made him put them all in this sack. This burlap sack, right?" Phillip didn't want the answer to his question. He just wanted everyone to settle in to what he was saying.

"So he puts them in there—there's like what, ten or something?"

"Seven," I whispered.

"And he has to throw the sack into this pond out on their farm, so he does, you know, puts these baby kittens in this sack and knots the top and throws them out in the pond."

Candy had closed her mouth, but she wouldn't look at me. She was staring at Phillip and Phillip was smiling as though this was the funniest fucking story he had ever told, and he was taking his time getting to the punch line.

"The only problem is, though," Phillip took a swig from his bottle and ran the back of his hand across his mouth. "His grandma didn't tell him that he had to weigh the bag down. You know, put some rocks in it or something. So when he throws it out there, it just floats on the surface with all of these kittens screaming and trying to swim, but they're trapped in that bag, you know."

"Screaming?" Candy said.

"Fucking screaming. All ten of them. Roy told me that it was like hearing babies cry."

"But he swam out and got them, right?" Candy asked. She turned toward me at the table and her thigh touched my leg. "You swam out and got them right?"

Veronica had the same look on her face that Phillip did, and I realized that they were meant for each other and it was perfect that she'd found him.

"There was nothing I could do," I said.

"But you could swim out and get them," Candy said.

"My grandma wouldn't let me."

"His grandma wouldn't *let* him. Fucking Nazis." Phillip slammed his bottle down on the table and beer foamed and ran over the top.

"What happened?" Candy asked.

"They died," Phillip said. "What do you think happened? He and his grandma stood there and watched the bag thrash around until they finally drowned."

"God," Candy said. She was looking down at the table, and there was something in her voice that made me want to put my hand over hers and let her know that I was just as sorry as she was. "How long did it take?"

Everyone around the table looked at me. Veronica had her head cocked against Phillip's shoulder.

"Twenty minutes," I whispered.

No one said anything. I could remember watching that brown sack take on water, and I could remember how the pond smelled with all of its black mud and fish and water grass and the summer heat pulling mosquitoes off its surface. I had started to take off my shoes and wade in to get the bag, but Grandma Hannah had put her hand against my arm and stopped me. She didn't say "no" or "stop." She just kept her hand on my arm, not tight, not gripping, just present, and we stood there and watched the sack together and listened to the kittens crying on and on until one by one they tired and drowned and the last one that held the sack above the surface finally gave up and went down with the weight.

Candy's thigh was warm against me. I couldn't remember what she was wearing, if she had on jeans or not. The more I thought about the weight of her thigh, the more I could feel her taking up the table beside me, spilling over the invisible line down the middle, until she absorbed me.

Phillip leaned his head in toward Veronica's and whispered something in her ear, and she laughed and pulled back and hit him lightly on the chest, but did not move away from him. She stood up slightly so she could lean across the table and cupped her hand around Candy's ear, and Candy nodded and pulled at the disintegrating label on her bottle, and when Veronica sat back down, there was a spark that jumped around the three of them and I was the one breaking the circuit.

I was picking at my bottle label and trying to peel it off in one piece because I could, and Candy put her hand over mine and I let her, and she squeezed my hand and I could tell that her palm was cool and damp and soft and so much different from the thigh pressed tight and hot beside me. Phillip and Veronica were kissing; I could see the silhouette of their tongues moving back and forth between them.

"You ready?" Candy asked. "We're first," she said.

I took a swallow of beer and it was warm and hard to get down. The table was covered in bottles and I tried to line them up in rows like fence posts. I didn't look at Candy. "First?"

"Phillip said we can have the car first."

For a minute I was confused, and I was back in my living room and in the corner by the front door were two black garbage bags with the sheets and the hot-water towels that we had used to soak up what had come from our mom, Christy and me, before anybody came, and the first thing I had to do was get rid of them, throw away the evidence, everything except the narrow bottle in my front pocket.

Phillip pulled back from Veronica and there was a glazed look in her eyes that threw back the overhead light like the wet road had done up the mountain. He dug the car keys out of his front pocket and slid them across the table toward me. "Thirty minutes," he said. He smiled at me, and then Veronica slipped her hands around his neck and pulled him back toward her and her mouth.

Candy slid out of the booth and stood waiting for me to follow. The keys were cold and I looked at each of them and knew what they were meant for—the car, the front door, the door to my grandmother's house. I could tell the difference just by touch. Candy took my hand as we walked across the empty floor. When we were outside and the door closed behind us, the Eagles were muffled and the night air hit us. I took a deep breath and swallowed the taste of rain and pine and forest. Underneath it all I could smell a campfire, and I wondered how far away it was and wished that I could sit beside it.

The gravel crunched and shifted under our shoes, and I walked toward the car and led her behind me, leashed with my arm. "It's cold," she said. There were no cars on the highway, no distant drone of a truck coming through. I wanted to run down the white center line as fast as I could, run between the trees and suck down the air until my lungs burned and I had to run with my mouth open just to keep my breath.

When I put the key in the door, Oscar jumped up off the backseat and started barking and lunging at the glass, and Candy screamed and jerked her hand out of my grip, but then Oscar saw that it was me.

"My God, that scared the shit out of me," she laughed. "Is that your dog?"

"He was my mom's dog," I said. The past tense had caught up with me and it had taken only a day and a night and already it came second nature.

"He's cute," Candy said. She knocked on the glass and Oscar let out a sharp whine and tried to lick her hand through the closed window.

I opened the door and Oscar jumped over the seat and tried to jump on me. Candy kept holding her hand out toward him and saying things in a singsong voice that I couldn't understand. "He probably has to pee," I said. I hooked my fingers into his collar and pulled him down from the seat, and when he was out of the car, Candy started rubbing his head and scratching behind his ears, and he rolled over in the dirt.

"He is so sweet. I love him. What's his name?"

"Oscar," I said. I gave a sharp whistle and Oscar jumped to his feet and tried to sit without touching the gravel. "Go on. Go pee," I said. I pushed at him with my knee and pointed him toward the brush that edged the parking lot in front of the car. There was a low scrub of bushes and tree trunks, and then the land sloped up and away from the parking lot and became a hillside and then a mountainside as the ground cover fell away in favor of rocks. Oscar put his nose to the ground and disappeared toward the trees.

"Go ahead," I said. I pulled the driver's door wide and swept my arm toward the seat.

She sat down behind the steering wheel and tried to slide to the other side, but there wasn't an inch of slide to be had and she was firmly wedged between the wheel and the seat. To get her to the passenger side from there was going to take a lot of pushing. "We'd be more comfortable in the back," I said quickly, and I reached around her and pulled the lock on the back door. She stood up and smoothed her shirt front, and then she was able to get herself onto the backseat and with some hard breaths and a few kicks against the floorboards was able to move to the other side and make room for me.

I shut the door, and we were in the quiet, and the car smelled like dog and dog food. The combination reminded me that my stomach was full of nothing but cheap beer and distant handfuls of Doritos, and my stomach did a slow turn that made me swallow hard. I reached for the window crank and then remembered that it was broken off. "Can you roll your window down a little?" I said. She turned the crank a couple of times and the air came in and cooled the car and cleaned out the smell in one breath. Outside the car I could hear Oscar's tags rattling and the occasional sound of snapping brush as he walked around in the bushes.

Candy put her hand on the seat between us, and in the half-light from the parking lot I could see how white her skin was. I reached out and touched it with my fingertips. It was warm, and I could feel the uneven ridges of veins, but they were soft and rolled away from the pressure of my fingers and I knew that I would have to press hard to find her pulse.

Candy turned toward me, but there was a lot of her that had to come between us and it was going to be hard for me to reach her with my mouth if kissing was the next thing to do. I would have to get up on one knee on the seat and climb up a little, but she seemed okay with that and helped me get into position, and I closed my eyes and fumbled through the best that I could. Her lips were nice, and she was comfortable and slow and when she kissed me I stopped thinking about all of the things that were demanding my time. She slid her hands down my ribs and pulled at the bottom of my T-shirt, and for a second I thought that I would feel her hands on my skin, but then they dropped my shirt hem and moved down and she fingered the fly on my jeans and her left hand started rubbing at the crease, and then it moved to the right and started squeezing the bottle in my pocket up and down and up and down and I knew the rhythm she was trying to rub and I realized that what she had in her hand was not what she thought she was gripping.

I pulled back from her and she tried to keep me from going but I rolled back enough to get a hand down to my jeans, and she put her hands on my shoulders and pulled me back toward her and said, "It's okay, it's okay."

I fished the pill bottle from my pocket and held it up to her. The light from the single pole in the parking lot caught the amber and made it flash like a turn signal. She took it from me and squinted at it to read the label. "Oxycontin?" she said. Candy held the bottle up to the shaft of light. "Who's Sharon O'Donnel?"

I leaned my head back against the seat and wished that there was no top on the car and I could look up at the stars and find Orion because he was always there when I needed him. I could always take comfort in the three stars for his belt. "Sometimes my mother," I said.

"Was she sick?"

I remembered the nights of crying in the bedroom, the muffled sound of her pillows taking the brunt of her sobs while Christy and I sat in the living room, inches apart, the TV on in front of us, blank-screened and throwing back light, and the only thing we moved was our eyes.

"Yes," I said.

I nodded and stared out the windshield toward the tree trunks and buckthorn that I knew were somewhere in front of me.

She handed the bottle back to me but I couldn't make my fingers close around it, so we held it between us together. "She's been dead for twenty-six hours," I said.

She was quiet for a minute and when she spoke it was barely a whisper. "Phillip told me," she said. I felt her hand slide up to my wrist. She took the bottle from me and I let her. "Come here," she said.

She pulled me in toward her and undressed me in layers, and she was so careful and soft that I hardly felt her. I closed my eyes and let her move me, lift my arms one by one, raise the T-shirt, pull it over my head, take the jeans and the socks and the shoes. Every time she took something off me, she pulled me closer to her so that the heat from her body held me like a blanket. I tried to talk to her, tried to apologize, but every time I found my voice, she said *shhhh* against me and lifted a finger to my lips.

When I was undressed, she unbuttoned her shirt and pulled me to her and wrapped the open sides of the shirt around me, and she slid down against the door so that we were both lying across the seat and I wasn't so much against her as settled into her, pressed in below her surface. When I opened my eyes, she was looking up at me, and I could see the creases in her brow, the lines on her face, and I knew that the parking lot light was showing her age. She raised her head a little and kissed both of my eyes and went back to work moving me, burying me, guiding me, drowning me, and from that height above the seat rocking and rocking, I could see over the door panel and out into the darkness, and smell the mountain grape and deer brush leaking in. Far away I could hear a dog barking, faint clips of sound breaking the heavy stillness of the highway and moving away from me. I knew that soon Phillip would be at the car, and he would want inside, and I would have to come to the surface again. I didn't know for just how long I could stay.

PERMISSIONS

Carolyn Abram, "It's All Performance." © 2013 by Carolyn Abram. Reprinted by permission of the author.

Jodi Angel, "A Good Deuce," *Tin House,* Summer 2011. © 2011 by Jodi Angel. Reprinted by permission of Tin House Books.

Gustavo Arellano, excerpt from *Taco USA: How Mexican Food Conquered America* (Scribner). © 2012 by Gustavo Arellano. Reprinted with the permission of Scribner, a division of Simon & Schuster, Inc. All rights reserved.

Poe Ballantine, "Free Rent at the Totalitarian Hotel," *The Sun,* June 2012. © 2012 by Poe Ballantine. Reprinted by permission of the author.

Jen Bergmark, "Boyle Heights," *Puerto del Sol,* Summer 2011. © 2011 by Jen Bergmark. Reprinted by permission of the author.

Mark Cox, "Palm Springs," *Inlandia: A Literary Journey,* Fall/Winter 2011–12 (first published in *The Café Review,* 2006). © 2006 by Mark Cox. Reprinted by permission of the author.

Elizabeth C. Creely, "Daire Nua: The New Oak Grove," *New Hibernia Review,* Winter 2011. © 2011 by Elizabeth C. Creely. Reprinted by permission of the author.

Rachelle Cruz, "Serving Oysters to M.F.K. Fisher," *Muzzle,* Spring 2011. © 2011 by Rachelle Cruz. Reprinted by permission of the author.

Natalie Diaz, "The Last Mojave Indian Barbie" from *When My Brother Was an Aztec* (Copper Canyon Press). © 2012 by Natalie Diaz. Reprinted with the permission of Copper Canyon Press, www.coppercanyonpress.org.

Joan Didion, excerpt (chapters 11, 16, and 17) from *Blue Nights* (Knopf). © 2011 by Joan Didion. Used by permission of Alfred A. Knopf, a division of Random House, Inc. Any third party use of this material, outside of this publication, is prohibited. Interested parties must apply directly to Random House, Inc., for permission.

Steve Erickson, excerpt from *These Dreams of You* (Europa Editions). © 2012 by Steve Erickson. Reprinted by permission of Europa Editions.

Tania Flores, "California Was Never Kansas," *ChicoSol,* August 28, 2011. © 2011 by Tania Flores. Reprinted by permission of the author.

Linda Norton, "Stanzas in the Form of a Dove" from *The Public Gardens: Poems and History* (Pressed Wafer). © 2011 by Linda Norton. Reprinted by permission of the author.

Geoffrey G. O'Brien, "Bohemian Grove" from *Metropole* (University of California Press). © 2011 by the Regents of the University of California. Reprinted by permission of the University of California Press.

Julie Otsuka, excerpt from *The Buddha in the Attic* (Knopf). © 2011 by Julie Otsuka. Used by permission of Alfred A. Knopf, a division of Random House, Inc. Any third party use of this material, outside of this publication, is prohibited. Interested parties must apply directly to Random House, Inc., for permission.

Ismet Prcic, excerpt from *Shards* (Black Cat). © 2011 by Ismet Prcic. Used by permission of Grove/Atlantic, Inc. Any third party use of this material, outside of this publication, is prohibited.

Zara Raab, "Artemis in the Barnyard" from *Swimming the Eel* (David Roberts Books). © 2011 by Zara Raab. Reprinted by permission of WordTech Communications, LLC.

Jess Row, "The Dispatcher," *The Threepenny Review*, Summer 2011. © 2011 by Jess Row. Reprinted by permission of the author.

Greg Sarris, "Maria Evangeliste" from *West of 98: Living and Writing the New American West* (University of Texas Press, 2011), ed. Lynn Stegner and Russell Rowland. © 2011 by Greg Sarris. Reprinted by permission of the author.

Shanthi Sekaran, "Imperfect Eulogy for Elmer Morrissey," *ZYZZYVA* (weblog only), April 25, 2012. © 2012 by Shanthi Sekaran. Reprinted by permission of the author.

Susan Straight, "Geometry of the Winter Desert: Field and Home," *KCET,* March 6, 2012. © 2012 by Susan Straight. Images © 2012 by Douglas McCulloh. Reprinted by permission of the author and the photographer.

Cheryl Strayed, "Transcend" from *Tiny Beautiful Things: Advice on Love and Life from Dear Sugar* (Vintage Books). © 2012 by Cheryl Strayed. Used by permission of Vintage Books, a division of Random House, Inc. Any third party use of this material, outside of this publication, is prohibited. Interested parties must apply directly to Random House, Inc., for permission.

Alexandra Teague, "The House That Doesn't Grow" from "The Winchester Series," *The Seattle Review*, Volume 5, Number 1, 2011. © 2011 by Alexandra Teague. Reprinted by permission of the author.

Lysley Tenorio, "L'amour, CA," from *Monstress* (Ecco). © 2012 by Lysley Tenorio. Reprinted by permission of HarperCollins Publishers.

David Rains Wallace, "Point Reyes: Renewed by Fire," *Bay Nature,* July–September 2012. © 2012 by David Rains Wallace. Reprinted by permission of the author.

AUTHOR BIOGRAPHIES

CAROLYN ABRAM is the author of *Facebook for Dummies* (Wiley, most recent edition 2012).

JODI ANGEL is the author of *The History of Vegas* (Chronicle Books, 2004). Her second short story collection is forthcoming from Tin House Books.

GUSTAVO ARELLANO is the author of *Orange County: A Personal History* (Scribner, 2008) and *Taco USA: How Mexican Food Conquered America* (Scribner, 2012). Editor of *OC Weekly*, he also writes the nationally syndicated column "¡Ask a Mexican!" His website is gustavoarellano.net.

POE BALLANTINE is the author of two essay collections and two novels, and his work has been published or anthologized in *The Atlantic Monthly, The Sun, The Best American Short Stories,* and *The Best American Essays.* His forthcoming memoir is *Love and Terror on the Howling Plains of Nowhere* (Hawthorne Books, 2013).

JEN BERGMARK's fiction has appeared in the *Indiana Review* and *Puerto del Sol.* Her website is jenbergmark.com.

MARK COX's most recent poetry collection is *Natural Causes* (University of Pittsburgh Press, 2004).

ELIZABETH C. CREELY's essays have appeared in the *Mississippi Review,* the *New Hibernia Review,* and the anthology *Eccentricities of Geography* (Western Press Books, 2012).

RACHELLE CRUZ is the author of the chapbook *Self-Portrait as Rumor and Blood* (Dancing Girl Press, 2012). Her website is rachellecruz.com.

NATALIE DIAZ is the author of *When My Brother Was an Aztec* (Copper Canyon Press, 2012).

JOAN DIDION's most recent book is *Blue Nights* (Knopf, 2011). *The Year of Magical Thinking* (Knopf, 2005) received a National Book Award.

STEVE ERICKSON is the author of nine novels, most recently *These Dreams of You* (Europa Editions, 2012). His work has appeared in *Esquire, Rolling Stone, Salon, LA Weekly,* and the *New York Times Magazine.* Also a film critic, he is the editor of the literary journal *Black Clock.* His website is steveerickson.org.

TANIA FLORES's blog, *Pitaya and Parachute Sketches,* can be found at taniarabelleart.blogspot.com.

VINCENT GUERRA's poetry has appeared in the *Boston Review, Denver Quarterly,* the *Indiana Review, Narrative Magazine, FIELD,* and *Pleiades.* He is the poetry editor of *Juked.*

STEPHEN D. GUTIÉRREZ is the author of the short story collections *Live from Fresno y Los* (Bear Star Press, 2009) and *Elements* (Fiction Collective Two, 1997). His website is stephendgutierrez.com.

ROBERT HASS's collection *Time and Materials: Poems 1997–2005* (Ecco, 2007) won both a Pulitzer Prize and a National Book Award. His most recent publication is *What Light Can Do: Essays on Art, Imagination, and the Natural World* (Ecco, 2012).

KEVIN HEARLE is the author of the poetry collection *Each Thing We Know Is Changed Because We Know It* (Ahsahta Press, 1994). His website is kevinhearle.com.

BILL HUTCHINSON is a senior writer for the *New York Daily News* and the author of the memoir *Sushi and Black-eyed Peas* (TheWriteDeal, 2012).

MICHAEL JAIME-BECERRA's most recent publication is the novel *This Time Tomorrow* (Thomas Dunne Books, 2010).

DANA JOHNSON is the author of *Elsewhere, California* (Counterpoint, 2012) and *Break Any Woman Down* (University of Georgia Press, 2001). Her website is danajohnsonauthor.com.

CLAIRE KAGEYAMA-RAMAKRISHNAN is the author of the poetry collections *Shadow Mountain* (Four Way Books, 2008) and *Bear, Diamonds and Crane* (Four Way Books, 2011).

CHIEUN "GLORIA" KIM's poetry has appeared in the *Porter Gulch Review.* A student at Cabrillo College, she is the winner of the 2013 *New California Writing* Student Award.

MICHAEL LEWIS, a contributing editor to *Vanity Fair,* is most recently the author of *Boomerang: Travels in the New Third World* (W.W. Norton, 2011).

SYLVIA LINSTEADT's blog, *The Indigo Vat,* can be found at theindigovat .blogspot.com.

DAVID MAS MASUMOTO is most recently the author of *Wisdom of the Last Farmer: Harvesting Legacies from the Land* (Free Press, 2009). The website for Masumoto Family Farm is masumoto.com.

JOSEPH MILLAR's most recent poetry collection is *Blue Rust* (Carnegie Mellon University Press, 2012). He won a Pushcart Prize in 2008 and can be found on the web at josephmillar.org.

DONNA MISCOLTA is the author of *When the de la Cruz Family Danced* (Signal 8 Press, 2011). Her website is donnamiscolta.com.

JUAN VELASCO MORENO is the author of the poetry collection *La masacre de los soñadores/Massacre of the Dreamers* (Editorial Polibea, 2011) and the novel *Enamorado* (Ediciones Miraguano, 2000).

KEENAN NORRIS is the author of the forthcoming *Brother and the Dancer* (Heyday, 2013), winner of the James D. Houston Award. His website is keenannorris.com.

LINDA NORTON is the author of *The Public Gardens: Poems and History* (Pressed Wafer, 2011). Her blog can be found at thepublicgardens. blogspot.com.

GEOFFREY G. O'BRIEN's fourth poetry collection is the forthcoming *People on Sunday* (Wave Books, 2013).

JULIE OTSUKA's *The Buddha in the Attic* (Knopf, 2011), her second novel, won the PEN/Faulkner Award for Fiction. Her website is julieotsuka.com.

ISMET PRCIC'S first novel, *Shards* (Black Cat, 2011), won the Art Seidenbaum Award for First Fiction, a *Los Angeles Times* Book Prize. His website is ismetprcic.com.

ZARA RAAB'S second poetry collection is *Swimming the Eel* (David Roberts Books, 2011). Her website is zararaab.com.

JESS ROW's second short story collection is *Nobody Ever Gets Lost* (Five-Chapter Books, 2011). His website is jessrow.com.

GREG SARRIS is the chairman of the Federated Indians of Graton Rancheria. His short story collection *Grand Avenue* (Hyperion, 1994) was made into an HBO movie.

SHANTHI SEKARAN is the author of *The Prayer Room* (MacAdam Cage, 2009). Her website is shanthisekaran.com.

SUSAN STRAIGHT's eighth novel is *Between Heaven and Here* (McSweeney's, 2012). *Highwire Moon* (Houghton Mifflin, 2001) was a National Book Award finalist. Her website is susanstraight.com.

CHERYL STRAYED's most recent book is a memoir, *Wild: From Lost to Found on the Pacific Crest Trail* (Knopf, 2012). She is also the author of the "Dear Sugar" advice column at *The Rumpus*. Her website is cheryl strayed.com.

ALEXANDRA TEAGUE's first book of poetry, *Mortal Geography* (Persea Books, 2010), won a California Book Award. Her website is alexandra teague.com.

LYSLEY TENORIO's debut collection of short stories is *Monstress* (Ecco, 2012). His website is lysleytenorio.com.

DAVID RAINS WALLACE's most recent book, *Chuckwalla Land: The Riddle of California's Desert* (University of California Press, 2011), won a California Book Award.

ABOUT THE EDITORS

GAYLE WATTAWA is thoroughly addicted to contemporary literature and is always maxing out her allowable holds at the Berkeley Public Library. (Even so, she sometimes suspects that she reads more book reviews, literary journals, and lit news blogs than actual books.) She is the founding editor of the New California Writing series and editor of *Inlandia: A Literary Journey through California's Inland Empire*. She has supervised the assemblage of many literary anthologies as Heyday's acquisitions and editorial director. She has bachelor's degrees in English literature and mathematics from the University of California, Berkeley.

KIRK GLASER is a senior lecturer in the Department of English at Santa Clara University, where he teaches writing and literature and serves as faculty advisor to the *Santa Clara Review*. His poetry has been nominated twice for the Pushcart Prize, won several national awards, and appeared in such publications as the *Threepenny Review, Cerise Press,* and the *Berkeley Poetry Review*. He is currently working on a young adult science fiction novel entitled *The Runner Between Worlds,* as well as circulating a poetry manuscript, *Leaf of Ash*. He earned his B.A. from Dartmouth College and his Ph.D. in American literature at the University of California, Berkeley.

ABOUT THE SERIES

N EW CALIFORNIA WRITING is an annual literary
anthology that collects fresh and thought-provok-
ing writing about California that has been published in
the previous year, with a special emphasis on Californian
writers, publications, and publishers.

Two special inclusions are the winner of the New California Writing
Student Award and a preview of the year's James D. Houston Award–
winning manuscript, to be published by Heyday and available in November.
(For more information about the James D. Houston Award, please visit
heydaybooks.com/houstonaward/.)

With *New California Writing 2013*, Heyday and the California Legacy
Project at Santa Clara University continue a partnership begun in 2000
under the editorship of Terry Beers in order to bring readers the best of
California writing.

We welcome and encourage your suggestions. For more information
about what we are looking for and how to submit material, please visit
heydaybooks.com/newcaliforniawriting.html.

For more on other California Legacy titles, events, or other information, please visit californialegacy.org.

HEYDAY
into California

About Heyday

Heyday is an independent, nonprofit publisher and unique cultural institution. We promote widespread awareness and celebration of California's many cultures, landscapes, and boundary-breaking ideas. Through our well-crafted books, public events, and innovative outreach programs we are building a vibrant community of readers, writers, and thinkers.

Thank You

It takes the collective effort of many to create a thriving literary culture. We are thankful to all the thoughtful people we have the privilege to engage with. Cheers to our writers, artists, editors, storytellers, designers, printers, bookstores, critics, cultural organizations, readers, and book lovers everywhere!

We are especially grateful for the generous funding we've received for our publications and programs during the past year from foundations and hundreds of individual donors. Major supporters include:

Anonymous (2); Acorn Naturalists; Alliance for California Traditional Arts; Judy Avery; James J. Baechle; BayTree Fund; S. D. Bechtel, Jr. Foundation; Barbara Jean and Fred Berensmeier; Berkeley Civic Arts Program and Civic Arts Commission; Joan Berman; Buena Vista Rancheria/Jesse Flyingcloud Pope Foundation; Lewis and Sheana Butler; California Civil Liberties Public Education Program; Cal Humanities; California Indian Heritage Center Foundation; California State Library; California State Parks Foundation; Keith Campbell Foundation; Candelaria Fund; John and Nancy Cassidy Family Foundation, through Silicon Valley Community Foundation; The Center for California Studies; Graham Chisholm; The Christensen Fund; Jon

Christensen; Community Futures Collective; Compton Foundation; Creative Work Fund; Lawrence Crooks; Nik Dehejia; Frances Dinkelspiel and Gary Wayne; Durfee Foundation; Troy Duster; Earth Island Institute; Eaton Kenyon Fund of the Sacramento Region Community Foundation; Exhibit Envoy; Euclid Fund at the East Bay Community Foundation; Furthur Foundation; The Fred Gellert Family Foundation; Wallace Alexander Gerbode Foundation; Nicola W. Gordon; Wanda Lee Graves and Stephen Duscha; The Walter and Elise Haas Fund; Coke and James Hallowell; G. Scott Hong Charitable Trust; Donna Ewald Huggins; Humboldt Area Foundation; James Irvine Foundation; Claudia Jurmain; Kendeda Fund; Marty and Pamela Krasney; Guy Lampard and Suzanne Badenhoop; Christine Leefeldt, in celebration of Ernest Callenbach and Malcolm Margolin's friendship; LEF Foundation; Thomas Lockard; Thomas J. Long Foundation; Judith and Brad Lowry-Croul; Kermit Lynch Wine Merchant; Michael McCone; Nion McEvoy and Leslie Berriman; Michael Mitrani; Moore Family Foundation; Michael J. Moratto, in memory of Ernest L. Cassel; Richard Nagler; National Endowment for the Arts; National Wildlife Federation; Native Cultures Fund; The Nature Conservancy; Nightingale Family Foundation; Steven Nightingale; Northern California Water Association; Pacific Legacy, Inc.; The David and Lucile Packard Foundation; Patagonia, Inc.; PhotoWings; Robin Ridder; Alan Rosenus; The San Francisco Foundation; San Manuel Band of Mission Indians; Greg Sarris; Savory Thymes; Sonoma Land Trust; Stanley Smith Horticultural Trust; Stone Soup Fresno; Roselyne Chroman Swig; Swinerton Family Fund; Thendara Foundation; Sedge Thomson and Sylvia Brownrigg; TomKat Charitable Trust; Lisa Van Cleef and Mark Gunson; Patricia Wakida; Whole Systems Foundation; John Wiley & Sons, Inc.; Peter Booth Wiley and Valerie Barth; Bobby Winston; Dean Witter Foundation; The Work-in-Progress Fund of Tides Foundation; and Yocha Dehe Community Fund.

Getting Involved

To learn more about our publications, events, membership club, and other ways you can participate, please visit www.heydaybooks.com.

ECO-FRIENDLY BOOKS
Made in the USA